Surviving Childhood Sexual Abuse

Surviving Childhood Sexual Abuse

Practical Self-Help for Adults Who Were Sexually Abused as Children

Revised Edition

Carolyn Ainscough
Kay Toon

Da Capo
LIFE
LONG

A Member of the Perseus Books Group

First published in Great Britain in 1993, 2000
Sheldon Press, SPCK, Marylebone Road, London NW1 4DU
This is the revised edition of the book originally published as *Breaking Free*.

North American edition © 2000 by Da Capo Press
Copyright © 1993, 2000 by Carolyn Ainscough and Kay Toon

Cataloging-in-Publication Data is available from the Library of Congress

ISDN 1-55561-225-3

Da Capo Press is a member of the Perseus Books Group.
Find us on the World Wide Web at http://www.dacapopress.com

Da Capo Press books are available at special discounts for bulk purchases in the United States by corporations, institutions, and other organizations. For more information please contact the Special Markets Department at Perseus Books Group, 11 Cambridge Center, Cambridge, MA 02142 or email jmccrary@perseusbooks.com

8 9 10—06 05

Contents

Preface

We first met in 1983 while we trained to be clinical psychologists. During our training, the words "sexual abuse" were hardly mentioned—certainly not in relation to adults who were experiencing psychological problems.

After finishing training, we both took jobs with Wakefield Health Authority. There we worked with adults, referred by general practitioners or other professionals, who were experiencing emotional difficulties coping with their lives. These clients came to us with a variety of problems (depression, anxiety, eating disorders, sexual problems, phobias) but as we talked with them, many began to tell us they had been sexually abused as children. This appeared to be a major cause of their current problems.

At first we worked individually with clients who had been sexually abused. In 1987, we set up our first Survivors group. We had already run anxiety groups together and our clients had found group work beneficial. They could share their problems and experiences with others in the same position, help and encourage each other and set up long-lasting support networks and friendships. We hoped Survivors would benefit in similar ways.

Since then, we have set up a psychology service in Wakefield for Survivors and have led many Survivors groups, as well as continued to work individually with people who were sexually abused as children. The groups meet weekly with us for between fifteen and twenty weeks and then continue to meet as self-help groups. In these therapy groups the Survivors can share the pain of their experiences, work through their feelings and begin to break free of their problems.

We decided to write a booklet on sexual abuse to help and encourage Survivors who were waiting for therapy. Some former members of the Survivors groups were eager to help by contributing writings they had done as part of their own therapy. Soon the booklet had expanded into a book. At the same time, A.C.T. (Abuse Counseling and Training), an action group of Survivors committed to helping other Survivors and working toward prevention, was formed. A.C.T. has now been superceded by Moving On—a support and discussion group for Survivors who have completed therapy with us.

Many Survivors have never had the opportunity to talk about what happened to them and how they feel about it. This book was written to share what we have learned, to reach out to all people who have been sexually abused as children and to help others take their first steps in breaking free from the past. It is not intended as an alternative to professional help; we hope this book will give Survivors confidence to seek the help they deserve.

This revised edition of *Surviving Childhood Sexual Abuse* now includes the experiences and writings of male Survivors, puts more emphasis on women abusers and describes the meaning and application of the term *false memory syndrome*. It also includes a new chapter in which some of the women who contributed to the original book describe what they have been doing in the intervening years and tell us how they feel now.

This book expresses our belief in the power of human beings to survive, to heal and to grow. It would not exist without those Wakefield Survivors who were prepared to share their experiences with us and to contribute their writings. All the events and people described here are real. The names have been changed for legal reasons or to protect family members, but not because the Survivors are ashamed. They know the responsibility for sexual abuse always lies with the abuser and never with the abused child.

Acknowledgments

The ideas in this book have developed from our work with the Survivors of sexual abuse who were brave enough to share their experiences with us, who have struggled to overcome their problems and break free from their pain and guilt. We would like to express our respect for these Survivors and our thanks for the knowledge we have gained by working with them. We would especially like to thank all the people who have contributed their writing to this book.

We would also like to thank Margaret Ainscough, Chris Bethlehem, Alistair Cant, Sharon Jackson and Diane Skinner, who have read various drafts and offered their suggestions and corrections; Chris Leach for his support and advice about writing and publishing; Jon Fraise for help with the word processing and Sally Pinnell for contributions from her research on our groups. We express our appreciation and gratitude to Bryn Thomas and Andrew Lister, who gave their support and cooked fortifying meals throughout the writing of this book. Andrew Lister also generously devoted his time to reading draft after draft of the book, rewriting problematic sentences and advising on punctuation.

Our special thanks to Erika Reinhold, not only for contributing her personal story to the book but also for all her hours of typing and retyping, and to members of A.C.T. for their unfailing enthusiasm and support for this project.

Carolyn Ainscough and Kay Toon
Clinical Psychologists

PART ONE

Sexual Abuse Changes Lives

1

Survival and Recovery: Sharing the Pain

Now I feel more powerful. I'm going to take care of this power and nurture it and I'm going to take charge of my life. I'm going to get out of this mess. I can see a different life. I can smell a better future. I'm not frightened any more. I'm breaking free. Lizzie

The sexual abuse of children is not a new problem. Generations of children have been sexually abused in secret and remained silent. The silence and secrecy are now being broken as Survivors of childhood sexual abuse begin to speak out about their experiences and break free of their past. Survivors of sexual abuse are learning that they are not alone and they are reclaiming their own power and self-respect.

Until recently, the sexual abuse of a child was thought to be a terrible but extremely rare event. Since the 1980s, however, an increasing amount of attention has been given to sexual abuse on television and radio and in newspapers and magazines. As more and more Survivors dare to speak out, it is becoming clear that many people have been sexually abused as children. Many Survivors, however, have carried the secret of their abuse to the grave; others still carry the burden of that secret and suffer in silence. We may never know the true extent of this problem. The shame and secrecy that surround sexual abuse and keep people silent make it difficult to estimate the number of people who have been sexually abused. The results of research studies vary but it is generally believed that at least one in 10 people has been sexually abused as a child. Even the most conservative estimates indicate that sexual abuse affects large numbers of people. It is a worldwide problem not confined to a specific country, race, culture or class. This means there are millions of people alive today who have been sexually abused as children.

Who is this book for?

This book is primarily a self-help book for adult Survivors of childhood sexual abuse. Sexual abuse has damaging effects on children but it can also lead to problems in adulthood. This book contains information about sexual abuse, the kinds of problems it can cause and ways in which Survivors can begin to deal with these problems. It is not possible to diagnose a past history of sexual abuse from current problems and symptoms. This book cannot tell you whether you have been sexually abused. We hope that friends and relatives of Survivors and people working in the caring professions will also read this book and gain insight into the difficulties Survivors face. However, we address this book to you, the Survivor.

The words we use

Sexual abuse. We use the term "sexual abuse" to mean any kind of sexual behavior by an adult with a child or any unwanted or inappropriate sexual behavior by another child. This includes sexual intercourse, oral sex, anal sex, being touched in a sexual way and being persuaded to touch someone else. It may involve inserting objects into the child's body or sexual acts with animals. However, sexual abuse doesn't always involve physical contact. Being made to watch other people's sexual behavior, or to look at their bodies or at sexual photographs or videos can also be forms of sexual abuse. Sexual abuse includes abuse by one person, abuse by a number of different individuals or by groups of people. The abuse may have happened only once or many times over a number of years. It may still be happening.

    Abusers. We often refer to abusers as "he," because the majority of abusers (at least 80%) are men. However, more Survivors are now talking about abuse by women. An abuser is anyone who has sexually abused a child. This could be a father, mother, brother, other family member, friend, person in authority, acquaintance, other child or a stranger.

Survivors. We use the word "survivors" to refer to people who have been sexually abused as children. They have had to find ways of surviving the trauma of sexual abuse but, with the help of this book, we hope they will go beyond simply surviving to living a fuller and happier life. Survivors are usually referred to as "she" in this book because when this book was first published, most of our work had been with women Survivors. However, many men also have been sexually abused as children. We have included stories and quotations from the men we have worked in this new edition. Survivors can come from any religious or ethnic background or any walk of life. Wakefield Survivors include teachers, housewives, policewomen, radio dispatchers, social workers, truck drivers, single parents, the unemployed, nurses, driving instructors, domestics, caterers, clerical workers and businesspeople.

Child. The word "child" is used here to refer to teenagers as well as younger children. Abuse can start as a teenager or in adulthood. This book is primarily for people whose sexual abuse started before they became adults.

This book is for men and women who have been sexually abused as children in any way by male or female abusers.

About this book

This book is intended to help you think anew about your experiences and feelings and to start to work through your problems. Survivors share with you their own experience of sexual abuse. Their comments appear throughout this book. They also describe the problems they have had since being abused and the ways they have found to overcome these difficulties. Each Survivor has had her own personal struggle but has been helped by sharing her pain with other Survivors and experiencing their understanding and support.

The book is divided into five sections. Part One, *Sexual Abuse Changes Lives*, contains accounts by Wakefield Survivors of their experiences. It illustrates ways in which sexual abuse affects people both as children and as adults. Part Two, *"It Must Have Been My Fault,"* considers the feelings of guilt and shame that Survivors experience. We look at the common questions that Survivors try to answer: "Why did it happen to me?" and "Why didn't I tell?" We also look at the signs children may show when they are being sexually abused and what happens when people do tell someone that they have been abused.

2

Survivors Speak Out

In this chapter Jane, Eileen, Anita, Graham, Pam and Dorothy speak out about the sexual abuse they suffered and how it affected them as children and adults. Each Survivor's story is different but many of the feelings and effects are similar. These stories are powerful and at times distressing, but also hopeful and positive. You may feel upset for the person whose story you are reading, and the stories might also trigger feelings about your own abuse. Use these stories to reflect on your own experiences and feelings. If you can, find a friend to whom you can talk about how you are feeling. Read the chapter slowly and stop when you want to. Do not feel you have to read these stories before going on to the rest of the book. Leave them and come back to them later if you wish.

Jane's story

I am in the bathroom staring at the light. I am lying on the floor next to the scales. I don't remember what my daddy said to me beforehand but I remember as he lay down on top of me. I wanted to push him away but he held my wrists to the floor on either side of my head. I remember his clothing rubbing against my naked skin. The contact hurt, the pressure hurt as he rubbed himself up and down over me. I remember his brown tie flapping around my face. Afterward he stood me up in the bath water. He told me not to tell, that my mother would not understand, it was our secret. The threats came later.

That was the first time my stepfather sexually abused me. I was seven years old. My parents split up when I was four. My natural father had always been a distant figure, and then for three years I had very little contact with any men. When my mother remarried, we became a real family. My little sister and I had a daddy.

As the family became older, my stepfather became more threatening and domineering. As I became older, I felt that I was walking on a tightrope between my two lives. I wanted to be liked and loved as me, but what if people knew what I was really like, what I allowed to happen, what I was involved in? My stepfather was very popular. He used to run errands for older neighbors, pick up prescriptions for the sick, move coal for people and clear snow. So I thought it must be me who was really bad. I must be responsible. Who would believe otherwise? My stepfather rewarded me with money sometimes, more money than my mother could spare, so I felt even more guilty. I felt that if my mother found out, her marriage would break up. It would be as if she was being punished, not me, whose fault it really was.

Sometimes I would screw up all my courage and refuse him, but whatever tactics I used, he would outmaneuver me. He would appear to go along with me, and then he would begin to be really nasty to the family. He would reduce my mother's housekeeping allowance. He'd threaten to throw us all out of the house. He would go to the bar straight from work and show up late for meals. He would fluctuate between totally ignoring one of us and picking on us for minor things and blowing them out of proportion. He had total control over the TV and would change the channel five minutes before the end of a program we were all watching. "My name is on the lease" was a popular phrase of his that would cause a lot of distress. Then he would come back to me and ask again. This would continue until I gave in. I felt guilty for giving in to him, and I felt guilty for causing all the misery to my family.

When I began to menstruate, I wanted to beg my mother not to tell him. I felt ashamed again, not in control of my body, but I didn't feel I had the right to ask her not to tell him. I wondered if this would change anything, but I guess since penetration wasn't involved, nothing did change. I still used to have nightmares about becoming pregnant through clothing.

Once I developed breasts (a word I didn't like, because he used to tell me I had beautiful breasts), I only had to strip to my waist. He would change into nylon trousers and then push his nicotine-stained tongue into my mouth and ears, and play with my nipples with his hard-cracked fingers. I would be on the floor, and as I cried silently the tears would collect in my ears. I could never figure out why the sight of tears didn't put him off. I would clench my fists on the floor and grit my teeth against his tongue and try to imagine myself out of my body. I lived in constant dread. I knew what would happen whenever I was left alone with my stepfather. Being ill and absent from school was not much fun at our house.

Keeping this big secret made me feel I was different. I had to pretend that I was normal and the same as everyone else. I kept to myself, not daring to risk close friendships nor to draw attention to myself in any way. I deliberately didn't take an active role in the classroom at school. I had friends at school but no best friend, no one to ask over to my house after school. The more I pretended, the more guilt I felt over the deception, and the more certain I became that people liked the "pretend me," not the real me. The friends I did have were mainly boys, because they were happy to play outside rather than inside and they weren't interested in being "gossipy." I found them less socially demanding. This became a problem with my stepfather when he began to see them as a threat. I was about fourteen at the time.

I have always been alone. I don't think I ever considered telling. I knew no one who could cope with sharing this awful secret. Now I know that it wasn't my secret and I no longer feel isolated. Having met other Survivors, I feel sad for what they have been through, but it has helped me realize that being abused wasn't my fault. I don't have to be ashamed. I know now I am not alone, that the feelings that I had were not abnormal, and that I am not crazy. Now I am free, and I am in control of my life. I know who I am. I am full of hope for the future.

Eileen's story

I think that my uncle must have sexually abused me from the age of two or three years old. I was told that I began to be a "naughty child" about this age. I was continually disruptive from then on. I thought that if I did something really naughty, someone might find out that my uncle was putting his hand down my panties and hurting me with his fingers. I played "dare games" with my friends in the hope I would get hurt and would be taken to the hospital and away from my uncle. My father was away in the military and mother was still suffering from the death of my younger sister and didn't notice anything beyond my attention–seeking behavior.

I started school on my fourth birthday. This was one year earlier than the usual age in those days. Being sent to school early was a form of rejection to me and I resented being there. As soon as the teacher turned her back I ran away. I arrived home before my mother by a different route. This was a daily routine for almost three years. The resentment built up in me even stronger because I was punished regularly. We lived one and a half miles from school and my mother spent most of her day walking back and forth between home and school, determined to get me used to it. I eventually did.

My mother and I visited my grandparents almost daily. I was sent regularly to deliver messages and to do errands for my uncle who lived on the same street. My earliest memories are of knocking on Uncle's door. The door would open and I would be quickly pulled into the house. He would lock the door and push me against the wall beside the window and put his hands down my panties and touch me. He told me that if I told anyone what was happening, I would be punished for what I had done wrong.

The feelings of guilt and fear increased in me. I felt very confused, helpless, dirty and disgusted. There was no one to talk to. I was very much alone and very lonely. I was desperately unhappy and cried silently for help, but no one could hear me. There was constant pain and soreness in my genitals, but no one noticed that either.

By the time I was eight years old, he was partially penetrating my body with his penis. Although he did not climax at this time, he gained great pleasure from the abuse. At the age ten, I was suffering from gross anxiety and displaying more behavior problems than ever. I had nightmares of his overweight, stocky body, his thick glasses and his aggressive manner in his excitement. His heavy breathing and his sweaty hands as he held me down repulsed me, and I would wake up in the night, crying, afraid and shaking with fear. I began to have frequent bouts of vaginal pain when passing urine. I was unaware at the time that I was suffering from cystitis and that this was connected to the abuse.

By the time I was eleven the feelings of guilt and unhappiness were very prominent. I cried every night and lived in constant fear of the next attack. My personal hygiene became an obsession in order to cleanse my mind and body of the dirty feelings from the abuse that was forced on me. I hated him for abusing me and gaining pleasure from it and causing me pain and misery. My vagina was constantly sore and the thought of his sperm seeping from my body following intercourse nauseated me. He obviously never stopped to think how I felt and only appeared to be concerned for his own selfish needs.

My schoolwork suffered despite the struggle to learn. The abuse was always first in my thoughts; learning came second. I was encouraged by the schoolteacher to take an advanced-placement examination. She said I had the ability but didn't apply it. I failed the exam miserably, possibly due to a lack of knowledge, but mainly through lack of concentration. I constantly hoped that the teacher would guess the reason for my misery and poor schoolwork. I was too young to realize that no one has a crystal ball in their head to read unspoken words and thoughts. I thought no one would want to help me, even if they could, because I was dirty, disgusting and unworthy of help. I was not even fit to be a human being because of the disgraceful things I did.

My abuse continued, until one day when I was fourteen, he attempted to attack me as though it was his lawful right. He tried to pull me to the floor and started to grope his hand up my skirt. I began to struggle and fight, hitting him anywhere my fist would reach while avoiding his hands in resistance. He was shocked at my reaction at first, but soon recovered when I hit him on the face with one hand and at the same time pulled his hand away from tearing at my underwear. It was a struggle because he was a very strong man, but miraculously I managed to get away from him. When I reached home I burst into a flood of tears and, very briefly, told my father what had happened. He went to see my uncle. I never discovered what action my father took to resolve the situation but the abuse never occurred again. My parents obviously thought it was a one-time incident. I was never asked, and I didn't tell them otherwise. Possibly the reason they didn't ask me was that the abuser was a family member, so it was kept quiet and covered up.

I carried the secret for fifty years because even in my adult life there was no one I could trust with my story. In the past years the press has publicized stories of rape and abuse and the females have often been accused of provocation and of being the guilty party. On the strength of that I felt no one would believe me either. I had pushed the experiences of the abuse to the back of my mind and pretended it had not happened, or so I thought. That is, until the nightmares and flashbacks pushed it forward again. Whenever child abuse was publicized I always felt very sympathetic toward the abused and extremely angry at the abuser. It never occurred to me that I understood because it had happened to me. It would have been too painful to remember my childhood experiences and associate them with others who were suffering the same. I felt unworthy, dirty, disgusted, ashamed and unfit to be a human being. I felt depersonalized, detached and I had lost my personal identity. I became a victim of life.

Wrestling throughout my life with the emotional misery and torment of abuse has been very difficult, but with determination and group therapy I have overcome the major difficulties in the emotional side of my life. The abuse has changed my personality and I have often wondered what or who I would have been without the traumatic experiences. I have been burdened by the misery of my emotions all my life up to the present time. I often think of the "other me" and what it would be like to have had not only a happy, contented childhood, but also a peaceful and happy transit into adult life. Now that I have been to a Survivors group and have told my story, maybe one day I will find the real me.

Anita's story

Looking back on my life and recalling events leading up to my abuse, I have no happy memories at all. I'm sure there must have been some good times, but I really can't remember any. I never felt loved and secure as a child. My father was always drunk and became very violent and abusive toward my mother. I was terrified of him. My mother was always tired and overworked, and I can't remember ever seeing her smile. Neither of them ever gave me love or affection, and I was desperate for a little love. I tried so hard to make them love me, but I always got everything wrong. I was a shy, clumsy child, and I was constantly put down and ridiculed at home and at school. As I grew older, I became more and more shy and insecure. I had no friends and was terribly lonely.

Eventually my father left home and moved in with a girlfriend. At first he came to see us, but gradually his visits stopped. My older sister moved out to live with him and that was the last I saw of both of them. My mom by this time was working every waking hour and I never saw her, either. Now that I was the oldest girl at ten years old, I came home from school to an empty house, did all the housework and made a meal for my older brother and younger sister.

Around the same time I became very ill and was diagnosed diabetic. I spent two months in the hospital with no desire to get better at all. The only visitor I had in all that time was my mom, and she found it really difficult to visit because she had to work. I felt very guilty because of this. My mom had had a terrible life and now that it was just getting better, I had to go and get sick and become an even greater burden than I was already.

While I was in the hospital, my mother remarried. When I came home, my stepfather made a terrible fuss over me. I felt so special! I had never had attention like this before and I loved it. In fact I made a point of showing off to my brother and sister. "I'm his favorite," I'd say, "He really loves me." I threw myself at him. Every time he sat down I'd jump on his knee and throw my arms around him. He'd kiss and cuddle me and I felt so special. I immediately began to call him Daddy and was sure at last that I did have a real daddy who really loved me. I soon began to realize that I didn't get cuddled as often when other people were around, but I put this down to him not wanting to make my brother and sister jealous. He began taking me for long rides in his car. He'd park in a lonely spot and then start to kiss me, but somehow the kisses weren't the same. They were sloppy and wet and I didn't like it. I didn't dare tell him, though. He also started touching me all over my body. This made me feel uncomfortable because I really didn't understand it. It was a really funny feeling and I wished he wouldn't do it. Each time we went out he did this more and more. He also started breathing funny and I began to feel frightened.

My mom was working most nights now, and he started telling me to wait after the others went to bed. He told me he loved me, but I couldn't tell anybody, because no one would understand and I'd get into trouble. We'd keep these special times secret just between us because he loved me so much. "And you do understand, Anita, it's because I love you so much that I do these things to you. Don't be frightened. I won't hurt you. You'll like it, I promise. I do love you." But he did hurt me. It was horrible. He did terrible things to me and I was so frightened. He talked to me all the time, telling me how wonderful everything was. "It's good, isn't it, Anita? You like this, don't you? I told you you would, didn't I?" I was so scared I couldn't move. My body was stiff and tears were rolling down my checks. Yet still he seemed to be in a fantasy world, believing I was really enjoying it.

He was so perverted. I feel sick at the thought of the things he did to me. As he became excited he began to slaver and dribble all over me, and he'd grunt just like a pig. I tried so hard to cry out. I opened my mouth but nothing happened. I had now become quite sick and withdrawn. All the teachers thought it was on account of my being diabetic. I didn't even think about my diabetes; I made myself ill on purpose. On several occasions I became so ill I was taken to the hospital for tests and re-stabilization. This was the only relief I ever got.

When I was fourteen, I had become such a freak at school I was a constant source of fun for the other kids. One day a couple of girls were making fun of me, referring to the fact I had never had a boyfriend and trying to embarrass me by asking me all sorts of silly questions about sex. Had I ever tried this or had that done to me? I became so fed up with it I broke down in tears and told them all to leave me alone, because in actual fact I had had more experience than all of them and knew more than they'd ever know. One girl, though, persisted and wanted to know what I was talking about, so I told her. She was shocked and then insisted on dragging me off to our school counselor.

I couldn't really tell the school counselor anything, only that my stepfather had done things to me, which is all I ever said to anybody. He then told my mother. I was terrified of facing her. I felt as if I'd wrecked her life once again. Her first words to me were, "Why didn't you tell me? Why did you tell someone else?" This seemed to have really hurt her and I felt guiltier than ever. She promised me it wouldn't happen again and that was an end to it. It wasn't mentioned again. It did stop for a couple of weeks and then one day he came in to tell me how sorry he was. He began to cry and he put his arm around me. As he did this, he began all over again. Later I told my mother he had started doing things again and she said she'd make him stop. By this time he seemed to realize he could get away with anything, and so now he didn't even wait for my mom to be out of the house. I never knew when he was going to appear next. I'd be certain he was out of the house so I'd risk running a bath and he seemingly appeared from nowhere.

My life was a nightmare. I decided the only answer to my problems was to end it all, so I overdosed on my insulin and put myself in a coma. Of course I was saved, and sent to a child psychologist, who told me all my problems were due to being called "matchstick legs" as an infant. After this episode, I was desperate and took it upon myself one day to try out a bar. I found that, with a little makeup and the right clothes, I looked attractive and got served easily. This became a way of numbing myself. I couldn't make the problem go away, but at least I could make it bearable. I stopped going to school. I'd just disappear into the park with a bottle of vodka. The teachers never seemed to notice. I started going out every night. I'd just walk into a bar and I'd always get served. I was fifteen by this time and had just stopped caring.

I started getting invited to parties. The first time I went to one I stayed out all night. When I got home, he was waiting for me. He began to hit me. I thought he would never stop. He told me I'd worried my mother to death and how dare I do this. After that first time it was much easier. I told my mom I was going out and I didn't know if I'd be home and she seemed to accept it. I went out almost every night. I was always drunk and I slept around. I just didn't care. I smoked dope and took LSD, anything so I didn't have to feel.

Then one day the guy I spent the night with seemed to have become crazy about me and asked me to marry him. I was now sixteen, so I said "Yes." My mom agreed and that was that. A month later we were married. Soon afterward I was rushed into the hospital with acute liver damage and was told I must consider alcohol a poison. I didn't take another drink for three years. Instead, I became obsessed with having a baby, and eventually, after losing a couple, I had a baby. This was the unconditional, natural love I'd been waiting for all my life, and it was all I wanted.

Our marriage was a joke. There was nothing between us. We led separate lives, and I wouldn't have sex unless I really couldn't get out of it. I made excuse after excuse. Luckily, the first time we did have sex after our daughter was born, I got pregnant again, so I didn't have to bother any more with sex until after the birth of our second child. After our son was born, I had a lot of illnesses and used this as an excuse. I eventually had to have a big operation. When I got over this, my husband became impatient. He came home drunk one night and raped me. From this our third child was born and immediately afterward my husband walked out and left us.

After this I became obsessed with dieting. After a short period of anorexia, I became bulimic (bingeing on food and vomiting), and it took over my life. It's the only way I have of coping with life, because deep down I really detest myself. I am desperately lonely and unhappy, and I just can't wait for life to hurry up and finish. I've had a couple of disastrous relationships since the breakup of my marriage. I just can't seem to make them work. I hate sex and men and find it difficult to make friends generally with anybody. I keep trying hard to make my life work. I adore my children and I don't think I give them what they deserve, but I keep on trying and maybe one day I'll get it right.

It seems everything I try I fail at, and the harder I try, the bigger the mess I make. I moved and tried to make a new start shortly after the breakup of my marriage. The first time I gave in and accepted a little practical help from a man, I ended up being held prisoner in my own home for three days, repeatedly raped and abused. Then I got into a relationship with a man so manipulative and possessive it was like reliving my childhood all over again. After so many horrific experiences, I wonder if maybe it's been me who has caused it all along. My own daughter was molested at age four by a man at a resort. I wonder if all men are abusers. Maybe they are normal and I am the one with a problem.

I have recently found a faith in God, which has kept me going and helped me believe in myself more. I am gaining confidence gradually now and hopefully beginning a whole new life.

Graham's story

My story is an account of the physical, mental and sexual abuse that I was subjected to starting from at least five years old. There are some memories from when I was even younger, but they are vague and I can't make sense of them. Apparently my aunt looked after me for the first year until my mother took me back, probably for the welfare benefits. I have always known that my mother didn't like me, but it's hard to think she didn't want me from birth. It probably would have been better if she had opted for an abortion rather than subject me to the life I have had.

For as long as I can remember, my mother has always tried to hurt and embarrass me in front of friends or whoever else might be around. She always called me "little bastard." When I was little, I drew on my face with a pen, and she scrubbed my face until it was bleeding. Once she tried to kill me. She tried to drown me in the bathtub, holding my head under the water. I think it was because I woke up with a soiled diaper. I can still see that face from under the water. She was slapping me and shaking her fist as though she was going to thump me in the face. My head was in the water with my eyes wide open and I could see the anger in her face. I tried to breathe but my mouth and nose filled with water. I can remember struggling, and then I was on the bathroom floor, coughing. She dragged me downstairs, pulled me across her knee, spanked me and told me not to do that again.

I was usually sent to bed at 7:00 P.M. and I cried myself to sleep. I never knew if I would wake up in my own bed or hers. She would go to bed around 11:00 P.M. and about half an hour later I would hear her pathetic voice calling me. I would pretend to be asleep, hoping she would stop. She never did stop. She would get louder and louder until I could detect her voice getting angry. I knew if I didn't answer her, she would come marching into my room and literally drag me from my bed into hers. If she saw I had wet my bed she would hit me. It got to a point that I answered right away and got into her bed so I wouldn't be spanked for wetting the bed until the next morning. When I got into her bed she cuddled me. I didn't like this because I knew what was coming next. She would slowly rub her grubby hands all over my body. She would squeeze me closer to her and I would try to turn my head away from the smell of tobacco and beer. She would rub baby lotion between my legs and bottom. She would gradually get more aggressive, touching my genitals and squeezing them in her cupped hand. She would move her other hand under me and push her fingers into my bottom. It hurt me but I knew I had to try not to cry or she would get angry and hit me. After this she would move to the bottom edge of the bed and position herself rather like a woman having a baby. I can't get myself to say what happened next. I cannot cope even thinking about this, let alone living with it.

It is f—ing disgusting to me to live my life knowing she made me have sex and oral sex with her. It is so degrading and I try to forget. It hurts so much because she is my mother.

Her boyfriend used to come and stay for days on end. If I didn't do something they wanted me to do, she would make me sleep naked in a cupboard all night and tell me Jack Frost or Dickie Dark was waiting for me. One night when she went out with her friends, he stayed in to baby-sit me. As soon as he was alone, he sat me on his knee and put his hand under my bottom. He ended up with one of his fingers in my bottom. He put some sort of lubrication on his penis and had full anal sex and I screamed. It made me soil the bed and he slapped me for that and for crying because he hurt me. Until then I had never experienced such pain. He gave me some pin money and told me this was our secret.

I am disgusted that I was often taken into their bed and told to do things to both of them. The things a decent parent wouldn't think of. I didn't know that having sex with her or with him was wrong because I'd never known anything else, but I never understood why it used to hurt so much. It continued until she died, and I am sure that if she was still alive it would still be going on now. I wished someone would help me and stop them from hurting me. I tried to do what they told me to do because sometimes they were nice to me if I did it properly.

She used to let him take me to his house on Friday nights and he would take me back home on Sunday nights. She used to do some kind of preparation for when he came. She would pull my pants down and put me over her knee. She would put two suppositories in my bottom and tell me to sit on a potty. After a while she stopped using suppositories and would lay me on a table in the bathroom. She fixed a tube to the tap and put the other end up my bottom. She would turn the tap on and my abdomen used to swell up and it hurt like hell. She wasn't careful with me and she often made me bleed from my bottom, which frightened me. She didn't care and made me wear a diaper, even to school, to stop the blood showing through my pants. It didn't stop either of them from having sex with me and penetrating me.

I didn't like going to his house. There were always other children there and one of the worst parts was being stripped naked and left with the other children in a toy room. There was also loads of adults. Some of them were nice but the others didn't even talk. I had to do some things to them like oral sex. Sometimes they would spank me, others pushed things into my bottom even though they knew it hurt me. There were a few who just wanted to treat me as their baby. My mother knew I was being taken to his house and used as a child prostitute with men, women and other children.

When I was about nine years old I ran away. After two days my mother phoned the police, who brought me home from the railroad station where I'd been sleeping. I wish I'd told the police why I'd run away, but I was scared of what they would do to me and I knew it was all my fault and no one would believe me. When the police left, my mother and her boyfriend made me strip naked, then beat me all over my body with a belt until my body was covered with belt marks. From then on I did everything they told me to do, no matter how dirty I thought it was.

My mother had many suicide attempts and I was always having to phone for an ambulance. She eventually killed herself when I was fifteen years old. The last time I saw her boyfriend was when I was seventeen. I was on my way home after a night out. He and three of his friends trapped me in a public toilet and decided to rape me, with two girls chanting and egging them on. They threw me around, punched me and kicked me and I couldn't do anything but beg them to stop. He used the same phrase he always used: "Are you going to be nice to me? We've got a lot of catching up to do." He started to undo his pants and the other three dragged me over and literally tore my trousers and underpants off me. The two girls started to join in, chanting "f–k him, f–k him." I will never forget that as long as I live. They anally raped me and made me perform oral sex. They left me bleeding and naked on the floor and told me they would find me if I reported it to the police. I locked myself in my studio for three weeks and was eventually committed and kept sedated in a psychiatric hospital for a year.

I don't know what it is like to have a mother. A mother who would show me affection and occasionally put her arms around me to make me feel safe and cared for. I hate myself and I have tried to get this out of me. I have washed, scrubbed and torn my skin to get the abusers off me. I take laxatives to get it all away from me but it won't go away. I feel ashamed and unclean and never feel as if my body or the house is clean enough. I have tried to kill myself many times, but I won't do that now because I have children to care for. At times the abuse seems to come flooding back to me. Even though my mother is dead, I still can't go into the bathroom without hearing her calling my name and I feel her pushing me. In addition to these hallucinations I have nightmares, flashbacks and panic attacks. The abuse has left me unable to show affection to my wife and children. I hate the torment I've put my wife and children through, shouting at them and shutting everyone and everything out of my life. I spent days on end secluded in my own room. I was punishing myself through a sea of bad memories.

A couple of years ago I got very depressed. I was going through a bad crisis in my life, and I was getting no help or support from anywhere. My wife searched for help for me and found all the help was aimed at women. It made me feel that it is okay to rape a man and use a boy as a child prostitute. I eventually got a referral for clinical psychology. I dreaded seeing the psychologist and needed a lot of pushes from my wife but it wasn't as bad as I thought it would be. I felt a lot of relief. Since then I have been receiving weekly therapy sessions. It makes me feel better, knowing that just talking to someone I trust frees me of some of the bad thoughts I had about myself. I feel a lot better in myself and, although I'm not at the end of my therapy yet, I am coping and can deal with life a lot better.

Pam's story

My mom and dad had to get married because I was an unexpected arrival. Throughout my childhood I felt this was why they both treated me so badly. They never bought me clothes, shoes, school uniforms, etc. They made me baby-sit my brother and two sisters and I had to do the housework, washing and ironing. I was a stand-in housewife in more ways than one.

One Saturday in August when I was twelve years old, my mom went shopping and as usual my father was left to look after us all. I went upstairs to wrap my mom's birthday present. I couldn't quite do it, so my dad came upstairs into my brother's bedroom, supposedly to help. As I was walking out the door my dad grabbed me, pulled me onto the bed and ripped my shirt out of my skirt. I began to shout and scream and kick. Nobody came to help me.

He started fondling my body and sucking my breasts and then he pulled my pants down. I was still shouting and screaming and kicking. My brother came upstairs demanding, "What's going on?" My dad threatened him with a beating, so my brother went back downstairs, none the wiser.

My dad kept trying to shut me up. He said I would enjoy it. After he had finished he walked off, leaving me crying into the pillow. He came back fully dressed shouting, "Hurry up and get dressed before your mother gets back." I walked into the bathroom. My father came in and pulled my bra back down and then left me.

For years my dad had made sexual comments to me, and tried to put me on the pill as soon as my periods began, but this was the first time he'd raped me. It went on for another two years.

I had nightmares and "daymares" all the time. I became withdrawn, defiant and snappy. I felt as if my whole body was crawling. I felt so dirty and used. The same kind of thing had happened to me before, but with a different, older, member of the family. This left me wondering if I was different from everybody else. I was all alone. Fears of becoming pregnant constantly ran through my mind.

I mentioned the rape to the social worker who was visiting our family at the time. He wasn't interested. My mother commented on my change of behavior, so I told her. She said I was a liar and should have been drowned at birth. Nobody was willing to help, so I ran away and took an overdose, but it didn't work and I ended up back home.

At seventeen, I met and fell in love with my first husband, who was twelve years older. I left home to live with him and we got married eventually, but he couldn't accept what had happened to me and also decided he didn't want any children. He turned out to be just like my father—he beat me regularly—so I left him and filed for divorce.

After my divorce, my faith in men disappeared completely and the nightmares continued. Then eighteen months later I met my second husband, who guessed there was something wrong between me and my father, so I told him the story. He was the first person whom I had told and who had understood. Six months later I was pregnant and we had a son. One year later we married. Then I started suffering from depression and agoraphobia. I thought this was a buildup of trying to cope with a baby, work full time and having a falling-out with my parents. After seeing my doctor, I realized my problems had to do with the sexual abuse. She referred me to a psychiatrist, who wasn't much help because he was a man, but he referred me to a clinical psychologist who ran a support group for women who had been abused as children.

During the group sessions, emotions ran high. I relived the entire horrible episode again, often beating my husband in my sleep, shouting and screaming at my father in my nightmares. I became very depressed. After about ten weeks of the group, I confronted my mother and father by locking them in my house and telling them how much I hated them and why. At last my mother believed me. As soon as they went home I felt so much better for getting it off my chest. Now the healing process could begin.

I am now in control of my emotions. I don't have nightmares any more and my marriage is even better for having gone through this trauma. I don't think I could have done it without the love, understanding and thoughtfulness of my husband, whose love and devotion spurred me to get treatment in the first place.

I have now forgiven my father, although I will never forget. He knows this, my mom knows this and now we get on OK. We understand each other, and keep our distance. My life has meaning for the first time and I can honestly say, there is life after abuse.

Dorothy's story

(Dorothy has never attended a Survivors group. She came to see us only once, after she had taken an overdose, and then sent us her story. She wrote, "I am sorry that my spelling is so bad, but that's what happens when you haven't had much schooling. I began to tear this letter up but decided it might be useful to others." We think so too. We found her letter so powerful we asked if we could publish it in full.)

As far as I am concerned, my life began at the time my daughter was conceived. If I go back to my childhood or my teenage years, I am only filled with sadness. I would rather die than live those years again.

I have been told that I was a perfect baby and a very bubbly child who loved being around people. I was a tomboy who enjoyed school and was very bright and always eager to please. I was a chatterbox with a constant giggle and was loved by everyone. Around seven or eight years old I suddenly changed and became sullen and withdrawn. I was always alone and would not talk to anyone or smile. I wouldn't go to school. I was truant, and if I did go to school I was disruptive. I ran away a lot and spent most of my time alone in secluded fields and isolated areas.

I began to have fits and blackouts and memory loss. No one could understand why my personality had changed so suddenly— no one but me and my older brother.

He was the one who abused me time after time after time. I never told anyone what was happening to me, and I grew more insecure and afraid as time went by. I now remember well what my brother did to me. I remember the cold bathroom floor, my hands tucked tightly under my chin and the fear and silent tears. I remember well the pain as things were pushed inside me, things left inside me and the blood between my rigid legs. I remember the penis in my body and in my mouth. I remember the taste. I remember the throbbing inside my head and my ears, and I remember always waking up under a pile of coats in a dark lobby.

I think my teens were the worst. In my early teens, I wanted to be like other girls, who all seemed to have boyfriends. Lots of boys asked me out and I did go with one or two, but as soon as a boy touched me, I froze. I would just run, often for miles without stopping, only to fall down in a dead faint. I soon became known as Miss Ice or Miss Fits. It was hard to cope with life and I often tried to hide from it by running away and sleeping under bushes.

Even though my brother had married and didn't live at home any more, I still hated being at home and I would do anything to get away from it. I even pretended to go to sleep in people's houses, hoping they might let me stay over. I hated my body so much that I cut it with glass and razor blades. I put pepper into my eyes so I wouldn't have to look at anyone. I withdrew more and more. I rarely left my bedroom. I started writing stories, but the stories developed a sordid quality. I wrote about little girls being sexually abused and I drew pictures to go with the stories. When my parents found my stories they forbade me to go to my room until bedtime. I hated not being able to go to my room, having no place to hide, to feel safe and at peace. I ran away and ended up in another city, where I sat all day by a lake. Eventually someone found me collapsed in the middle of a busy road. I was taken to a hospital late at night. Two days later, when they discovered who I was, I was transferred to another hospital.

Eventually I got a job close to home, as a nanny to a 7-month-old boy. The baby became very dependent on me because his parents weren't around much. I loved this baby and was very happy. I had my own room with a lock on the door and my own warm bed. I loved the job and I was never sick in all that time. Suddenly it ended. The baby and his parents were moving to the coast. They wanted to take me with them, but my parents said no. I was depressed at the thought of going back home, and I missed the baby more than I thought possible. Once I was back home, I withdrew again and the fits started.

When I was seventeen, I met and married a 17-year-old boy. We found a cozy little house and made it really nice. I loved that little house and cleaned and polished it all day long. I loved to cook and try new dishes, but soon my sparkling little house was gone and my bubble burst. Within the year the marriage was over, it was never consummated and had no real love in it. I was back home and my parents sold all the contents of my home.

I couldn't take it any more. I had had enough of life and hated fighting it all the way. I felt my life was meaningless and would never go anywhere. I took a massive overdose and ended up in a light coma. I lost most of my hair and became more depressed than ever. I ended up in a psychiatric hospital, where I was given shock treatments. Then I was taken to a different hospital and put into some sort of sleep that let me go back in time, back to being a little girl. I got to the age of eight and went into convulsions and this treatment wasn't used on me again.

No one ever knew what had happened to me, though doctor after doctor tried in vain to find out. I must have put up a block that no one could penetrate, not even the best doctors. From the age of fourteen to the age of nineteen I had lots of electric shock treatments and so many doctors that I never got used to one. Still I told no one. The fits continued, the depression, the attempts on my life. My fear of men grew stronger, and I grew more and more withdrawn, until I rarely ever left the house and only spoke when spoken to.

One night I woke and heard my mother talking to dad. She was wondering what would become of me and how it was a shame I'd been born. Dad said I would go into a home when they were old. I couldn't believe my parents had given up on me, even though I'd given up on myself. Over the next few weeks I began to try, by baking and sewing and going for walks on my own. Soon after, my mom introduced me to the man I married. He was fifteen years older than me, needed somebody to look after him, was very lonely and very undemanding. I made a good wife and was determined to prove to everyone that I could make it. I had to show them that I wasn't abnormal like they thought, that I wouldn't end up in some home, that I was capable of doing anything other women did. I knew I could cope; I had to show others, too. My husband wanted for nothing. He had little sex drive, so we had no problem in that area. We made a nice home and I was fairly happy. I longed for a child.

As a young teenager, my mother took me to several doctors, who always give me an internal examination. I never knew why and I never asked, but I always blacked out before the examination was completed. Now I was married and longing for a child but it wouldn't happen. I went to my doctor who gave me yet another examination. This time I didn't black out, but I nearly did when he told me I'd never be a mother. I couldn't accept this. I wouldn't give up hope. I cried every month when I had my meaningless period. I would go through anything for a child and asked for more medical help. In the hospital I underwent long and almost unbearable examinations. I was told I'd never be able to conceive and also asked if I'd been interfered with as a child. I went home in tears. For the next two years I went into every church I could find.

Eventually I did get pregnant. While I was in labor I had some sort of flashbacks. I saw pictures of myself as a little girl. I was frightened and I tried to push it away, but with each pain came a picture, a picture so clear it was lifelike. I saw myself on the bathroom floor and my brother too. By the time my daughter was born, I had completed the jigsaw but I was so preoccupied by the gift of my child that I put it in the back of my mind again. I just wanted to concentrate upon this perfect extension of my life. Later when my daughter was less dependent upon me, I began to reflect again upon my childhood pictures and my jigsaw puzzle. I began to analyze myself and my problems. I realized that I had never been abnormal, just a victim of circumstance. What my brother had done to me had left me scared and insecure. I couldn't trust those who were close to me and couldn't trust men. My father had never hugged, kissed or touched me. In fact, I had never felt really loved by any man, not even my husband, who was never romantic, never loving or warm. He was a selfish man and cruel in many ways to my daughter and me.

After my daughter's birth I was told never to become pregnant again, but twelve years later I gave birth to a son. Things had been getting worse with my husband, and when our son was just two years old, I left him. The next two years were a nightmare. I've never felt so isolated. I moved to a new house and a new town, and I didn't only lose a marriage but also my friends and family. My son was always sick and I didn't know anyone.

Now four years later I have a happy home full of warmth and love and laughter. My daughter is almost eighteen and my best friend. She's engaged to a good boy and I look forward to having him extend my family by becoming my son-in-law. My daughter works hard and enjoys life. She thinks a lot of her 5-year-old brother. It's not easy to be a mother to a young boy when you reach middle age and have no man in your life, but it's an adventure I wouldn't want to miss. My son is full of energy and loves to bring me slugs and worms and gets me to climb trees with him, and put on my rubber boots and take him fishing. My daughter and my son are the reason I live and my reason for being born. I've gotten so much love from these two young people that I could never lack love again.

The sexual abuse was very dirty and painful, and so I associate pain and fear with sex and with men. I blacked out because I didn't know how else to deal with it. I became distrustful of all people and I've isolated myself most of my life. Now at 43 and alone, it is harder and I do get lonely. I do often wonder what it would be like to be held by a tender, loving man. To be able to do what others take for granted. I would like to have confidence and be able to walk out of my home without feeling the whole world is looking at me.

My brother is free—he had his childhood and his teens, his marriage and he got no punishment. I am a prisoner in my own body, I was denied my childhood and my teens and I've lost two marriages. I sometimes hate my brother and wish he were dead, but most of the time I just feel nothing toward him. I try not to think about it, but every now and then I have nightmares, always the same. I'm always sobbing, always bleeding, always in pain, with him forcing things into my vagina. I understand myself now, I was abused terribly for some years, damaged in mind and body, I needed my parents but they weren't there. I have been paying all my life for my brother's crime.

Further reading

Other accounts of sexual abuse can be found in the books below.

General

The Memory Bird: Survivors of Sexual Abuse. Linda Farthing, Caroline Malone and Lorraine Marce (eds). Philadelphia, PA: Temple University Press, 1997.

Autobiography

Angelou, Maya. *I Know Why the Caged Bird Sings.* New York: Bantam Books, 1983.

Armstrong, Louise. *Kiss Daddy Goodnight: Ten Years Later.* New York: Pocket Books, 1987.

Chase, Truddi. *When Rabbit Howls.* Jove Publications, 1990.
The story of a woman who developed multiple personalities to survive her abuse.

Fiction

Harrison, Kathryn. *Thicker Than Water.* New York: Bard Books, 1998.

Morris, Michele. *If I Should Die before I Wake.* New York: Dell Publishing Co., 1982.

Vachss, Andrew. *Shella: A Novel.* New York: Alfred A. Knopf, 1993.

Walker, Alice. *The Color Purple.* New York: Washington Square Press, 1983.

3

The Damage Caused by Sexual Abuse

I n the last chapter, Jane, Eileen, Anita, Graham, Pam and Dorothy
shared their experiences of being sexually abused as children.
Each Survivor's story is different. They were abused in different
ways, by different people and for different lengths of time. Linking
each Survivor's experience, however, is the pain they have
suffered, the damage that has been done to them, and the ways
they have struggled to survive. Each Survivor is at a different stage
of working through his or her difficulties, but each has found
courage and hope. Each has come to realize that, as Pam says,
"there is life after abuse." After the first meeting of a Survivors
group, group members say they feel relieved and surprised to find
they are not alone. They discover other people have had similar
experiences and have suffered similar problems as a result of being
abused. By the beginning of the second meeting, the Survivors
have usually found some reason why they think they are still
different from the rest of the group and shouldn't be there:

+ I was only abused once.
+ I was abused by a woman.
+ I had more than one abuser.
+ The abuser didn't have intercourse with me.
+ I was a teenager when I was abused.
+ It started when I was a baby.
+ The abuser wasn't a family member.
+ I enjoyed the sexual stimulation.

+ I've never tried to kill myself.
+ What happened to me doesn't seem as bad as what happened to everyone else.

Many Survivors feel frightened and distressed when they see how sexual abuse has damaged other Survivors. By focusing on the differences between their experiences and other people's, they may try to convince themselves that they haven't been affected as badly. Survivors often feel guilty, ashamed and worthless, so emphasizing these differences may be a way of saying, "I don't deserve to be helped." Feeling different is also a lifelong habit for many Survivors.

All of the women in chapter 2 were abused by male family members (a father, two stepfathers, a brother and an uncle). Most abusers are men, but up to 20% of abusers are women. Some women abusers, like Graham's mother, sexually abuse their own children. Abusers can be male or female relatives, friends, strangers, older children and people in positions of authority. Abuse includes many different types of physical acts or may not even involve physical contact. The physical acts of abuse described in chapter 2 include exposing genitals, fondling, masturbation, intercourse and penetration with objects. The acts are different, but they are all acts of abuse. Sexual abuse may also involve animals, group sex, rituals and torture. Sexual abuse can occur on a regular basis over many years by one or several abusers, or it may happen on only one occasion.

Jane, Eileen, Anita, Graham, Pam and Dorothy have all had different experiences but they have all been sexually abused. Try to remember what you were thinking as you were reading chapter 2. Were you emphasizing the differences between your experiences and theirs? Your story may be quite different from theirs, but if you have had an inappropriate or unwanted sexual experience, you have suffered abuse.

The Survivors in chapter 2 all have been affected both as children and as adults by being sexually abused. Some Survivors develop serious problems in many areas of their lives and are unable to cope. Some have support and resources when children and adults that enable them to overcome the effects of their abusive experiences. Others may appear to cope well on the surface, but are struggling with fears and insecurities underneath. Table 1 (page 37) shows the most common long-term effects of sexual abuse. Frequently Survivors do not realize the extent to which they have been affected by being sexually abused.

> Before I joined a Survivors' group, I felt confused—did the abuse really happen? I even thought I'd come through it unscathed; it hadn't really affected me. I was blindfolded; everything has been affected—me, my personality, my sexuality, my relationships with everyone—parents/adults/friends, male and female. Who was I? Who am I? Jocelyn

Before Jocelyn joined a Survivors' group, she felt sometimes that getting depressed, having feelings she couldn't cope with and not liking to make close friendships was just part of her personality. She was amazed to find that the other women in the group had similar feelings and difficulties. Gradually the patterns began to appear and she realized that her present difficulties were connected to her childhood abuse.

Like Jocelyn, Survivors often think

+ That's just the way I am.
+ I'm not lovable, that's why I keep having disastrous relationships.
+ I'm not very smart, that's why I didn't do well at school.
+ I'm a loner.
+ I'm a weak person.
+ I'm not very nice.
+ I was a difficult child.

Many survivors find it difficult to accept that being sexually abused as a child can continue to affect them years later. Researcher David Finkelhor has tried to explain how sexual abuse affects a child and leads to long-term problems. He suggests four ways in which childhood sexual abuse causes problems: 1. traumatic sexualization; 2. stigmatization; 3. betrayal; 4. powerlessness.

Wakefield Survivors have found this model useful in helping them understand how sexual abuse can affect a person's life in fundamental ways. The process of stigmatization, betrayal and powerlessness apply also to people who have been physically and emotionally abused. We look more closely at this model next.

Finkelhor's model: Four ways in which sexual abuse causes problems

Traumatic sexualization

Children usually feel frightened, confused or distressed when they are being sexually abused and may also experience physical pain. Their early experience of sexual behavior and sexuality are traumatic and inappropriate. The physical and emotional pain involved in sexual abuse means that sex becomes associated with bad feelings. These feelings can continue into adulthood and lead to fears and phobias about sex, and a dislike or avoidance of sex, touching or intimacy. Survivors may have difficulties in becoming aroused or reaching an orgasm, and may experience "flashbacks" to the abuse during sex. In chapter 2, Anita and Dorothy describe their dislike of sex and the ways they tried to avoid it. Graham said he didn't know it was wrong to have sex with his mother and her boyfriend. He also described how painful it was.

However, not all children experience such distress at the time they are being abused because not all abusers are brutal. Anita loved the kisses and cuddles she received from her stepfather at the beginning. Sometimes children enjoy parts of the touching and many experience sexual pleasure and orgasm.

> My father would put his hand between my legs and rub my clitoris (I didn't know what it was then). I would always feel a lot of shame later because what he was doing felt nice. Sandra

However "nonbrutal" the abuse is, when children are sexually abused they are exposed to sexual experiences that are inappropriate or too advanced for their age or level of development. They are also given confusing and incorrect messages about sexual behavior.

As a result of their inappropriate sexual experiences, Survivors can grow up confused about their own sexual feelings and normal sexual behavior. Their sexual experience, knowledge and identity are not allowed to develop naturally. This leads to sexual difficulties in adults ranging from fears and phobias about sex to preoccupation and obsessions with sex. Survivors, like Graham, who were abused by someone of the same sex may have concerns about their sexual orientation. Sexual difficulties are discussed in more detail in chapter 12.

Stigmatization

Some children who are abused may believe for a time, like Graham did, that what is happening to them is "normal." However, at some point most victims feel something is wrong and shameful about the abuse, even when they don't understand exactly what is happening. The abuser may blame the child for the abuse, tell her to keep the abuse secret and frighten her into silence. This secrecy makes the child feel that she has something to be guilty and ashamed about. Other people who are told or who find out about the abuse may be shocked and blame the victim or put pressure on her to remain silent. This can add to the feeling of shame. Jane and Dorothy kept the secret of the sexual abuse all through their childhood. Although no one threatened them, they felt the stigma of the abuse and knew they had to remain silent. Adult Survivors often continue to keep the secret because they are afraid of other people's reactions and because they feel ashamed.

Many Survivors blame themselves for the abuse and continue to feel responsible and guilty for anything bad that happens to them or to other people they know. Survivors often feel bad about themselves and different from other people. They isolate themselves from other people and avoid making close friendships. Graham secluded himself in his bedroom. Eileen has spent most of her adult life feeling dirty, disgusted, ashamed and unfit to be a human being. She has never made close friends and has always felt different from other people. The feelings of shame and guilt can lead Survivors to abuse and punish themselves with drugs, alcohol or through self-mutilation and suicide attempts. Dorothy's feelings of stigma and shame were so great that she mutilated her body with glass and razor blades and by putting pepper in her eyes so that she wouldn't have to look at anyone. She also tried to kill herself. Dorothy still keeps her distance from other people and feels the whole world is looking at her when she leaves the house. Graham felt ashamed and unclean and self-harmed, abused laxatives and cleaned his body excessively. Some Survivors feel so different that they see themselves as outsiders in society, unable to care about what happens to them or what they do. Survivors who feel like this may start to behave in criminal or antisocial ways and end up in court or prison. Feelings of guilt and shame are dealt with in Part Two.

Betrayal

When a child is abused, especially by a relative or someone she knows and likes, her trust in that person is betrayed. Abusers often build trusting relationships with a child and may make her feel wanted and cared for before abusing her. They manipulate her trust and vulnerability and disregard her well being. The child may also feel betrayed by her mother or other nonabusing adults if they do not support and protect her.

Anita was vulnerable. She received very little attention from her real parents and was overwhelmed by the affection shown by her new stepfather. She soon trusted him but the kissing and cuddling turned to abuse; Anita's trust was betrayed. Furthermore, Anita's mother betrayed Anita by failing to protect her from the abuse. Jane's stepfather also betrayed Jane's trust in her "real family" and her new daddy by abusing her. Despite Anita's and Jane's tears and obvious distress, their abusers continued to abuse them. Their well being was disregarded, and they were treated abusively by the very people who were supposed to love and protect them. Graham was abused by his mother, who also allowed him to be used as a child prostitute.

Betrayal can be experienced as a feeling of loss—loss of a trusting and loving relationship. This leads to feelings of grief and depression, or anger and hostility. Fear of betrayal can lead to mistrust of others, especially men, and cause Survivors to withdraw or feel uncomfortable in close relationships. In chapter 2, Dorothy describes her grief at not being able to trust and to form intimate relationships. At 43, she has resigned herself to being alone. On the other hand, some Survivors become extremely dependent and clingy.

Betrayal by the very people one would expect to trust can make it difficult for Survivors to judge how trustworthy other people are. Trustworthy people may be mistrusted, and trust put in those who do not deserve it. This in turn makes the Survivor vulnerable to further abuse and exploitation of herself and her children.

Pam married young and was physically abused by her first husband. Anita experienced further physical and sexual abuse as an adult. Graham was raped as a young adult. Survivors do not ask to be abused again and are not responsible for the abuse. However, sexual abuse may leave Survivors more vulnerable to further abuse, especially if they are unable to judge trustworthiness or feel compelled to cling to bad relationships. Relationship problems are discussed in Part Four.

Powerlessness

A child experiences an intense sense of powerlessness when she is sexually abused. Her body is touched or invaded against her wishes and this may happen again and again. The abuser manipulates the child or forces the child into abuse. Even if she tells someone else, she may not be able to make them believe her. The child repeatedly experiences fear and an inability to control the situation.

Many children attempt in their own way to try to control the situation and stop the abuse, but their attempts are often useless. Jane sometimes managed to say "No" to her stepfather, but he then behaved badly to the whole family until she gave in again. Jane felt no one would believe her if she tried to tell what was happening because her stepfather appeared to be such a nice man. She was trapped. Anita's mother stopped the abuse for two weeks but then it started again and continued even when Anita's mother was in the house. Anita had nowhere to turn; she was powerless. Pam had been unable to stop the abuse despite shouting, screaming and kicking, nor could she get her mother or the social worker to believe her. Older boys especially believe they should have been physically strong enough to stop the abuse. Feeling powerless leads some children to seek out the abuse in an attempt to feel they have some control over what is happening. Unfortunately this action results in reinforcing their beliefs that they are responsible for the abuse.

The powerlessness experienced in sexual abuse can lead to long-term feelings of being unable to take action or change situations. Survivors thus feel powerless to prevent further abuse. They may end up feeling like victims all their lives. Powerlessness also results in fears, anxiety, phobias and nightmares. Survivors may try to escape from their fears and feelings of powerlessness by running away from home or from school, or by withdrawing emotionally. Emotional withdrawal can take the form of depression, blanking out or blacking out, or living in a fantasy world. Dorothy ran away from home and was truant from school. She suffered from anxieties and nightmares and later retreated into depression, fits and blackouts. Pam suffered from nightmares, depression and agoraphobia when she was nine years old. Graham ran away from home at nine and slept in a train station. Pam's healing really began when she confronted her parents and was able to feel powerful and effective again.

Survivors may also react to feeling powerless by attempting to take control and by making themselves feel more powerful in some way. Eating disorders often involve a desperate attempt to exert some control, by controlling one's food intake and body weight. Some Survivors try to feel more powerful by aggressive behavior, or by bullying, being abusive and controlling other people.

Researchers suggest that women Survivors tend to react passively to this feeling of powerlessness, whereas male Survivors frequently react by trying to exert their own power. If this is true, we would expect more women Survivors to become anxious and depressed, and more male Survivors to become controlling, aggressive or abusive. Anxiety, depression and eating disorders are discussed in Part Three.

Making the connections

Survivors are often affected by being sexually abused not only as children but also in adult life. Many Survivors do not realize that their present problems are connected to their past experiences. David Finkelhor describes four processes by which sexual abuse causes problems. Some of these processes are common to other types of abuse or trauma. Physical abuse by a parent can also cause a child to experience a sense of powerlessness, betrayal and stigmatization. In accidents and disasters, victims frequently experience an overwhelming sense of their own powerlessness and, without help, this can develop into a problem or difficulty. When disasters happen, counseling services are usually brought in to help victims and rescuers deal with the terrifying experiences they have been through. Being sexually abused is like being involved in a disaster, a disaster that may be a one-time incident or may be repeated over many years. Sexual abuse also has the added impact of traumatic sexualization not found in other types of abuse or disasters. Sexual abuse has immediate and long-term effects. Without help, these problems can continue indefinitely. With help, Survivors can and do overcome these problems.

Table 1: Effects of Sexual Abuse

- fears
- anxiety
- phobias
- nervousness
- nightmares
- sleep problems
- depression
- shame
- guilt
- feeling like a victim
- lack of self-confidence
- feeling different from others
- feeling self-conscious
- feeling dirty
- feeling unable to act or change situations
- obsessed with cleaning or washing
- constant worry
- suicide attempts
- self-harming
- blackouts
- fits
- not remembering what has happened for hours or days (blanking out)
- binge-eating
- self-induced vomiting
- compulsive eating
- anorexia nervosa
- no interest in sex
- fear of sex
- obsessed with sex
- avoiding specific sexual activities
- feeling unable to say "No" to sex
- aggressive sexual behavior

- flashbacks
- hearing the abuser's voice when he or she isn't there
- seeing the abuser's face when he or she isn't there
- confusion about sexual orientation (homosexual or heterosexual)
- confusion about sexual identity (male or female)
- unable to get close to people
- marrying young to get away from home
- marital problems
- unable to love, or show affection to, children
- excessive fear for children
- alcohol problems
- drug problems
- employment problems
- being re-victimized
- criminal involvement
- needing to be in control
- delinquency
- bullying
- clinging and being extremely dependent
- abusing others
- aggressive behavior
- anger
- hostility
- problems communicating
- distrusting people
- working too hard
- difficulty in judging people's trustworthiness
- physical problems

Survivors are damaged to different degrees by their experiences. This does not depend on what has happened physically. A Survivor who has been raped will not necessarily be more damaged than a Survivor who has been touched. The degree of damage depends on the degree of traumatic sexualization, stigmatization, betrayal and powerlessness that the child has experienced. This in turn depends on a number of factors, such as

+ who the abuser was
+ how many abusers were involved
+ if the abuser was same-sex or opposite-sex
+ what took place
+ what was said
+ how long the abuse lasted
+ how the child felt and how she interpreted what was happening
+ if the child was otherwise happy and supported
+ how other people reacted to disclosure or discovery of the abuse
+ how old the child was

This book aims to help you understand how your current problems are linked to the abuse and how they can be overcome. For now, just try accepting the idea that being sexually abused will have affected you in some way. This isn't intended to make excuses for your problems; it's a way of trying to understand them and overcome them. You deserve that understanding and help. No matter how small your problems are, they are worth working on; no matter how big your problems are, you can overcome them.

For many Survivors, accepting the connection between sexual abuse and their present problems can be distressing and frightening. They don't want to believe that after all these years the abuse is still affecting them. Accepting the connection, as Jocelyn found, can also be enlightening and hopeful. Problems that could not be explained become understandable, and with understanding comes the possibility and hope of healing.

Exercises

Before doing these exercises, read the notes on writing in chapter 1.

1. Look at the effects of sexual abuse listed in Table 1 and check any that apply to you.

2. Write an account of how you feel you have been affected as a child and as an adult by being sexually abused. It is impossible to know for sure, but use what you have read in this chapter to re-examine your life and make the connections between the sexual abuse and what has happened since that time.

Further reading

Finkelhor, David, and Sharon Araji. *A Source Book on Child Sexual Abuse*. Los Angeles: Sage Publications, 1986.

PART TWO

"It Must Have Been My Fault"

4

Why Me?

Christian
I wanted it

Many survivors have asked themselves the question, "Why me? Why did he choose ME to abuse?" They often answer this question by blaming themselves for what happened:

+ I must have been flirtatious.
+ It must have been something bad in me that she could see.
+ Maybe I led him on.
+ I was big for my age and well developed. — *I was too needy, I did something too kind*
+ It happened because I was the youngest.
+ It happened because I was the oldest.
+ I sat on his knee and snuggled him, and liked it.
+ It's my fault because I was so quiet and shy—it wouldn't have happened if I'd been noisy and outgoing like my sister.
+ I must have acted like I was gay.

Sometimes the abuser has given a reason for the abuse:

+ It happens because you don't show your feelings— I'm teaching you.
+ You look like your mother.
+ You're too friendly with your girlfriends—I'm stopping you from becoming a lesbian.
+ I'm punishing you for being naughty.
+ You gave me signals that you wanted it.

40

A child might well believe such excuses, and adult Survivors may continue believing these explanations and blaming themselves for the abuse. These beliefs keep the Survivor silent and add to feelings of guilt and shame.

Elaine's story

Susan, Anne and Elaine are sisters. All three were sexually abused by their stepfather when they were children. At the time, each one thought she had been specially chosen to be abused. They didn't realize their stepfather was abusing all of them. Susan thought she had been abused because she looked like her mother. Anne had been told by her stepfather that she was frigid and he was teaching her about love. Elaine, the youngest of the sisters, blamed herself for being so quiet and shy: "If I'd been more confident and outgoing like Susan, it wouldn't have happened." Each girl felt she had been singled out to be abused because of her looks, her behavior or her personality. None talked about what was happening to them.

When Elaine was 27, she became deeply depressed and tried to kill herself. For the first time, she told Susan what had happened to her. She couldn't believe what Susan said—that it had happened to her too. When they discovered that Anne had also been abused by their stepfather, all three sisters began to look again at why it had happened to them. They began to think it might not have been their fault after all and to see that it was their stepfather who was responsible for the abuse.

Survivors usually blame themselves for what has happened. But sexual abuse doesn't start with a child; it starts with an abuser. There is nothing special or strange about a child who is being abused. It could happen to anyone. So why does it happen to one person and not another?

Finkelhor's model: Four steps before abuse occurs

We have already looked at David Finkelhor's model about the effects of abuse. Finkelhor has also studied the situations in which sexual abuse occurs and found that four things must happen before a child is abused.

1. There is a person who wants to abuse.

2. The person overcomes inhibitions about abusing.
3. The abuser gets the child alone.
4. The abuser overcomes the child's resistance.

We will discuss each of these steps below.

There is a person who wants to abuse

First, and most important, a victim must have come into contact with a person who wants to abuse a child. It is still not known why certain people want to abuse children. Some abusers have authoritarian and controlling personalities. They do not see children as other people, but as objects they can use for their own benefit. An abuser may be someone who feels socially and sexually inadequate and insecure with other adults. He wants to abuse children to get sexual gratification without risk of rejection. Some abusers are sexually aroused by children. Studies have found that some child abusers show a greater sexual response to photographic slides of children than to slides of adult women, although many child abusers are also in sexual relationships with adults. An abuser may be someone who himself has been sexually, emotionally or physically abused as a child or adult. He may try to make himself feel more powerful by victimizing someone else.

The above are ways of trying to understand why a person wants to abuse a child—they are not excuses or justifications. The abuser is still responsible for the abuse. It is probable that a variety of factors combine to produce a person who wants to abuse but for now we have no clear answers. What we do know is that it is not a case of a person coming into contact with a certain child and suddenly becoming an abuser. Before the abuse occurs there is usually a period where the abuser fantasizes about what he is going to do to a child. The abuser's desire to abuse is not created by the child—it is there before the child appears.

The person overcomes inhibitions about abusing

People who want to abuse know that it is wrong to abuse children. At the very least they know it is illegal. Before they can put their fantasies into action, they have to deal with any thoughts they may have that abusing is wrong. Abusers attempt to do this in a number of ways. Many abusers drink alcohol before abusing. Alcohol lowers inhibitions and people then do things that they already want to do but might not dare to do when sober. It has been found that in 30 to 40% of abuse cases abusers have drunk alcohol before abusing, and 45 to 50% of child molesters have had drinking problems. Drinking alcohol does not cause a person to sexually abuse a child, but if he already wants to abuse, drinking alcohol or taking drugs may release his inhibitions and allow him to act out his fantasies.

Many abuses try to justify what they are doing:

+ I'm just loving her.
+ It's not intercourse, so it's not abuse.
+ It's sex education.
+ He's too young to remember anyway.
+ I'm not hurting her.
+ He enjoys it.
+ The law doesn't understand the special relationship I have with my daughter.
+ He's my stepson, not my real son, so it doesn't count.
+ I'm keeping the family together.
+ I was abused and it didn't hurt me.
+ She seduced me.

They manage to convince themselves that what they are doing is acceptable. They often justify their behavior in the same way to the child they are abusing and may even convince the child that they have a good reason for abusing. Whatever an abuser says, there is no good reason for abuse. Abuse does not benefit the child.

In certain groups of people or families, the sexual abuse of children may have become so common that it is thought to be normal. Child pornography, although illegal in this country, is available in the form of videos and photographs. Looking at child pornography, discussing it and exchanging it with friends encourages people to think that it is acceptable to use children for sex. The recent increase in sex tourism—people going abroad specifically to have sex with children—also makes child abuse seem more acceptable. Pedophiles (people primarily sexually attracted to children) have publicly argued that sex with children should be legalized and that children are capable of giving informed consent to sex at the age of four. In this climate, a potential abuser can convince himself that sexually abusing a child is a form of sexual liberation.

Child abuse is sometimes highly organized. Abusers know each other and may abuse together either in families or in groups of friends. Abusers sometimes help and support each other by protecting each other, swapping information, and helping each other get employment where they have access to children. They create an environment for themselves where child sexual abuse is seen as acceptable.

The abuser gets the child alone

For abuse to occur, the abuser must get a child on her own or at least away from adults who would protect her. For fathers, mothers, stepfathers and other family members, this is easy—bath time, bedtime or whenever the other parent is out of the house. Abusers often plan ahead to get children on their own by, for example, taking the child on an outing or encouraging the mother to go out for the evening.

Children may be especially at risk if one of their parents is absent or ill for a period of time, or if their mother is in the hospital having a baby. The abuser is often a trusted person, a family friend or family member, so it is usually easy for him to get the child alone without anyone being worried or suspicious. Abusers often work on becoming a "trusted person" by befriending the family and gaining their confidence as well as the child's.

Many children may have come into contact with abusers but have not been abused because the abuser did not get the opportunity. Children who are abused are unlucky enough to have been alone with an abuser or away from people who could protect them.

The abuser overcomes the child's resistance

The child does not come into this situation until the end. The scene has already been set. The person is ready to abuse as soon as the right opportunity arises. He only has to make sure he can overcome any resistance the child might show. It isn't difficult for an abuser to make sure the child does what he wants. Many children are taught that adults know best and that they should do as they are told. They don't attempt to resist. It's hard for a child to object to what is happening or to disobey. The child may not even be clear that what is happening is wrong because the abuse may start at an early age, when the child is too young to understand what is going on.

Abusers make sure children don't try to resist by using persuasion ("It's our special secret"), rewards (money, candy, gifts or simply not being in a bad mood) or by getting the child sexually aroused. Making children feel they are participating in the abuse can result in their feeling trapped and unable to resist. It can teach children to actively seek out the abuse themselves. Abusers also use threats ("You'll be sent away") and when the abuse has happened once, this in itself can be used as a threat ("I'll tell what you did"). Physical violence may be threatened and in some cases used. Children soon learn to lie still if the choice is between being sexually abused or being sexually abused and beaten up. Some children are given alcohol or drugs before they are abused.

Why did the abuse happen to me?

You may blame yourself by feeling you caused the abuser to abuse you or because you think you should have stopped him. A child does not cause abuse, an abuser does. For abuse to happen there has to be an abuser who wants to abuse and who has overcome any misgivings he has about it. Then he must find a place and time when he can abuse undisturbed and frighten or persuade the child into doing what he wants.

When Ron married Elaine's mother, he came into daily contact with three young girls. He fantasized about touching them and carefully planned how he could put his fantasies into action. One night he had a few drinks, his wife was working a late shift and it was easy to get Elaine alone in her bedroom. Afterward he told himself he hadn't hurt her and she wouldn't remember anyway, so he hadn't done anything wrong. He told Elaine not to tell anyone or she'd never see her mother again.

Elaine hadn't been chosen because she was quiet and shy. She was abused because she was unlucky enough to find herself on her own with a man who had a desire to abuse children sexually. As Susan, Anne and Elaine talked to each other, they began to realize that they hadn't caused their stepfather to abuse them. He was an adult who knew what he was doing was wrong. He was responsible.

"I have been abused by three different people, so it must have been my fault."

Survivors who have been abused by more than one person often feel that this proves that it's something about them that caused this to happen.

> I was abused by so many people that I thought I had been put on this earth to be abused. Graham

However, it is not unusual for Survivors to have been abused by more than one person. Half the Survivors in the Wakefield groups have been abused by more than one person, and research has found that approximately 43% of abused women have been abused by a number of different men. Steps 3 and 4 in Finkelhor's model show why it is so common for a child to be abused more than once.

Step 3: The abuser gets the child alone. The child's situation may make it easy for abusers to get access to a child. Jocelyn's parents took in renters. She lived in close contact with a succession of men. This made her vulnerable to abuse. Having parents who are regularly absent or ill can also increase the danger.

Step 4: The abuser overcomes the child's resistance. As we discussed in chapter 3, children and adults who have been sexually abused are often vulnerable to further abuse. Sexual abuse results in a child feeling powerless and unable to protect herself. It is easy for another abuser to control a child who has already learned to do as she is told and remain silent. Some children feel so helpless and have been abused so often that they begin to accept abuse as a "normal" situation that has to be tolerated or which they are taught to seek out.

"It must be my fault, because he didn't abuse my sisters and brothers or anyone else."

Sometimes abusers do abuse just one child in a family. They often find ways of isolating that child from their rest of the family by making him or her feel different or special. The abuser might favor that child by giving special attention, treats or presents, or the abuser might blame and ill-treat the child, and convince the child that he or she is bad. The abuser finds ways of making the child feel responsible for the abuse in order to manipulate the child into keeping silent. Even if you were the only victim, your abuser is still responsible for the abuse.

However, most abusers do not usually select one "special" child to abuse and then stop. They go on abusing children whenever they get the opportunity or can create one. As Elaine's story shows, sisters (and brothers) may each spend years believing they are the only one in the family who has been abused. If one person has been keeping the abuse secret, other people have probably been doing the same thing. Survivors frequently discover that other family members have been abused by the same person. Thirty years after her own abuse, Sandra discovered that three of her brothers had also been abused.

> I have now learned that three of my four brothers have also been abused. All those years I kept quiet, my brothers did too. Maybe if we had shared our secret, we may have been able to work together to end the violence that was inflicted on us. We have all had difficulties in forming lasting relationships, and now we all lay the blame at our father's door. Sandra

Discovering that other family members have been abused can be distressing, but it does show that one person wasn't specifically chosen to be abused.

> I was sexually abused by my uncle from age six or seven (maybe earlier), and I was convinced, until I turned 21, that I was the only person he had abused. I always wondered why he chose me to abuse and presumed that it was because I was the oldest. My sister was two years younger and almost always in the same bed as me while the abuse took place, but I always thought she was asleep and didn't know about it. I thought maybe my uncle was under the impression that I enjoyed what was happening.
>
> I was glad when the abuse stopped. I thought he would never abuse again in case he was found out. He then went on to sexually abuse my sister and my cousin. I found out about what had happened to my sister when I was 21. Everything finally came into the open when I was 22 years old and my cousin told me about what he was doing to her. It broke my heart because I felt I could have done something earlier to prevent it from happening to her in the first place. Sonia

In the Wakefield's Survivors groups, at least 40% of the women's abusers are known to have abused other children.

Finally, this is how one Survivor now answers the question, "Why did it happen to me?"

I was young, I was vulnerable and I was in the wrong place at the wrong time. I am not ashamed of what happened. I was not to blame. Jocelyn

Exercises

1. We have seen that Survivors usually think of reasons why they were chosen to be abused; for example, "I was quiet and shy." Write down any reasons why you think you might have been to blame for being abused or why you might have been chosen.

2. Abuse starts with a person who wants to abuse, not with a child. Write down your answers to these questions (see Finkelhor's steps 3 and 4):

   ✦ How did the abuser manage to get you alone or in a position where he or she could abuse you?

   ✦ How did the abuser get you to do what he or she wanted?

3. Finally, look at your answers to question 1 again and ask yourself if you really are to blame for being abused.

Further reading

Finkelhor, David, and Kersti Yllo. *Child Sexual Abuse: New Theory and Research.* New York: Free Press, 1984.

5

Why Didn't I Tell?

Most Survivors feel ashamed and guilty about the sexual abuse they suffered as children. They may feel especially guilty if it went on for months or years. Kate was sexually abused almost every week by her father from the age of two until she left home to get married at eighteen.

By the time I was twelve I knew it was wrong, but I still didn't tell anybody. Why didn't I stop him? It must have been my fault. Kate

Many adults who were sexually abused as children believe they should have stopped the abuser. But how? A child is powerless in relation to an adult. Adults are physically more powerful than children and could resort to physical violence if necessary. Even if the abuser is the child's brother or sister, or a child of a similar age, there are many reasons why she doesn't stop the abuse.

Abusers rarely need to use physical force to coerce children into sexual relationships; they can exert power in other ways. Children are brought up to obey and respect adults, and so all adults, especially relatives, have sufficient authority to make children do whatever they want. Adults and older children are also able to manipulate the child's feelings. They can use threats and promises to gain access to the child's body and to keep the child quiet. If a child can't stop the abuser herself, then her only way out is to tell someone else.

"Why didn't I tell?" is one of the first questions Survivors ask. Some Survivors were abused only once, but many Survivors were abused repeatedly for periods ranging from a few months to more than twenty years. Repeated abuse can lead Survivors to believe they must have been at least partly to blame because they "allowed" it to continue and didn't stop the abuser themselves or tell someone else what was happening.

Why don't children tell?

If a child cannot stop the abuser herself, why doesn't she tell someone else about it? The child may have no one to tell, or she may not know what to say. She may be frightened about the consequences if someone does believe her. She may feel so guilty and confused that she can't risk telling anyone because she feels the above is her fault. Table 2, below, lists some of the reasons why children keep the secret and continue to suffer the abuse. We will look at some of these reasons in the rest of this chapter.

Table 2: Why Children Don't Tell

1. **Whom to tell?**
   Parents dead, ill, absent.
   Parents involved in the abuse.
   No trustworthy adult around.
   No opportunity to talk alone with a trusted adult.
   Caregivers do not listen, involved with own problems.
   Frightened of parents.
   Parents discourage talk about sex.
   No friends.
   No one to tell.

2. **What to say?**
   Child too young to talk.
   Child doesn't know how to describe what's happened.
   Child too embarrassed and ashamed to say what happened.

3. **Fears about consequences of telling**
   (a) **Threats from the abuser**
       No one will believe child.
       Child will be put into a home/taken into foster care.
       Child will not see her mother again.
       Family will be split up.
       Affection and love will be withdrawn.
       Family and friends will reject child.
       No one will want to marry her.

continued ...

Threatened or actual physical violence to child, her family or pets.
Abuser will kill himself or go to prison.

(b) Fears concerning other people's reactions

No one will believe child.
Mother will feel guilty.
Family will be hurt.
Mother/father will be upset.
Mother will reject child.
Other people will think child is to blame
Other people will think child is dirty, contaminated or disgusting.
Child will be rejected and abuser supported.

(c) Fears for the abuser

Abuser will be hurt and rejected.
Abuser will be put in prison.
Abuser will get beaten up.
Abuser will kill himself.

(d) Fears that telling won't help

Nothing will change.
No one can stop it.
Events will go out of control.
Fear of the unknown.
It might get worse.
Abuser is too powerful and can't be stopped.

4. *The child's confusion: Feelings and thoughts that prevent children from telling include:*

Feelings of guilt, self-blame, shame and embarrassment.
Confusion—is it really happening? Is it wrong?
Thinking the abuse is normal.
Not understanding what is happening.
Believing she is the only one this has ever happened to.
Feeling dirty, contaminated, polluted.
Trapped by the secrecy.
Feeling she is being punished and deserves it.
Hoping the abuse won't happen again.
Blocking off all memories of the abuse.
Feeling sorry for abuser.
Not wanting to betray abuser by telling.
Feeling it's her fault because she took candy, money, toys or other rewards from the abuser.
Feeling it was her fault because she learned to seek out the abuser.
Enjoying the sexual stimulation.
Enjoying the affection, warmth or closeness.
Thinking "I didn't tell when it first happened, so how can I tell now?"

Whom to tell?

I didn't tell—There was no one to tell. Nobody listened or paid any attention. Of course I never said anything out loud. I cried and I always had a "tummyache," I ran away from school, I even begged not to go out with the man who abused me, but none of these things changed anything. Circumstances stopped the abuse, not me. I couldn't stop it. Jocelyn

A child may be worried and distressed about the abuse she is suffering and decide to tell someone about it. Whom can she tell? She can't tell just anyone about something she finds so confusing and shameful. The only people who may be able to help are parents, a trusted adult or someone in authority

I don't really think I could have told anyone other than my mom because the secret was so big. Jane

Some children do tell their mothers when they are being abused. Other children do not have a mother or close caregiver to whom they can talk about the abuse. The mother may have left home, be in poor health, dead or in the hospital. She may be the abuser or involved in the abuse. Mothers who are physically present may be preoccupied with their own problems or not have the time or patience to listen. Some children do not have an adult with whom they have a close and confiding relationship.

Looking back, I know I would not and could not have told anybody. The reasons I kept quiet were very real ones. The relationship I had with my parents was not stable or loving enough to give me confidence and trust in them. They would have considered themselves and others first; what was best for me would not have crossed their minds. My father would go crazy over minor, needless things. What would he have done faced with this? My mother never listened to us. That stands out in my mind. When I was crying and pleading with her not to send me out one day with the abuser, she said, "Why? Don't be silly, go on, go!" Never, never listened, would ask "Why" and then not wait for an answer. Jocelyn

Even if the child has a good relationship with her parents, there are many reasons why she might not tell them about her abuse. In some households sex is a taboo subject. The parents are very strict, so children are too frightened to bring up the subject of sexual abuse. Embarrassment alone prevents many children from talking; the shame and stigma that surround sexual abuse make it a very difficult subject to talk about.

Children who are being abused often withdraw into their shame, distrust people and avoid getting close to anyone in order to prevent their secret from being discovered. They don't have a friend to tell.

What to say

Even children who do have a good relationship with a trusted adult may find it impossible to tell them. How do you tell? What do you say? Many children are abused from a young age, too young to talk or too young to know what is happening to them. Older children may not know how to talk about what is happening to them. They may blurt out, "Daddy keeps touching me." They know what kind of touching they mean, but the adult they are talking to does not and may assume it is tickling or some innocent form of touching.

> I never told anyone about my abuse, although at one point (when I was about 11) I decided to do something about it because my uncle actually tried to have intercourse with me. I couldn't take it anymore. I tried to tell my mother, but all that came out was that I didn't want to stay at my uncle's anymore (I stayed at least once a week usually). I told her he used to come into the bathroom while I was undressed or in the bath and generally made me feel uncomfortable. I never actually revealed that he had touched me, although I tried to drop hints. Sonia

Even teenagers find it very difficult to talk about their sexual abuse. They may feel too ashamed and embarrassed and not know how to introduce the subject. They may not have listened to any sex education because of their bad associations with sex and so they do not understand what is happening or know how to talk about it.

Fears about the consequences of telling

> I have often asked myself, "Why didn't I tell anyone about my sexual abuse?" Now I can actually think of a number of reasons. I didn't tell out of fear of what might or, according to my abuser, what would have happened. I was always being told that I'd be

put into a home and that once word got out, no one would want to have anything to do with me. I would never, ever have a boyfriend. According to the abuser, my mother would not have anything to do with me. Because I didn't have a good relationship with my mother, I didn't find this hard to believe.

I do believe deep down that if I had come out and said what was happening in a straightforward way to my mother, the result would have been just the same. I am beginning to realize that I have been torturing myself with the question for no good reason. I only wish I had realized a lot sooner. Joanne

Even if a child does have a trusted adult she can talk to, and does know how to describe what has been happening to her, she still may not tell because of fears about what possible consequences. These fears are discussed below and include threats from the abuser, fears that she might not be believed, fears about other people's reactions, fears about what might happen to the abuser and a fear that nothing will change.

(a) Threats from the abuser

My dad would say, "You'll be sent away and I'll be sent to jail if you tell." Dad also said, "It will be our secret. Mommy and Daddy will not love you anymore if you tell." So part of my fear, why I didn't tell Mom, was because it would upset her and the family would break up. I cared about my mother and I couldn't bear to upset her. I had nobody else that I could tell at that time and I was frightened. Lucy

Children of all ages fear being rejected by, or separated from, their mothers. The abusers, especially fathers and other family members, play on this fear and often tell the child it will be her fault if the family breaks up or if her mother is upset. The child is left feeling responsible for keeping the family together and saving her mother from being hurt, even though it is the abuser who is causing damage to the family. Graham was sexually abused by his mother. The only person who showed him any affection in his childhood was his grandmother.

My mother always told me the police would think I was a "dirty little bastard" if I told them, and they would take me away to a children's home and I would never see grandmother again. Graham

Other threats can be equally powerful. "No one will want to marry you if they find out what you've been doing with him" (Joanne's abuser). Abusers often tell children that if they tell anyone they will be rejected, blamed and not believed.

Kirsty's stepdad often beat her and her brothers, even when they had done nothing wrong. Kirsty was therefore very frightened when he began forcing her to have sex with him and threatening her with violence if she told anyone.

> At first I was afraid to tell because he said if I told anyone I would
> be taken away from my mom and she wouldn't want to know me.
> Then came the threats and the beating, and if you knew what
> type of violent man he was, just the threats were enough, never
> mind the hitting. I was scared of what he would do to me, and
> also I couldn't stand the thought of being parted from my mom.
> Kirsty

Some abusers do use physical violence to force their victims to have sex with them. Others threaten the child with violence toward the child, or toward other people. The abuser may threaten to beat the child's mother or brothers and sisters or to torture or kill her pets. "If you tell anyone what is happening, you will never see your dog again." An abuser may even frighten the child by threatening to kill himself if the secret is revealed. Violence and threats of violence are easy ways to frighten children into silence, although threats concerning the consequences of telling for the child or the family are more common.

(b) Fears about other people's reactions

> I knew it was all my fault and nobody would believe me. Graham

Children often do not tell about the abuse because of they fear how other people will respond. The most common fear is that no one will believe them. The abuser often reinforces this fear. It is a child's word against an adult's, and the adult may be well liked and respected in the community. Nowadays, because of television and newspaper coverage, people are aware that child sexual abuse does happen. In the recent past it was thought to happen rarely, so even if there were trusted adults around for a child to tell, the adult probably would have found it hard to believe and would have had little idea what to do about it.

Children often fear that telling will hurt other people, particularly their mothers and families. They may also fear that other people will think of them as dirty and contaminated and will not want to know them anymore.

> I couldn't tell anyone because I was so ashamed, and I was afraid I would be sent away. When we were very little, before I started school, four of us were caught comparing our genitals. Mom said if we ever did it again we'd be sent to a naughty boys and girls home. I'll never forget that. Luke

Their own feelings of guilt and shame cause them to fear that they will be blamed and that others will support the abuser, not them.

(c) Fears for the abuser

Many children love their abuser, despite the abuse, and do not want their abuser to be hurt by the abuse becoming known. They are concerned that their mothers and families will reject and punish the abuser. Children also fear that if they tell about the abuse, the abuser might be put in prison, be beaten up or even kill himself. They continue to put up with the abuse rather than put their abuser in danger.

(d) Fears that telling won't help

The child may feel that even if she does tell, nothing can be done to stop the abuse.

> Our family lived with my grandfather and an aunt in a small apartment. I had to share my mother's bed for the first five years of my life. My brother, the abuser, slept in the same bedroom as my parents and me. Because there was no space for either him or me to move out of our parents' bedroom, I saw no way the abuse could stop. When bedtime came and he wanted to abuse me, I was there. There was nowhere to go. Pretending to be asleep did not help either. No way out - he said he'd kill me if I told anyone. Ingrid

Ingrid believed the sleeping arrangements at home made it impossible for anyone to stop her brother abusing her. In chapter 2, Anita and Pam described how they told their mothers and others about the abuse, but their mothers took no steps to stop it. The child's own feelings of powerlessness may also make her feel that no one else could change the situation.

Many children only want the abuse to be stopped and are frightened that they will make the situation worse if they do tell. They fear they will have no control over what happens next. Other people may be told, Social Services may need to separate family members, the police may be brought in. They are afraid they will have no say in what happens and that the situation could get worse. These are rational and realistic fears.

Often children do not tell about the abuse because they fear the consequences. Many of these fears are rational - the child may not be believed, she may be put into foster care. Often, though, it is the child's perception of the abuser's power that keeps her from telling. She believes nothing can stop the abuser, that he will punish her and that everyone will be persuaded to believe him. The abuser used his adult authority and cunning to manipulate the child into a sexual relationship, which leaves the child feeling powerless and unable to protect herself. It is difficult for a child in this situation to understand that other adults may not be powerless in relation to the abuser.

The child's confused feelings

I wondered if what was happening was normal or if I was imagining it. Jane

A child who is being abused is put in a frightening and confusing situation. They may never have heard of anything like this happening. Nobody has told them it is right, but nobody has told them it is wrong. Everyone may like and respect the person who is doing these things. It may be daddy. They may think, as Jane did, "Maybe it isn't happening at all, maybe I made it up," or "Everyone else likes him, so he can't be bad - it must be me."

Children are brought up to trust adults (especially family members and friends) and to do as they are told. Abuse plunges the child into confusion.

One of the main reasons I felt that I couldn't tell anyone was that I had lived for the first seven years of my life trusting my mom and doing what I was told. Now there was a man who was my new daddy and whom mom said I could trust. A major factor for me was the confusion I felt between doing what I was told by him, being obedient and not telling my mom; and being disobedient and telling my mom. In the past I had kept secrets for my mom and she had been proud of me for doing so. Maybe this was another secret to keep. Jane

Abuse often begins gradually, as an affectionate cuddle progressing over weeks or years into touching, intercourse and oral sex. Children may enjoy and encourage the initial warmth and contact, but then feel frightened and guilty as the abuse progresses and they find it unpleasant or realize it is wrong. In this situation, children often feel they have encouraged the abuse. They feel they have implicated themselves and only got what they've asked for. How can they tell when telling will mean revealing their own guilt?

> When it first started, he would just push up against me. I was too young to think anything was wrong. When he started touching me I began to get a little sexual pleasure, not knowing that he was indecently assaulting me. It wasn't until I got to high school that I realized he was doing something wrong. I felt sick inside and guilty for letting it go on for so long. Anthony

If the abuse starts suddenly, children are often too frightened or stunned to say anything. They hope it won't happen again. When it does, how can they tell when they didn't tell before?

> When it began, I didn't tell because of the initial guilt, shame and confusion. The longer it continued, the more incriminated I felt. Jane

Other ways children have of coping with the trauma of sexual abuse is to block out their thoughts about it, to pretend it isn't happening, or to retreat into a fantasy world.

> I don't remember how the abuse began. I was too young. I think it must have happened gradually, otherwise I would remember the first time. But when it became more serious, before I entered school, I had to find a way to escape the abuse. I could not escape physically, but although there was nowhere to go for my body, I could send my mind away. Again, I do not remember how it started, but I clearly remember how I developed my own fantasy world in which to escape while I was being abused. This fantasy became as real to me as if I were there physically. During the abuse I sent my mind there, where I was liked by everyone and felt safe. I left my body behind to be used. Sometimes the deception was so great that I could hardly feel what was happening to me. Katarina

Children can't tell others if they've convinced themselves the abuse isn't happening. Children can block off the abuse so completely that they do not think of it at all when it isn't actually taking place.

*I blocked out the whole thing as if it had never happened, so I
never told anyone because in my mind it hadn't happened. That is,
until a few years ago, when I started to have flashbacks. I can't
remember if I was blackmailed or threatened or told it was a
secret. I felt detached from it all somehow, as though I watched
and it wasn't really me.* Margaret

After the abuse has ended, many people block out the memories.
They forget all about it until something triggers the memories.
Some abusers give candy, money or other rewards to the child after
the abuse, and this confuses the child even more. She feels it was
her own fault because she accepted a reward, so she cannot tell
anyone. Mary was given some marbles after she was abused -she
didn't dare tell her mother about the abuse because she wasn't
allowed to play with marbles. Shirley was abused by a shopkeeper
who gave her candy afterward. She couldn't tell her mother
because she knew she wasn't supposed to take candy from
strangers. Giving a child money or presents often leaves the child
feeling confused about her role in the abuse. The bribe makes it
difficult for her to tell anyone about the abuse.

Abusers may make sure the child becomes sexually aroused
during the abuse. Children who get enjoyment from the sexual
stimulation often feel that because they felt some pleasure they
encouraged the abuse and therefore cannot tell anyone. Boys often
get erections during sexual abuse either as a reflex or as a response
to sexual stimulation and this cannot be hidden from the abuser.
This obvious sign of arousal makes them feel they must be
involved in and responsible for the abuse.

*I was already feeling isolated when the abuse started. I tried so
hard to get my mother to love me but I couldn't get through to
her. Then here was someone giving me something, yet taking a lot
more. All I wanted was to feel loved, but instead I was used. It all
started so innocently. I liked the feeling of touch and I felt equally
responsible. But then he wouldn't stop. My head knew something
was wrong and it didn't want this, yet my body did. When he
touched me I got a hard-on and wanted to touch him back.
Afterward I felt so dirty and ashamed. Feelings of shame and guilt
increased—my body had let me down, betrayed me. He stole
something from me. He wanted sex and he used me. I couldn't
tell because I felt so filthy, so fucking guilty.* Luke

Children do not enjoy being sexually abused, but they may enjoy some of the things that go with it. They may enjoy the attention or affection, especially if they get very little elsewhere. They may enjoy the physical stimulation and sexual arousal. Sexual abuse, however, involves more than affection, attention and physical stimulation. It also involves betrayal of the trust a child has in an older person, the manipulation of a child's feelings and inappropriate sexual contact. The feelings of guilt and shame surrounding sexual abuse are enough to prevent most children from telling anyone what is happening to them. They may feel dirty and polluted. They may feel guilty because they enjoyed the physical contact or the attention or because they accepted money or candy. The child's attempt to make sense out of a situation she does not understand usually leaves her feeling confused and ashamed and unable to tell anyone about the abuse.

Breaking free from the guilt

You may have been feeling ashamed and guilty for many years, blaming yourself for not stopping the abuse. After working through this chapter, you may begin to realize it was impossible for you to stop the abuser yourself and that there were many good reasons why you couldn't tell someone else about the abuse. Understanding your reasons for not telling will not make the guilt and shame disappear overnight because you have been carrying these feelings for a long time. You may understand intellectually that you couldn't stop the abuser but may still feel guilty. It can take a while for your feelings to catch up with your thoughts. Work through the exercises at the end of this chapter and do them again every time you start to blame yourself for the abuse. In time, the feelings of shame and guilt will fade.

Here is Anita's description of why she didn't tell:

> In the beginning, I was very young and I didn't understand what was happening. As I grew up and began to realize things weren't right, I felt more and more uncomfortable. I didn't know how to tell. At first I thought maybe I was imagining things. Then I thought nobody would believe me because it was all so unbelievable. Things like this just didn't happen. As I got a little older and now knew for sure it wasn't my imagination, I wanted to tell, but now it had gone on for some time, and I'd let it.
>
> At first when my stepdad cuddled and kissed me, I'd longed

to feel like I did. I missed my daddy so much and my mom had never been affectionate. I kissed and cuddled him back and felt really special, but when the touching started I felt uncomfortable. But I couldn't tell because I felt so ashamed and guilty. I've craved love and attention and I had finally had it, so therefore I'd brought it all on myself. It was all my fault and I deserved to suffer. My mom had already had one bad marriage. Now she was happy with my stepdad and I couldn't ruin everything by telling her what he was doing to me.

It went on and things got worse and worse: he'd appear from nowhere, he seemed to be everywhere at once, at every corner I turned in the house. And every time I passed, his hands would be touching me. Each time I was alone he'd be there, and each time he'd do more and expect more and more. Every time I swore to myself it wouldn't happen again I'd tell, but how? What could I say, where would I start? I would hurt my mom so much and probably make her hate me. He'd also started telling me I could never ever tell because no one would ever understand and lots of bad things would happen to both of us if I ever did. Anita

Exercises

Doing these exercises may help you deal with the feelings of guilt, self-blame and shame.

1. You may wonder why you didn't stop the abuser. Adult Survivors often forget how small and powerless they were in comparison to their abuser. Doing this exercise helps you remember the differences in physical size and strength between you and the abuser at the time of the abuse.

    ✦ Find photographs of yourself and (if possible) the abuser at the time the abuse began.

    or

    ✦ Draw a picture of yourself and the abuser at that time.

    or

    ✦ Compare the difference in size between adults and children of the age you were when the abuse began. Would it be physically possible for a child to prevent a bigger child or adult from harming him or her? Remember that the difference isn't just one of physical size and strength, but of power and authority too.

2. Look at the list of reasons (Table 2, page 50) why children don't tell that they are being abused. Check any reasons that applied to you. You may be able to add to the list.

3. Write down your story of why you didn't tell anyone at the time the abuse was occurring.

6

Silent Ways of Telling

The last chapter looked at how children are usually unable to tell anyone that they are being sexually abused. They try to hide their secret and suffer in silence, but usually they are experiencing strong feelings inside: fear, depression, guilt, shame, anger, confusion, helplessness and despair. It's hard for a child to hide feelings like this completely. They tend to "leak out" in some way, in changed behavior or mood. People may notice the changes without realizing that they are signs of distress. Instead, the child may be thought to be "going through a phase," to be bad or even angry. We have called these signs "silent ways of telling" because, although the child remains silent about the abuse, the signs are there for anyone who is able or willing to read them. Today, with more knowledge of sexual abuse, we are learning to pay attention to children's bad or strange behavior and to ask, "What are they trying to say?"

> As a child I would refuse to eat, isolate myself and throw myself down the stairs. I thought I was going crazy and didn't deserve friends or family. I tried running away from home, and I spent hours alone crying. My head was full of questions, trying to find out what was wrong with me. I thought I wasn't normal. Graham

Looking back at their childhoods, the Wakefield Survivors can now understand their own behavior. Many of them had thought they were "difficult" children, but now realize they were reacting to the abuse, attempting to protect themselves and "silently telling" about the abuse. Some of the signs children show at the time they are being abused or in the years afterward are shown in Table 3 (below).

Some Survivors showed few signs or experienced only mild problems as children, while others showed a whole collection of severe problems and symptoms. It is important to recognize that children who are not victims of sexual abuse may also experience some of the difficulties described in Table 3. This table is intended only to help Survivors recognize the signs they were showing in their own childhood rather than as a method of "diagnosing" sexual abuse.

We will discuss some of these signs in more detail. Many behaviors that abused children develop to protect themselves or show distress continue into adulthood. Looking at why certain childhood behaviors developed can help an adult Survivor understand and accept the child she was and the person she is now.

Table 3: Silent Ways of Telling— Childhood Signs of Sexual Abuse

The following signs suggest a child is being sexually abused:

+ displaying too much sexual knowledge for age
+ inappropriate sexual behavior, e.g. tongue kissing
+ writing stories about sex or abuse
+ drawing pictures about sex or abuse
+ sexually transmitted diseases

The following signs do not necessarily mean a child is being sexually abused. They indicate that something is upsetting the child:

+ eating problems	+ wetting
+ refusing to eat	+ bed-wetting
+ overeating	+ retaining urine
+ compulsive eating	+ soiling
+ bingeing and vomiting (bulimia)	+ constipation
+ abusing laxatives	+ diarrhea
+ anorexia nervosa	+ retaining feces
+ excreting problems	+ smearing feces
	+ behavior or mood changes

continued . . .

- ✦ withdrawing from people
- ✦ fearful of being alone with particular people
- ✦ not making close friends
- ✦ depression
- ✦ anxiety
- ✦ phobias
- ✦ nightmares
- ✦ difficulty sleeping
- ✦ constantly tired
- ✦ suicide attempts
- ✦ obsessional behavior or thoughts
- ✦ tantrums
- ✦ clinging to adults
- ✦ acting younger than their age
- ✦ running away from home
- ✦ disruptive behavior at home
- ✦ disruptive behavior at school
- ✦ truancy
- ✦ school underachievement
- ✦ school overachievement
- ✦ bullying
- ✦ fighting
- ✦ fire-setting
- ✦ aggressive or violent behavior
- ✦ stealing
- ✦ frequent illnesses; e.g. stomachache, rashes, sore genitals
- ✦ frequent "accidents"
- ✦ self-mutilation or self-abuse; e.g. slashing, scratching
- ✦ alcohol/drug abuse

Eating and excreting

Children who are sexually abused experience a sense of powerlessness. Their bodies and feelings are invaded. They are unable to protect themselves or control what is happening to them. Feeling out of control is usually a frightening experience and people often react by attempting to take back control in some way. Children have few ways of taking control, but eating and excreting are two ways in which they can control their bodies. Mothers of young children know all too well that battling with children over food and "potty training" is rarely successful. Disturbances in eating and excreting are therefore obvious ways in which children can consciously or unconsciously attempt to take back control over their bodies and show their resistance to adult authority.

The part of our nervous system that controls digestion and excretion is affected by stress, depression, fear and anxiety. Symptoms of depression and anxiety include lack of appetite, overeating, gastric problems, nausea, diarrhea and constipation. Changes in eating and excreting patterns are common signs of distress.

Excretion problems

These problems include bedwetting, day-wetting, soiling, constipation and retaining urine. All children wet and soil themselves
when they are young. Remaining dry at night may only happen
very slowly with some children. However, wetting and soiling that
reappears after a period when the child has been dry and clean, or
goes on for an excessive length of time, often indicates some form
of distress. When the child is being sexually abused, wetting and
soiling can also be a conscious or unconscious attempt to keep the
abuser away by making herself dirty and smelly. Adult Survivors
sometimes still experience problems with bedwetting. Excreting in
inappropriate places may also be a way for a child to express his or
her anger or distress.

> I used to soil in sinks, on toilet seats and on the floor of the toilets
> in junior high school. Danny

Eating problems include a refusal to eat, undereating and overeating. In teenagers this can develop into eating disorders such as
anorexia nervosa, bulimia and compulsive eating (see chapter 11).
Eating helps blot out bad feelings and memories: as the food is
swallowed, so are the feelings. Overeating is an attempt to use
eating to cope with bad feelings. As with wetting and soiling,
overeating can be a conscious or unconscious attempt by the child
to protect herself from the abuser. She may feel that, if she makes
herself fat and unattractive, she will be left alone.

> The look of disgust on my brother's (the abuser's) face when he
> looked at me is still fresh in my mind. So I thought, "If he hates me
> fat, maybe he won't abuse me any more if I get fatter." So I began
> to eat huge amounts and gradually put on weight. It didn't stop
> the abuse but it increased the humiliation. Katarina

Not eating can be a way of attempting to regain control, but can
also be an attempt at self-protection—becoming too thin to be
attractive, fading away, ultimately dying.

Inappropriate sexual behavior

Young children usually have very little knowledge of sexual
behavior. Children who have been abused sometimes act out what
has happened to them with their toys, with other children, with
adults, or show it through their paintings and stories. If this

activity is not recognized as a sign of sexual abuse, the child may be blamed and thought to be rude or abusive.

When Kate was four years old, she was caught acting out the sexual behavior she had learned from being abused, and she was accused of sexually abusing a boy of her own age. Dorothy (see chapter 2) wrote stories and drew pictures about sexually abused girls and was punished for her "bad" behavior by being forbidden to spend time in her bedroom.

Sudden changes in behavior or mood

When a child is being sexually abused, her behavior may change suddenly. The outgoing child becomes quiet and withdrawn; the well-behaved child becomes disruptive; the easy-going child becomes sulky and moody. Adults who do not understand that this is a sign of distress may criticize or punish the child. Children can come to believe that they really are bad and therefore deserve to be abused. These same feelings may continue in the adult. Some of these changes in behavior and mood are discussed in more detail below.

Withdrawing

Sexual abuse by a known person is a betrayal of a child's trust. As a result, the child becomes unable to trust other people and keeps herself apart so she cannot be hurt by anyone else.

> I was reclusive. I never wanted to go out and play. Rhys

Many Survivors describe being loners as children or being friendly with other children and then dropping them when the friendship started to get close.

> I would make friends pretty easily but I would soon start to avoid them. I didn't want to get close to anyone. I didn't want to open up to anyone. Jocelyn

This barrier is also created because the child feels different from other people, even dirty and ashamed. The child does not allow anyone to get close to her in case they find out what she is really like or discover her secret.

> I used to hide from everyone because I hated myself. I thought I wasn't worth talking to. I spent hours alone in my room, sat on the floor at the back of my closet. I felt safer being hidden. It was like my personal sanctuary. Graham

For some children, withdrawing is the only way they know to cope with the trauma of their everyday lives and the burden of the secret they carry.

Emotional problems

Many sexually abused children suffer from depression throughout their lives and into adulthood. Anxiety, phobias and a general nervousness and watchfulness may also result from being abused.

> *After the abuse began I couldn't sleep without the light on, even now I need the TV or radio on to go to sleep.* Rhys

Suicide attempts may be a way of trying to escape from the abuse and pain, or of drawing attention to the problem.

> *I think I was about seven the first time I tried to kill myself. I tried to cut my wrist but the knife I chose wasn't very sharp. I didn't really want to die, I just wanted to be loved. I tried to cut my wrists three or four times when I was in junior high school. I've still got one scar, although it's really faint. I think I needed to cut deeper, not just the little veins I could see under the surface. After my abuser died, I was raped by someone else. Five months later, when I was fifteen, I tried to hang myself. I hanged myself from the window with the cord that's used to open it. The other kids laughed at me so I let myself down.* Paula

Adults may not notice a child's anxiety or depression or she may receive treatment for her symptoms without the real problem ever being uncovered. In chapter 2, Dorothy describes how she attempted suicide and received five years of psychiatric treatment, including many courses of ECT (electroconvulsive therapy) without anyone discovering that she had been abused. Chris was put on Valium® tranquilizers at the age of seven because she stabbed her father when he was abusing her. Like Dorothy and Chris, some Survivors may have been further abused by the mental-health system. If emotional problems are not recognized or are treated inappropriately, Survivors may reach adulthood believing they are strange, unstable or even crazy.

This sounds like a very bleak picture. However, some children experience only mild emotional problems and heal themselves with the help of family and friends. Others receive good and appropriate help and don't carry their problems into adulthood.

Difficult or disruptive behavior

The sexually abused child may show behavior that is interpreted by other people as difficult or disruptive. The child may simply be trying to avoid being left alone with the abuser. Kate tried to avoid going out with her father (the abuser) by having screaming tantrums and by pretending she was frightened of their car. Kate was told she was difficult and naughty.

Tracy recalls clinging to her mother at the bus stop and then screaming and holding on to her when she attempted to get on a bus without Tracy. The bus driver had to help pull Tracy away from her mother. This kind of behavior is often interpreted as the child being clinging, demanding or willful.

Difficult behavior is often simply an expression of the anger and upset the child feels.

> It wasn't until I was older, in my early teens, that I felt my behavior may have been an attempt to ask for help. I remember having bad tantrums, which were attributed to my having a temper (taking after my real father, who had a violent temper), but they always occurred in a nonconfrontational situation. These attempts were made at home and were always ignored by the rest of the family. Jane

Survivors frequently continue to believe as adults that they were silly, difficult or disruptive children. Moreover Survivors learn from this experience not to trust their own feelings. As children, their strong feelings had been disregarded or treated as trivial. As adults, Survivors often keep disregarding their feelings and dismiss feelings of anger, distress or pain with, "I'm just being silly."

Aggression and violence

Difficult behavior and tantrums are an outward expression of anger and distress. They are the opposite of depression, where the feelings are turned inward and not expressed. For some Survivors, disruptive behavior can turn into violence and aggression. Danny was physically and emotionally abused by his mother and stepfather:

> I sniffed glue, took amphetamines and attacked people. When I was ten I hit a classmate over the head with a half-brick. I trashed thousands of dollars' worth of property. Danny

Chris's story shows how anger can turn to violence and continue into adult life. Chris was abused every Sunday by her father from the age of seven or earlier.

> I ran away when I was ten. I was only out one night and I was found 16 miles from home. I just walked and walked. But I still didn't tell anyone. I always used fight at home, with everyone. I had urges where all I wanted to do was kill people, get revenge. I remember tons of bad things that used to be said to me. Then I'd carry out my revenge by waiting and waiting. And I'd always get my revenge. Chris

Chris started getting drunk and fighting at school. Then she attacked her mother, smashing her head into the fireplace and fracturing her skull.

> I was always in court for something. I got locked up on my thirteenth birthday and that was it. From then on I was nuts. I was always in trouble and locked in a special cell. Chris

She constantly fought and stole. She was sent to a psychiatric hospital, where she stayed for two years. As soon as she was let out, she attacked someone else "to pay him back," and was sent to prison. When she was released, she stabbed someone else and was sentenced to an additional three years. Finally, Chris was sent to a Secure Unit for mentally disturbed offenders. She was released from prison at 23 years of age. In ten years, she hadn't been locked up for only five months.

School problems

Signs that a child is being sexually abused may occur at school even when there is no real problem with the school. Truancy from school is common.

> I used to run away from junior high. I used to have a stomachache but my mom would still send me to school. There I'd ask for a bathroom pass. I'd grab my coat and run. I can feel myself running, trying to get away, away from everything. I always thought (or maybe it's because I was always told) that I ran away because I didn't like the nuns who taught us, but now I realize it was because of the abuse. I can feel myself as a child confused and wanting to do something and not knowing what I could do. Running away was the only step I ever made toward telling or doing anything. Jocelyn

School may be the only place the child can let out the anger and distress he or she feels. The child may be badly behaved or disruptive, arguing with teachers or other children, and fighting.

> *I used to drink after playing team sports at school, and I used to get drunk all the time. I was always fighting at school with anyone who stood in my way. I eventually got sent to a special school.*
> Chris

> *In middle school I was reprimanded on several occasions for biting other children. At boarding school, I got in a lot of fights the first few years. I was often teased about my hair and clothes and fighting was the only way I knew of defending myself. Oddly, I don't ever remember putting up a fight against the abuser.* Paula

> *I was truant from school. I terrorized other children at school. I locked one teacher in a storeroom and spat at another one. I set fire to the girls' bathroom because a male teacher came into them. Looking back, I now realize that my abuser had such a hold over me that I had to be in control. I wouldn't allow anyone to have any power over me. I rebelled against anyone who tried to control me or pin me down.* Carla

Bad behavior at school also interferes with school work and earns the child a bad name. School work may get worse as the child becomes unable to concentrate or ceases to care what happens to her. Survivors may grow up believing they are "stupid" because they didn't do well at school.

On the other hand, some sexually abused children are excessively well behaved at school and "clingy" with teachers in an attempt to get the love and protection that lacking at home. Some children become overachievers at school as they strive to escape from the pain of their feelings by concentrating their mind on work.

Frequent illnesses

Children who are being sexually abused may be ill frequently or complain of not feeling well. Illnesses may result from sexual abuse in a direct physical sense; for example, urinary infections from sexual contact. Illness can also be an indirect result of sexual abuse arising from the stress and trauma of what is happening in the child's life. Commonly children complain of stomach pains when no physical cause can be found. Headaches, skin problems and failure to grow properly are also reported. Jane lists a whole range of physical problems, which she now thinks might be related to the abuse:

> Not long after I remember the abuse starting I had to have my tonsils out. After that, I developed a persistent earache. I was referred to the ENT (ear, nose and throat) clinic, but my family doctor told me it was all in my head. Then I was diagnosed with a slight scoliosis and referred to the orthopedic clinic. They recommended that I take very hot baths which, unfortunately, my stepfather (the abuser) oversaw. After this, apart from feeling generally lethargic and tired and being checked for anemia periodically, I can't remember any illnesses until I was seventeen, when the situation was bad again, mainly because my stepdad stopped me from going out with my friends. I told my doctor the surface problem. He prescribed antidepressants, which I didn't take. I had also been to see my doctor on a few occasions for period pains. During my ultrasound professional training I couldn't cope and, due to my symptoms, glandular fever was suggested, although not confirmed. Jane

Physical well being is closely linked to mental and emotional health. If children are emotionally traumatized they are unlikely to remain physically well.

> At about the same time the abuse started (when I was about four years old), I developed asthma and eczema. I only remember the asthma vaguely, but I do remember it was pretty bad at times. I don't remember getting treatment for it. However, the eczema was bad. I developed it on my wrists and the backs of my knees. I had my tonsils out when I was five. The constant taste of pus in my mouth is still with me. The doctor said later it was the worst case he had dealt with in years. Ingrid

Sometimes children pretend they are ill or unwell in order to keep someone with them to protect them or in order to avoid being sent to see the abuser.

Frequent accidents and self-abuse

Similarly, children may hurt or injure themselves on purpose in order to protect themselves from the abuser. Mary recalls getting on her bicycle and deliberately riding it down a hill and into a lamppost. She knocked herself out and fractured her skull. She went to the hospital, where she felt safe. Lucy had an appendix operation when she was twelve years old. Although the operation was successful, her wound didn't heal for two years. She realized later that she had been opening the wound in her sleep. While the wound remained open, she was not sexually abused.

Ingrid scratched the eczema whenever it began to heal.

> Bedtime for me meant having bandages put all over my hands, arms and legs, and gloves put on to stop my fingernails from reaching the wounds. I even remember some nights when my hands were tied to the bed frame to prevent me from reaching the sores in my sleep. I always got free and literally tore off the flesh again. I still remember the tears and the pain.
>
> My mother would sit with me and hold my hand for three or four hours every night. She stayed until I was fast asleep and often then, when she tried to loosen my grip to get away from me, I woke up and she had to go through a long wait again. But because of my mother's devotion to helping me to avoid scratching the sores (which, I never did during the day) I was not "available" for abuse when my mother came to bed in the same bedroom. I found a way out. Ingrid

Self-injury and self-abuse are also expressions of self-disgust and forms of self-punishment. Children who are ashamed and blame themselves for the abuse may slash themselves with knives, burn themselves, hit or slap themselves or bang their fists or heads against the wall. Physical pain can bring relief from emotional suffering.

> I used to slash my face open with my hands. I broke a glass jar and slashed my arms and neck. I'd slash myself until the physical pain was greater than the pain I felt inside. Chris

In her pain and anger, Fiona smashed her fist through glass windows on many occasions. At least half of the Survivors we have worked with have harmed themselves in some way.

Summary

Children often do not tell that they are being abused. However, they usually show signs that there is something wrong and we have called these signs "silent ways of telling."

Adults frequently do not understand these signs. Instead of offering help and care, they label the child as naughty, silly, difficult, stubborn, mad or bad. Sometimes outside social services, such as mental-health workers, are brought in to help. In the past, when sexual abuse was little understood, this has sometimes resulted in a further abuse and labeling of the child by the system. Many Survivors grow up believing the labels, believing they are mad or bad.

Today we are becoming more sensitive to children's emotional problems and their causes. Unfortunately, adult Survivors have rarely been treated with such care in the past.

Once the links have been made between the childhood behavior and the sexual abuse, these labels can be left behind. The behavior of sexually abused children is not mad or bad—it is simply a way of coping with strong feelings of fear, distress and anger that cannot be expressed directly.

The exercises below are designed to help you look back over your childhood and understand and care for the child you were.

Exercises

1. Look at the list of childhood signs of sexual abuse in Table 3 and check any signs that you showed.

2. Write down what you think the adults around you thought about your behavior as a child. Include parents, teachers, social workers, psychologists or anyone else who is relevant. What did they say or do to you? Did they think you were distressed or did they think you were difficult, bad or mentally ill?

3. Write an account of how you felt as a child and the ways in which your behavior was affected by being abused. Try understanding and accepting the child you were rather than judging and criticizing yourself.

7

What Happened
When I Did Tell

I n previous chapters, we looked at reasons why children don't tell
anyone when they are being abused. We considered the silent
ways they show their distress. Some of the Wakefield Survivors *did*
tell someone about the abuse when they were children, and they all
told someone when they were adults. They frequently heard
negative reactions from those whom they told, which made them
feel more ashamed and afraid to tell anyone else. Ultimately,
however, someone reacted positively, enabling them to get help
and take the first step by breaking the silence.

The children who tried to tell

Until recent years, few people had heard about the sexual abuse of
children, even though it was happening to many children. It was
still a closely guarded secret. Survivors who are now adults did
sometimes tried to tell another person about their abuse when it
was happening, but they were often not believed; no one spoke
about sexual abuse and people just didn't believe it happened,
especially to someone they knew.

> I didn't realize it was wrong. I thought it happened to everyone. I
> told my school friends and they called me a liar. When they acted
> shocked and were going to tell the teachers, I realized it was
> wrong and so I pretended I had lied. I was frightened. They acted
> disgusted and shocked. It frightened me and I never mentioned it
> again to anyone. Margaret

Some children, like Margaret, tell other children, who don't believe it because it is outside their own experience and who are too young to be able to help. Katarina told a 7-year-old playmate, who probably could not even understand what she was hearing.

> The first time I remember clearly telling anyone was while my brother was still abusing me. I was about eight and I told a friend. For weeks I had prepared what I was going to say. She was the little sister of my brother's best friend. When I told her about the abuse, I expected her to be shocked and show some sympathy. Because of my brother's threats I knew the abuse was wrong. My friend did not say she didn't believe me, she said nothing, but while I was still telling her about what was so important to me she just shrugged her shoulders, turned and went off to play with some other children. I was in the middle of a sentence when she walked away, and I felt for the first time the feeling of total emptiness.
> Katarina

The response to children's disclosures is often that children "make up fairy tales," "have very active imaginations," or will do anything to get at their parents. Children can make up stories but so can adults, and adults make much better liars than children. Young children have no knowledge of sexual activity unless they have come into contact with it in some way. They cannot make up stories about something they know nothing about.

Pam approached two trusted adults when she wanted to talk about her experiences:

> I did tell someone when I was twelve years old. Around the time my father raped me, I approached my mother and tried to explain what I thought she already knew. But she refused to believe it. She said I was lying—did I realize it was my father I was accusing? She said I just wanted attention. She threatened me and told me not to tell anybody else about this "absurd" lie. I also approached my social worker, who was no better. He tried to worm his way out of it by pretending it never happened. When my parents found out I'd told the social worker I got a good whipping. After that I never told anybody. I kept myself to myself. I closed myself and my thoughts within a cocoon. Pam

Often when people are told about sexual abuse they cannot cope with the information. They don't want to believe it's actually happening or they don't know what to do about it. What mother wants to believe her husband, father, sister or son is an abuser? Sometimes it's not that people *don't* believe the child, rather that they *are afraid to* believe the child because then they would have to do something about it. Pam says that her mother, *"refused to believe me."* Pam's father was a violent man, and her mother probably was too frightened to stick up for her daughter and accuse him. This does not justify her mother's actions—Pam was left unprotected in an abusive situation—but it indicates some of the pressure her mother may have been under.

Pam also says that the social worker justifies not taking any action by *"pretending* it never happened." Doctors, teachers, psychiatrists, psychologists or anyone in the helping professions may also not want to believe that it's true. Believing may mean having to take action, rocking the boat; having to deal with the pain of the victim and the reaction of her carers; and having to confront one's own pain and anger. At least one in ten adults have been sexually abused as children. This includes all kinds of people—mothers, doctors, teachers, counselors, clergy—all of whom may hear disclosures. They may disbelieve a Survivor's story because they are still denying what happened to them. As human beings we have the ability to persuade ourselves that what we don't want to be true isn't true.

> When I was little I did tell my sisters that I didn't like my Grandad because he stuck his fingers up my bottom   at which I was slapped in the face by my sisters and told never to say it again.
> Polly

Polly's sisters did believe her, but they reacted like this because it was happening to each of them, too. They'd all been told to keep it secret—Polly had broken the promise.

> At that point, my two sisters realized it was happening to all of us. One of my sisters told my stepdad what Grandad was doing. He came up to reassure me and promised me it would never happen again. He would protect me. It continued to happen. He didn't protect me. He also said we couldn't tell my mom because it would upset her. I believed him and never mentioned it. Perhaps if I had told my mom it would never have happened again and I would have got help earlier and not be the mess I am today. I might even have liked myself. Polly

Many children who do manage to talk about their abuse are either not believed, like Pam and Margaret, or are believed but remain unprotected, like Polly. Some children get a more positive response and are believed and protected.

A child who is disbelieved when she tries to disclose can feel very frightened and confused. As we have seen in chapter 5, Survivors may already doubt themselves. Did it really happen? Did I make it up? Did I dream it? To be met with disbelief strengthens these doubts. Abusers often act normally after the abuse, "as if nothing has happened." This adds to the child's feelings that *she* must be mistaken.

Disbelief also adds to a child's feelings of helplessness and vulnerability. How can she ever stop it if she can't get anyone to believe her? If a child is disbelieved, by implication, she is accused of lying. Sometimes the child is told outright that she is lying and her disclosure is met with anger and insults. The sexual abuse is therefore compounded with further abuse and the child may feel betrayed by the lack of support.

The adults who tried to tell

Even as adults, Survivors may not be believed or taken seriously when they try to tell.

> The first person I told was my first husband. I don't think he thought it was true. He said, "Well, it's over now." He made me feel as though it was my fault for letting it happen. When I told my mom I think she felt helpless and maybe guilty. She didn't really want to know. She must have been blind not to see what my dad was doing all those years. Rachel

Many people find it very hard to cope with a disclosure of sexual abuse, sometimes because they don't know what to do to help. Pam's parents-in-law avoided her when they were told:

> When Brian told his mom and dad about my abuse they didn't telephone or visit for months - they thought it couldn't happen to anybody so close to home. However, they now understand why I hate my mom and dad so much. Pam

Graham hoped to get help from a doctor:

> Somehow I found the courage to approach my doctor, who was totally unsympathetic. She said, "I don't know what I can do" and

changed the subject. I could see a change in her expression and I tried to hurry the end of the consultation. I was on my way to a nervous breakdown and I came out even more depressed than I was when I went in. Graham

Although eventually Graham did get referred to a psychiatrist, he was still not given a chance to talk about what had happened to him.

Joanne's stepfather abused her throughout childhood. As an adult, she made sure her own children didn't come into contact with him by avoiding visits to her mother's when he was around.

Around four years ago my mother asked why we didn't visit her with our children while my stepfather was in the house. At that time he had just been released from prison after serving a sentence for abusing his natural daughter. I was so angry when my mother told me that my stepfather himself was asking as well. My anger made me tell my mother what my stepfather had been doing to me throughout my childhood. We both stayed remarkably calm under the circumstances. She looked surprised or kind of shocked at my disclosure although I do believe she already knew and was only acting shocked.

The next week when we saw her she even seemed protective of my stepfather, saying they hadn't actually had a big fight over it and, to my amazement, "He doesn't want any trouble at this point in his life." Joanne

Joanne's mother had believed her. Joanne believes her mother knew about the abuse while it was happening. She certainly knew he had abused his natural daughter. Joanne's mother chose to support the abuser and protect her own life, leaving Joanne feeling upset and betrayed.

Rhys also suffered when his mother didn't react to his disclosure:

My mother reacted as if it was nothing. I'm sure she knew, because she knew my sister had been abused. Rhys

It is difficult for Survivors to anticipate what kind of response they might get to a disclosure, as Anthony discovered:

I couldn't tell anyone about the abuse because I was afraid no one would believe me, and also because I was afraid of being rejected by my family. I decided to be open about my abuse years

after it had happened with people outside the family. The
responses were divided—some people understood and other just
didn't want to know. Anthony

Disclosure of sexual abuse may also be used to blackmail
Survivors. Lucy disclosed her childhood sexual abuse to her
psychiatric nurse. He used the information to keep her silent about
the sexual abuse he then inflicted on her.

Why do people react in these negative ways?

Many survivors, adults and children, received negative responses
when they talked about their abuse. Responses included: disbelief,
not being taken seriously, being believed but not protected, shock
and disgust, and being ignored. In recent years Survivors have also
been told that they are suffering from "false memory syndrome."
People react in these negative ways because they find it hard to
believe that sexual abuse really happens, they have not dealt with
their own sexual abuse, or they are frightened of the consequences
if they do believe and support the Survivor. Many people have also
been confused by the publicity about false memory syndrome (we
discuss this in chapter 17).

The emotional problems caused by sexual abuse can be made
worse by these negative responses to disclosure.

People I told often changed the subject because they didn't know
how to respond. Overall I felt I got mostly bad responses, so I
stopped telling because it only reinforced more negative feelings
about the abuse being my fault. Luke

Polly felt betrayed again when a trusted adult (her stepfather)
failed to keep his promise to protect her from the abuser. Margaret
felt guilty and ashamed about her schoolfriends' reactions of shock
and disgust. Pam felt powerless when neither her mother nor her
social worker responded to her cry for help. Being ignored can be
the most damaging response as once again the Survivor is treated
as if her feelings and experiences don't exist or matter.

Positive responses

It is possible to get useful and supportive responses from people
too. Sometimes it may take some persistence. Although Rachel had
received unhelpful responses from her mother and her first
husband, she was not put off from trying again.

After I was divorced I met Paul, and I thought I would tell him at the beginning so that I could try to sort out my feelings. He was really understanding and has supported me ever since. I also told Paul's mom. She was understanding and helped me try to see things in a different light. I also told a really good friend. She has helped me a lot and made me realize just what problems I had because of the abuse because I always blamed my unhappiness on other things.

I told my sister and she was understanding and told me she has always felt abused by my dad as well. I think other people didn't believe me in the past because they questioned whether things like this really happen. It always happens to someone else.
Rachel

Although Luke had had many negative responses to his disclosures, he decided to confide in his partner:

When I told my partner, she was extremely supportive and understanding of the issues. She maintained that she was my partner, not my counselor. Luke

Rhys also felt supported when he disclosed to his partner:

After I told my girlfriend, I expected her to be disgusted and not want any contact with me, but she was very concerned and to my surprise wanted to get close to me. Rhys

Pam had not been believed when she told as a child. She went on to have an unhappy first marriage and a divorce; then she met Brian.

I didn't tell Brian about what happened to me in my childhood, but to my surprise he told me he had already guessed what had happened to me. From his own job he knew the symptoms, reactions and effects too well not to notice. So I spilled the beans. Since then he has been my mainstay. Without his support I would have been a wreck. He is understanding, considerate, compassionate, sympathetic—everything I need. Pam

Graham eventually did get the response and the help he was looking for:

It just so happened that a documentary about sexual abuse came on the TV and they broadcast telephone helpline numbers for anyone who had been abused. I phoned and spoke to a

38-year-old man who had been abused, which made me feel a little better. He gave me numbers to call that would offer support and literature for self-help groups, and that's how I eventually was referred to professionals who counsel abused men and women. Graham

Why tell anyone?

Many Survivors had bad responses the first time they told someone of their abuse. So why encourage victims to tell? How will they benefit? The answer is, a child or adult who doesn't talk about the abuse is still keeping the abuser's secret and suffering in silence. All Survivors deserve the opportunity to release the heavy burden of the secret and to learn to feel better about themselves.

When I finally did tell, I cannot describe the relief I felt the next day. I was sitting quietly at my desk at work, and I remember realizing that I'd actually told someone at last. I'd told my boyfriend, my husband-to-be. I marveled at the fact that nothing terrible had happened. Joanne

Sharing the secret can be a first step to getting help for yourself and breaking free from the shame, guilt and pain.

I told my husband and he really tries to understand. Telling the bulimia group (eating-problems group) was the most useful thing for me, because now I can get help. I feel like I am not going to spend the rest of my life as a victim of people who want to use me. Shirley

Being able to tell people who listened meant that Shirley could get help for herself and learn to deal with abusive situations in her adult life.

Telling the right person can result in feelings of relief and liberation and be the first step on the path to overcoming your feelings about the past *and* your problems of today. Many Survivors have received treatment for years of depression, eating problems, "nerves," and so on, but improvements in these areas rarely last unless they get to the root of the problem.

Some Survivors decide to talk about their abuse in order to protect other children from the abuser, or to help themselves deal with worries about their own children. Often they meet a sympathetic partner and want to "come clean" and have an open and honest relationship.

When you feel ready to talk about the abuse, be aware that, for different reasons, the person you tell may not react sympathetically. The important thing is to persevere. Nearly all the Survivors we have worked with received unhelpful responses before they found someone ready to listen and to help them find a way to overcome their problems.

Once Survivors stop feeling ashamed and blaming themselves for the abuse, they begin talking about it to other people. Survivors are frequently surprised to find that many of their friends and family tell them that they too have been sexually abused, sometimes by the same abuser.

Nowadays the sexual abuse of children is in the news. More people know about it. More people are ready to listen and act to protect children and help adults. People are still around who won't listen, won't believe, will deny it, won't protect, and will abuse. However, there are more and more people around who *will* help. Try to find one of these people.

Ingrid's story

Ingrid first told a childhood friend about the abuse and wasn't believed. She continued to tell different people for more than thirty years until, at last, she got a sympathetic response and some help:

I think I may have told some friends at school when I was still a child, but I don't have a clear memory of that. I know that later I told my first husband, before I married him, when I was seventeen. I didn't like sex and thought it may have had something to do with my past. He believed me, but put little importance on the fact I had been abused. He beat me and took me in a sexual way that showed no love, no concern, no care for me. During my seven-year marriage to him, my problems increased. At times I became introverted and tried to analyze my problems to find a way to solve them. I couldn't do it on my own. I knew that only outside help could help me get rid of the memories that still haunted me. Very early in my marriage I realized I wouldn't get help from my husband, so I went to my primary-care doctor in Germany and told him, asking him to help me. His words: "Too bad, but forget about it, it's in the past." I had trusted him completely before, but when he could not respond to my need, not even see my need, I lost that trust. It took a few months for me to recover from the shock of telling someone I trusted and being brushed aside, as if what caused me pain had little importance.

My husband had many affairs, which made me feel even more inferior, and again I realized that I needed to sort out my life before I could sort out my marriage. I made an appointment with a marriage counselor, not to complain about my husband's behavior, but to tell the female counselor about the abuse and my consequent dislike for sex. She said it what I liked or didn't like was not important, and if I wanted my husband to remain faithful I would have to satisfy him in bed. She thought it was silly of me to make such a fuss over something so long in the past.

Again I walked home feeling empty and degraded. I spoke to two more people in the medical profession, people who should have known that professional help was needed. Always the response was, "Forget about it. He won't do it any more, so why do you worry about it?" By then I'd realized that more problems had developed, not only my distaste for sex. Every time I tried to tell someone who might be able to help, I also explained the effects the abuse had had on me. I got no help. Maybe I told the wrong people? I asked my brother to help me, begging my abuser to help me overcome the damage he did, by keeping out of my way. I was trying to avoid him. He didn't help me. He came to my house when he wanted to. Because my first husband had become friends with him and the lover of my brother's wife (with my brother's approval), I saw him frequently. I could not tell my parents. I felt I had to protect them from knowledge of what their son had done. But I talked to my sister, two cousins and an aunt and told them what he had done. They may have believed me, I don't know, but they looked at me in disgust and said, "He's got his faults, but he's also got his good sides, you shouldn't always see bad in people. He is your brother!" I was made to feel ashamed for telling the truth.

I withdrew into myself for a while and wondered if it was worth the bother. By belittling something that I felt had destroyed the value of my life they belittled me. One problem increased—the feeling of being worthless and of no importance. Not even my closest family seemed to care about my pain, and nobody was willing to help me.

I stopped telling anybody for about two years after my divorce while I tried to find out who I was and what direction to take in my life. When I met my second husband and knew I was going to marry him, I told him about my childhood experiences. But he is a man who cannot talk about feelings, cannot help me because he does not understand why I have a problem. If he has a problem, he ignores it and pretends it goes away. He believes me but is completely unwilling to listen to me talk about the past or my problems. So again, no help.

Because my regular primary-care doctor in Wakefield wasn't available, I saw someone else in his office when I went in with a minor health problem. I had not spoken about the abuse for about three years, apart from when I told my second husband. It was time to try again, because I knew I needed help. I didn't want to risk this marriage breaking up because I was an unfeeling partner during lovemaking. I don't think the doctor even heard what I was telling him. He never looked up from writing a prescription. He didn't say a word. By now I'd learned that if I wanted to tell someone about the abuse, I had to put all those years, all the pain and all the effects the abuse had on me into two or three sentences. I never got more time than that to talk about it. I was always interrupted with some patronizing remark. This time I didn't wait to recover from being rejected in my need for help. Within days I saw a female doctor in the family planning clinic and told her the same story. Her advice to overcome my dislike of physical contact was to "satisfy myself" or to "use a vibrator" if I couldn't find pleasure with a man. To a victim of sexual abuse who looks on sex as dirty and degrading, this is the most unhelpful suggestion there is.

Every time I told someone, the emptiness in me grew. I was so eager to find some response, someone who would say, "Tell me about it, I'll help you." I knew what my brother did was wrong. I wanted reassurance that it was wrong, someone to reinforce my belief that it was his fault that I wasn't feeling the way other women feel.

I tried to talk about it a few more times to people, mostly friends. They hardly acknowledged what they heard; none of them was supportive. Then I gave up. I resigned myself to never being able to enjoy sex; always having thoughts that I was less worthy than others; never losing the fear that my son would abuse his sisters; and all the other problems that I knew resulted from the sexual abuse I suffered as a child.

Suddenly I had some personal tragedies, which had nothing to do with my past. They came within a few weeks of each other and I became depressed. After three weeks, I went to see one of the doctors in my doctor's office. I told her about my depression, expecting to get some drugs to help. I gave her all the reasons why I thought things were getting too much for me. Again I mentioned in two sentences that I was abused as a child. For the first time in my life someone looked at me with sympathy, encouraging me to keep talking about it. We talked for about ten minutes. Never before was I allowed to say so much about how I felt it had affected me all my life. She told me about the Survivors groups and asked if I would be interested in joining them. I almost cried with relief. Yes, I was interested!

The new group had just started, so I had to wait three months before I could join, but from that day onward I felt protected. I saw that even though more than thirty years had passed since I first looked for help, it was not too late. We can change our lives, no matter how long it takes. The hardest part for me was always the moments just after telling someone, when I was not believed or told to forget it. But whenever I felt close to giving up I thought that somewhere, someone must care. I just had to find that person. Now I think that perseverance was the right way for me. If I had given up trying, I would not be the woman I am now. I am happier now and more fulfilled than I have ever been before.

Perhaps each of us can also be ready to listen and believe if someone (male or female, child or adult) chooses to disclose sexual abuse to us.

Exercises

1. If you have had a bad response when you've talked about your sexual abuse, try writing down what happened and why you think the person responded in this way.

2. Think about talking to someone about what has happened to you. Look at the Resources section at the back of this book. It gives suggestions about who you can tell and how to get help. If you phone one of the helplines, someone will listen to you—you will be believed. If you don't get an appropriate response, find someone else to talk to.

3. If you want to know how to respond if a child or an adult discloses sexual abuse to you, or if you suspect abuse, see chapter 17, *Working toward Prevention.*

PART THREE

Tackling the Problems

8

Buried Feelings

The ability to experience and express many different emotions—happiness, sadness, anger, grief, love, hate, fear and joy—is a natural part of being human. Sometimes, feelings are too intense or painful to be experienced or expressed directly. Problems Survivors have in adult life can be caused by the ways they have tried to cope with their painful thoughts and feelings about the abuse. They may try to forget and find ways to push their memories and feelings away or unconsciously cut off altogether so they won't remember what has happened or have no feelings about the event. The capacity to "seal off" protects people from fully experiencing the horror of their situation.

Burying feelings and memories

Abused children often hide their anger and distress from other people so that no one will suspect they are being abused. They may also keep their feelings under control while they are being abused to protect themselves from feeling distress and pain or because they do not want the abuser to see how much he is hurting them. Many adult Survivors continue to cope by blocking feelings and trying to forget about the abuse. However, the feelings and memories that people try to bury usually surface in some form and cause physical or emotional problems. Facing memories and feelings can be painful, but by finding new ways to express and process your memories and feelings instead of blocking them off you can begin to heal.

Below are some of the ways Survivors consciously or unconsciously cope by blocking memories and feelings, and the kind of problems this can cause.

Avoiding

Survivors commonly find ways to avoid thinking about their childhood abuse or to avoid their feelings about what happened. They may stay busy and distracted or make sure they are never alone so they don't have time to think. Some Survivors do the same thing again and again when their memories and feelings begin to surface; for example, washing themselves, cleaning, counting or checking things.

Survivors often try to avoid whatever might remind them of their abuse and cause their feelings and memories to surface. In particular, they may avoid anything to do with sex or sexual abuse (television programs, conversations, books) or anything that reminds them of their childhood (photographs, people, places, children).

> A few years ago I got out all my childhood photos. My brother was in many of them. I tore up the parts of the photos with his image and destroyed everything that reminded me of him. Yet the memories remained. Katarina

Some Survivors avoid people who express strong emotions; for example, people crying or shouting, because they fear it will churn up their own feelings. They may or may not be conscious of this behavior. Some Survivors describe mentally locking away their memories and feelings in a secure box.

Often Survivors are encouraged to behave this way because friends or advisers tell them that the best thing to do is put the abuse behind and get on with their lives. However, the memories and feelings do not go away; they are still there. They may be less accessible and less troublesome for a while, but this method of coping can lead to many problems.

Avoiding memories and feelings by keeping busy, finding distractions or repeatedly counting, checking or cleaning can be very stressful and lead to high levels of anxiety, and to phobias and obsessions.

> I couldn't express my feelings because of the constant battle to hide my secret and contain my fears. I perpetually felt like I was

bottling up my feelings and would explode. I wouldn't let anyone near me. I always played the joker or the agony aunt—I talked to other people about them, not me. I was always trying to look normal. I also became obsessed about working out. Luke

I pushed away the memories and feelings by cleaning excessively, brushing my teeth ten times or more a day, banging my head, slashing my wrists and burning myself. Graham

Adult Survivors often become so expert at sealing themselves off from distressing feelings that they do this automatically.

No matter what bad thing happened in my life, I could not cry. I could not feel any emotions. For most years of my adult life I was emotionally dead. I was neither happy nor sad, neither depressed nor angry. I simply felt nothing. Even when I was abused almost daily during my first marriage, it did not cause me the pain it should have. Most of the time it didn't bother me. I was too frightened to accept feelings of any kind. Ingrid

At first I used to have to concentrate and force myself to push away the feelings and memories. I blocked them out with different thoughts. Now it just happens without any effort—it's automatic. I even managed to forget about the abuse totally for 12 years. Rhys

Fiona had learned to avoid her feelings about being abused, and later realized that she had also dissociated herself from all bad feelings.

When I was talking to my daughter about growing up, I started telling her about when I was seventeen and my mom left home. Suddenly something hit me: I had never really noticed that my mother had left my life. It was as if I didn't care. I must have been so hardened to pain or pushed my emotions so deeply away that I couldn't feel the full extent of the hurt. Looking back now I get the stab of emotions, the emptiness, the betrayal. My sadness now as a mother myself could be the scars I bear from the kind of emotional upsets I suffered growing up.

I never really grieved about a lot of things, like the death of my granddad. I missed my granddad. I couldn't stand the emptiness I felt inside. Many times I wanted to cry, but most times I wouldn't let myself. Even today I do this. I feel ashamed to cry. I feel I'm

attention seeking and feeling sorry for myself so I get angry with myself and afraid about what people will think. Fiona

Physical tension

Feelings and memories can be held in check by physical tension. Children learn early to hold back tears by tensing their chest and face muscles. Anger, grief and rage can also be held in by tensing any part of the body. We talk about people becoming "rigid with rage" or "bowed with grief." These sayings illustrate how unexpressed feelings can affect the physical body.

Tensing the body can become an automatic response. It requires a great deal of physical tension and mental energy to hold back feelings and memories. It saps energy and can lead to chronic tension, headaches, aches and pains and many other physical problems. It also keeps the body in a heightened state of stress, and makes people more vulnerable to anxiety, panic attacks, illness and injury.

Food, alcohol and drugs

Food, alcohol and drugs can be used as ways of blocking out bad feelings. Eating can bring immediate comfort and enable people to distract themselves from their feelings and eventually block them out completely. Alcohol and drugs (legal and illegal) work in a similar way by allowing people to block out the pain and cut themselves off from reality. Alcohol, drugs and food can seem like very attractive ways of dealing with distressing feelings, memories and situations because they are easy to take and quick to work. But they are only short-term ways of blocking out distress. They may also become serious problems in themselves.

> *I blocked out my feelings by drinking alcohol excessively. I used alcohol as an escape from my thoughts, although it only worked temporarily. I got into trouble with the police because of the amount of alcohol I was consuming. I was aggressive at times, had mood swings and got arrested for being drunk and disorderly.* Anthony

Dissociating

Dissociating or blanking out is another way in which people can escape from their painful thoughts and feelings. They separate part of themselves from what is happening and from their distress and pain. Children may learn to dissociate when they are being abused. They separate, or dissociate, themselves from their bodies so that they do not feel the physical or emotional pain.

Some children describe the experience of stepping outside their bodies and watching themselves being abused without experiencing any of the pain. Others retreat into a fantasy world every time they are abused. Sometimes children learn to split themselves into different parts or identities to deal with different feelings, experiences and situations to help them cope with the overwhelming experience of being abused. Sometimes the different personalities do not know about each other or think they are separate people with different bodies. Dissociating is a way in which children cope with continuing abuse and is a way in which adult Survivors seal off painful thoughts and memories of the abuse. The Survivor may not realize that this is what is happening.

Blocking thoughts can go further, to become an automatic response to *any* bad feeling, however minor. This coping strategy becomes a serious problem over which the Survivor has no control. Sometimes adult Survivors go into a dissociated state for hours or days at a time. When they come out of this state they are often confused about what they have been doing or how they got to be where they are. Often they have been going about their everyday tasks, but may have appeared a little vague or different than usual. Sometimes people in such states are thought to be drunk or on drugs. Survivors who dissociate themselves from physical pain as children may discover they cannot feel pain as adults. Some Survivors "lose" time or learn they have said and done things about which they have no memory. Survivors who have developed separate parts of themselves may discover that they feel and behave very differently at different times. They may realize they do and say things that seem out of character at those times. Dissociating can be a very frightening experience. Survivors may feel they are going crazy or that there is something seriously physically wrong with them. Many are sent to see neurologists or to have other physical examinations.

Blacking out

Some Survivors black out or faint when there is no physical reason for this to occur. A Survivor may have blacked out for the first time while experiencing abuse as a child. Blackouts can happen to adult Survivors because something triggers memories and feelings about the abuse. In blacking out, they fall into a state in which they can no longer consciously think or feel. When they wake up they may have no memory of what caused the blackout.

Blackouts are frightening and physically dangerous. Lucy blacked out when anything reminded her of the abuse or her abuser. The blackouts protected her from emotional pain, but they became more frequent, and often she injured herself. Eventually she couldn't work or lead a normal life and was referred to a neurologist. When the neurologist found nothing wrong physically, Lucy was referred to a psychologist. As she began to deal with her sexual abuse, the blackouts occurred less frequently and eventually they stopped.

In addition to the methods mentioned above, Survivors also often seal themselves off from their memories and feelings by compulsively caring for others, by sleeping or by injuring themselves. All such coping strategies that block off memories and feelings can develop into problems in their own right.

Memories and feelings surface

Survivors can't count on suppressing bad memories and feelings if the underlying cause, the sexual abuse, is not dealt with. They may find that memories and feelings come back through dreams and flashbacks or surface unexpectedly. Sometimes Survivors transfer their feelings about the abuse to other people and situations.

Dreams. Hidden memories and feelings can come back into consciousness through dreams. Some Survivors have nightmares about exactly what happened when they were abused. Often they have nightmares that aren't about the abuse exactly but that relate to their feelings and memories of it; for example, nightmares about their childhood, the abuser, death, sex, being chased or trapped.

Flashbacks. Flashbacks are vivid memories in which a person feels he or she is re-experiencing a past event. During a flashback, the Survivor feels as if she is a child again and relives her abuse. Flashbacks are another way in which blocked memories and feelings can surface. They can happen at any time; the Survivor has no conscious control over them. Flashbacks can be triggered by reminders of the abuse and therefore often occur during sex. Like all forms of memory, flashbacks and dreams are open to distortion and may not represent past events accurately.

Many things and events can remind Survivors of their abuse. They may not always be able to avoid the triggers. Survivors who try to suppress their memories are vulnerable to being suddenly reminded of the abuse. They may find themselves caught unexpectedly by vivid memories. This can happen in situations where it is very difficult to deal with the memories; Dorothy's memories came back when she went into labor.

Table 4: Events That Trigger Memories and Feelings about Childhood Sexual Abuse

Below are some of the events and situations that may reawaken blocked memories and feelings about the abuse.

- ✦ Birth of a girl
- ✦ Birth of a boy
- ✦ Child reaching the age the Survivor's abuse started
- ✦ Death of the abuser
- ✦ Death of the mother or caretaker of the Survivor
- ✦ Meeting or seeing a person who looks like the abuser
- ✦ Revisiting the place of the abuse
- ✦ Hearing or reading about another person's abuse
- ✦ Feeling vulnerable, ill or under stress
- ✦ Any situation in which a Survivor once again feels
  - – stigmatized, e.g., falsely accused of stealing
  - – betrayed, e.g., partner has an affair
  - – powerless, e.g., fired from a job
  - – sexually traumatized, e.g., rape

Painful feelings can also come flooding back. Survivors frequently fly into fits of rage or dissolve into floods of tears for no apparent reason. Survivors may be taken by surprise by their feelings and unable to understand where they are coming from and what they mean. Many believe they are at the mercy of their hormones, suffering from premenstrual tension, postnatal depression, menopause or an unidentified chemical imbalance. Survivors may be treated for these problems, or for anxiety and depression, for many years without making a connection between their feelings and being sexually abused.

Feelings that do surface may be transferred to other people or other situations, where they can be more easily expressed. Survivors who feel very little about their own abuse may find themselves crying profusely while watching a movie or reading a book, or they may become mad with rage at an injustice done to another person. They may find themselves getting angry at people for trivial reasons.

> I was angry but I didn't know at what, so it was vented at my husband, the dog, anyone close to me. Jocelyn

Difficulties in relationships and sexual problems are also often the result of feelings about the abuse or abuser. The Survivor's buried feelings about the abuse surface and are transferred to a current relationship.

Facing buried feelings—when and why?

Recent research has shown that 50% of women and 23% of men receiving psychiatric help have been sexually abused. As we have seen, many mental health problems—such as anxiety, depression, phobias, sexual problems, eating disorders, drug addiction and tension—can be the result of burying feelings and memories about the sexual abuse. Survivors have often received many years of treatment for these surface problems before the underlying problem of the sexual abuse is uncovered and dealt with.

Eventually Survivors come to a point where the old coping strategies of suppressing no longer work or are becoming serious problems in themselves. Feelings and memories may be popping to the surface despite attempts to bury them. At this point, Survivors may decide they have to get help and that they need to disclose the abuse. They may have carried their secret for 10, 20, even 50 years before this happens.

In some cases, specific events cause memories and feelings about the abuse to surface.

> Last year I had a little girl who only lived an hour and then died. I thought I'd coped with it well, but my mother had been no help at all—she only came to see me once. I felt as though she'd let me down—everything accentuated how I'd felt for a long time about myself. I didn't like myself at all. I was really depressed, and one day I told my nurse that I'd been sexually abused as a child. I hadn't thought about it a lot, but I realized then that this was my problem. The death of my little girl brought back that my mother wasn't there for me, all those years ago; she didn't protect me then, either. That's what triggered my depression. Jocelyn

Jocelyn had been abused by two men 22 years earlier. She had struggled with her feelings and memories all those years by trying to push them away, but the death of her baby and the lack of response from her mother meant she was no longer able to keep them at bay. This prompted her to disclose her sexual abuse and then get help by joining a Survivors' group.

> I don't think I could have asked for help before. There's a point when it's right to go—for me, it was my mother letting me down again, and I could see it this time. Before, although I felt so bad, I didn't realize I needed help or that anything could help. Jocelyn

Rhys's feelings and memories also surfaced because of events in his life:

> I got a back injury playing football. I was laid up and couldn't be present at my son's birth. I got depressed. More and more memories came up, and I was flooded with emotion. That's when my primary-care doctor recommended that I get help. Rhys

Sometimes Survivors seek help because the abuse is having an effect on their relationship:

> I went for help because I became aggressive and I could not go on shouting and snapping at my wife. Graham

Getting into a relationship may also mean the abuse begins to surface:

> I fell in love with an individual who refused to let me stay insular and demanded to know everything about me. Once I began telling, the pressure became intense. I felt close to a nervous breakdown, so I sought help. Luke

Survivors may have to reach a stage where they feel absolutely desperate or attempt to end their life before they start to talk about the abuse.

> I was getting suicidal. I felt I was totally losing control and that I didn't have the right to make decisions. I always used to feel in control at work but now this was starting to crumble, along with everything else. I went to see my doctor for a referral for psychological evaluation. Jane

Anthony's use of alcohol led to increasing problems with the police. Luckily his need for help was recognized:

I had been put on probation so many times the courts didn't know what to do with me. Then I told them about my abuse and my probation officer got help for me. Anthony

Lucy had kept her memories and feelings buried by blacking out, but when this coping strategy became a serious problem in itself she decided to get help.

I kept having blackouts and being admitted to the hospital. They couldn't find anything physically wrong with me and referred me to a psychologist. I was so desperate that I either had to do something and get it right or kill myself. I decided it was time I really got to the bottom of it. Lucy

Like Lucy, some Survivors eventually get psychological help after they have been through a range of physical tests and investigations. Their physical problems (blackouts, fits, numbness, pains, gynecological problems) are revealed to be the result of emotional distress caused by being sexually abused.

I never used to cry or even get upset; I'd always black out. During one Survivor's group meeting, however, I burst into tears. Crying made me feel better, and I felt as if I could talk about the abuse. Feelings of anger also came out in the group.

Before, I always said I was "fine" and didn't need help, but I kept having blackouts. I think I would have killed myself if I hadn't found help. Now I can say "I'm not fine," and I don't have to act brave. Lucy

Some problems caused by blocking feelings are discussed in greater detail in the following chapters. We discuss ways of dealing with these particular problems, but to overcome them you also need to find ways to express and process the underlying feelings and memories about the sexual abuse.

The return of powerful feelings and memories can be frightening and disturbing. However, it does mean that they can still be experienced and dealt with even if the abuse happened long ago. Allowing your buried feelings and memories to surface is the first step. Being truly in touch with your feelings not only helps to heal the past but also allows you to experience life more fully and openly in the present.

Exercises

1. Write a list of any ways in which you have tried to block your memories and feeling; e.g. avoiding (places, people, thoughts); keeping busy; distracting yourself; obsessively doing something (counting, checking, cleaning); using alcohol, drugs or food; sleeping; dissociating; blacking out.

2. Look at Table 4 (page 93) and check any events that have triggered your memories and feelings about the abuse.

3. Many Survivors have lost touch with their feelings. In order to help you get back in touch with your feelings, during the next few days keep asking yourself, "What am I feeling now?" Do this regularly throughout the day, and make a note of your feelings. Put a Post-it® note on your watch (or on something else you look at regularly) to remind you to make a note of your feelings every time you look at it.

9

Anxiety, Fears and Nightmares

When I had my first panic attack, I didn't know what was happening. I just felt a fear I had never experienced before. I was scared to tell anyone because I thought I was cracking up and they would think I was really stupid. Polly

Not being able to eat in front of people came on gradually—it just seemed to get worse and worse. It was as if everybody was watching me. Mavis

Many Survivors of childhood sexual abuse feel tense and nervous much of the time. Some Survivors cannot travel alone, avoid busy stores, are unable to eat in front of people, have panic attacks or think everybody is looking at them. Other Survivors have intense fears of specific things, such being in the dark or older men. These are all anxiety problems, and while many people suffer from anxiety, it is a particularly common problem for people who suffered abuse in childhood. They have experienced so much fear as children that even as adults their minds and bodies are still in a state of fear.

Anxiety

When people feel anxious, their minds and bodies are in a state of fear, although they are not in danger. Anxious people are usually tense and may describe themselves as "jumpy," "nervous" or "wound up." Anxiety has three parts: physical symptoms, changes in behavior and negative thoughts. Table 5 (below) contains a list of the more common symptoms of anxiety.

Physical symptoms

Anxious people experience the same physical reactions as people do when they are in danger. When people are in danger their bodies increase the production of stress hormones (adrenalin and cortisol). This is known as the "flight or fight" response, which helps people deal with dangerous situations by preparing the body for action.

Table 5: Common Anxiety Symptoms

Physical symptoms

- tension
- palpitations (awareness of heartbeat)
- "butterflies" in stomach
- trembling, shaking
- pins and needles
- feeling short of breath
- loss of appetite
- poor sleep
- sweating
- chest pain
- dry mouth
- weak legs
- aches and pains
- vomiting
- diarrhea
- blurred vision
- surroundings seem unreal
- nausea
- poor concentration
- dizziness
- churning stomach
- headache

Behaviors

- drinking too much
- eating too much
- eating too little
- taking drugs (prescribed or illegal)
- avoiding going places
- escaping from places where you feel afraid
- obsessive cleaning, counting or checking

Negative thoughts

- I'm going to have a heart attack.
- Everyone can tell what I'm really like.
- My children are going to have a bad accident.
- I'm cracking up.
- I'm going to end up in a mental hospital.
- Everyone is talking about me.
- People think I'm dirty.

Anxious people, however, experience these bodily symptoms even when they are not in danger. Many of the physical symptoms of anxiety, such as palpitations, butterflies in the stomach and dry mouth, are caused by the body's natural response to danger.

People often begin to breathe quickly or gasp for air (hyperventilation) when they are afraid. This rapid breathing causes changes in the chemistry of the blood, creating physical changes associated with anxiety (such as feeling short of breath, pins and needles, and dizziness). People also tense their muscles in response to fear and this can become a habit, resulting in aches and pains in many parts of the body.

Negative thoughts

When people are anxious, they have negative thoughts about themselves or other people. They often assume something awful is about to happen; for example, "I'll never see my children again." Anxious people often have negative thoughts about harmless events. They may, for example, notice somebody looking at them and think, "Everyone is looking at me. They can tell what I'm really like." The negative thoughts may be connected to the physical symptoms of anxiety.

Possible physical symptoms	Negative thoughts
Feeling dizzy	"I'm going to pass out"
Tingling sensation	"I'm having a stroke"
Blurred vision, things look unreal	"I'm going crazy—I'll end up in a mental hospital"

This kind of thinking is called *catastrophizing;* in this case, making a catastrophe out of the harmless (but uncomfortable) physical symptoms of fear.

Negative thoughts make anxiety worse by making the person become more afraid. This in turn produces more physical symptoms and starts a vicious circle of increasing fear.

Behavior changes

When people feel anxious, they often change their behavior in order to cope with their feelings. If they feel anxious in a particular situation, they may have a strong urge to escape, and sometimes they do run away. They may avoid that situation in the future because they fear they will become anxious there again. People also try to cope with feelings of anxiety by eating more, taking pills or drinking alcohol. However, avoiding confronting fear by using any of these coping strategies actually increases the fear. Unfortunately, all these ways of trying to cope with anxiety can become habits and, in time, develop into problems themselves, such as agoraphobia, compulsive eating, tranquilizer dependence, alcohol abuse and obsessive behavior.

Connections to sexual abuse

When people are anxious, they have often been in danger or experienced a great deal of fear in the past. Their bodies have continued to respond with the symptoms of fear even when they are no longer in danger. Children who are being abused may feel fearful for much of their childhood: afraid they will be sexually abused again; afraid the abuser will do something worse; afraid they are being physically damaged by the abuse; afraid they will get pregnant; afraid that people can tell they are being abused; or afraid of the consequences if someone finds out.

When children experience fear like this for long stretches of their childhood, it is unlikely this fear will just disappear when the abuse stops or they become adults. These children have learned to be fearful and will probably continue to experience the symptoms of fear until they understand why they are anxious and learn how to control their fear.

Nightmares

Survivors often become anxious when they start remembering or thinking about their sexual abuse. Their fears may be expressed as nightmares. Rachel felt so terrified by her nightmares that she made her fiancée walk the streets with her at night so that she could avoid having to go to sleep. Nightmares often illustrate fears and memories that are too frightening or painful for Survivors to face when they are conscious. But nightmares are not necessarily accurate pictures of past events.

Survivors often have nightmares about death, perhaps expressing the idea that it feels as though the sexual abuse killed something in them. Remembering her own sexual abuse may make a Survivor anxious about the safety of her children, and this may come out in her dreams.

My fears were really coming out in my nightmares. I dreamed I was in town and suddenly realized I had left my young daughter in someone's care where my abuser could get to her. I tried desperately to save her before he abused her. However fast I tried to go, I couldn't seem to reach her. The abuser was getting nearer to her all the time, right up to him opening the door to where she was—then I woke up screaming. Kate

Dreams can be terrifying, but they can also be a useful way for Survivors to process their memories about the abuse, to express their fears and to explore more difficult feelings.

Panic attacks

I had to go to the hospital to see a doctor. I took a taxi there and sat in the waiting room. The clock seemed to be ticking really loud and everything seemed very noisy. I was called into the doctor's office. He was talking to me but I just couldn't hear what he was saying. I started sweating and felt very hot. My hands were trembling, and I couldn't stop swallowing. My chest felt tight and I felt the room was closing in on me. I just had to get out. Polly

Panic attacks are an extreme form of anxiety, usually triggered by thoughts and memories. They are frightening because the physical symptoms are powerful and unexpected. People often react by thinking they are going to have a heart attack or die. These thoughts make people even more frightened and that increases the physical symptoms and the tension. In turn, this leads to more negative thoughts and causes the panic to build up and up. When people have panic attacks, they experience a very strong urge to run and may do so.

Survivors may have intense and sudden attacks of anxiety when they think about their abuse or are in situations associated with their abuse.

The first time I can remember having a panic attack was when I was about ten years old. I was at a Christmas party at my grandma's house. Three of my abusers were present at the party. I remember feeling very frightened and very dizzy. My heart was thumping very hard. I could feel all the pulse points in my body going and I started shaking all over. I felt very faint and weak. At the time I didn't realize what was happening. I didn't realize I was having a panic attack. Wendy

Some Survivors, like Wendy, started having panic attacks as children but many develop them for the first time as adults.

When I had my first panic attack, I was having flashbacks and nightmares about the sexual abuse by my grandfather. I tried to push the memories away and get on with my everyday life, but the panic attacks kept happening. Polly

Fears and phobias

Some Survivors are not only generally anxious, but also suffer from phobias—irrational fears of specific things or situations. People can develop phobias about situations where they have had traumatic experiences: people who have been involved in a car crash may become phobic about traveling in cars; or a child who is bitten by a dog may grow into an adult who is phobic about dogs. Some people, though, are not aware of how their fear began. People often develop phobias about situations (being in a supermarket, in a group of people, near a particular animal, in the dark) where they have felt anxious or had panic attacks. The initial fear can develop into a phobia if the person avoids getting into that situation again, thus allowing the fear to grow.

Being sexually abused is usually a traumatic experience and Survivors may develop fears and phobias. In this section we describe the phobias that are most commonly associated with sexual abuse.

Agoraphobia

The first panic attack I attributed to being tired and under stress, but they kept happening to me. They made me so frightened that I was scared to go out or do anything for fear of having one. If I went out, I would start feeling really shaky and my heart would be thumping. I would sweat and I felt dizzy, like I was going to pass out. I had to leave wherever I was. I just needed to run and get away, preferably home, where it would go away. I quit work and became a hermit. My friends and relatives tried to help but I wouldn't admit to them what was happening to me. I made excuses: too tired, headache, felt sick, anything to get out of going out. I tried going back to work but I was really nervous.

I seemed to cope for a while and then again, out of nowhere, I had another panic attack. I stopped working and became really

*depressed, thinking I was cracking up and would wind up locked
up in a nut house.* Polly

Agoraphobia is an intense fear of being away from the safety of the
home, being in busy places and feeling trapped. People who suffer
from agoraphobia often fear traveling on public transportation,
standing in a line, being in a busy place, being alone, or being out
of the house.

*I hate crowded places like supermarkets and shopping malls.
Sometimes I try to overcome this, but it is not easy for me.* Anthony

*Sometimes on a bus I feel like everyone is staring at me. I want to
run and hide - I feel threatened. I'm also frightened of spiders and
can't go upstairs if there is one around.* Rhys

Some people with agoraphobia feel safe enough to go outside if
they are in or near their car, or if they have someone else with
them.

Some Survivors of sexual abuse, like Polly, develop
agoraphobia. They may feel threatened and anxious when they are
outside their own homes and therefore develop a fear of leaving
them. Survivors have often felt trapped and out of control during
the abuse and these feelings may return whenever they are in
situations they cannot leave immediately; for example, waiting at
supermarket checkouts. Some Survivors do not feel safe when they
are alone because the feelings and memories of the abuse return.

Social phobia

Social phobia is a fear of meeting people or being in situations
where there are other people. Many Survivors suffer from social
phobia. They are self-conscious and think other people are looking
at them. Survivors often have negative thoughts that others can see
how guilty or dirty they are inside, or can see that they have been
sexually abused. They may feel particularly self-conscious when
they are eating in public. Some people feel they have a lump in
their throat or are going to choke. Survivors may have coped with
the abuse by isolating themselves from other people and feel
uncomfortable around others for that reason. They may avoid
other people because they are afraid of being abused or betrayed
again.

After Joan was abused by her sister's boyfriend in the
bathroom of her parents' home, she had to go back into the family

room and face her family. She felt ashamed and guilty and felt sure
they would be able to tell that she had been abused. As an adult,
Joan was shy and self-conscious, often blushing and trying to
avoid being the center of attention. She was too embarrassed to go
to the bathroom when she was at work or at a restaurant or other
public place, although she didn't understand why. When she came
out of a public restroom she thought everyone was staring at her.
She felt guilty, anxious, embarrassed and unsteady on her feet. She
coped by drinking as little as possible when she was out so she
wouldn't need to go to the restroom. Eventually she stopped going
to the restroom all day at work and avoided social gatherings. Joan
started off with a fear of public restrooms, but eventually
developed a social phobia.

Fears associated with the abuser

Survivors often have fears that are associated with the person who
abused them: fears of body hair, the smell of alcohol, cigarette
smoke, being kissed by older men, people with glazed-over eyes,
men generally.

As adults, both male and female Survivors who have been
abused by men may, as adults, be frightened of all men or a specific
group of men; for example, older men, or men with beards. Kate
was abused by several men, and as an adult she was frightened of
being alone with a man.

> When I went into a store I hated to have men wait on me.
> Sometimes I wouldn't go into a store at all unless I thought a
> woman would wait on me. Kate

Some abusers seem to go into a semi-trance while they are abusing.
Survivors often describe the glazed look in the eyes of their abusers
before or during the abuse, and often as adults they become fearful
if they see someone with eyes that look glazed over.

Fears associated with the abuse

Some fears and phobias develop because of their association with
the situation where the Survivor was abused or with objects used
during the abuse. Survivors often fear bathrooms, being in a room
with a closed door, the dark, being touched, washing their hair or
being alone at night. Abuse often occurs in the dark or behind
closed doors. Many children are abused in bathrooms; abusers who
are family members often take advantage of a child taking a bath

or washing their hair and use this as an opportunity to abuse them. Graham was raped in a public restroom by three men. He now has a fear of using public restrooms and a fear of being among men. Survivors develop fears of being touched in certain ways, on certain parts of the body or by particular people; these fears are usually associated with touch they experienced during the abuse.

Survivors may have fears relating to objects used during the abuse: knives used to threaten the child, bottles or other objects that were inserted into the child's anus or vagina. Lucy blacked out whenever ice cream was mentioned; her abuser had smeared her with ice cream. Some Survivors are manipulated or forced into sexual acts with animals. Moira had been forced into sexual acts with a dog and as an adult was very afraid of them.

> Before therapy I couldn't go near a dog without cringing and turning away, but now I can actually bathe my friend's dog without feeling ashamed and guilty about touching him. Moira

Claustrophobia (the fear of being in an enclosed space) can also develop from being locked in or feeling trapped during the abuse.

Fears associated with the abuser's threats

The threats used to silence some children are so terrifying that they develop lasting fears that the threats will be carried out. Sophie was raped on a grave when she was seven years old. The abuser said that if she told anyone, the rotting man in the grave would know and would find her. This threat was so terrifying for Sophie that she buried all memory of the abuse and, even as an adult, had nightmares about rotting bodies coming to get her and a phobia of dead bodies. Lorna's abuser said he would know, and would kill her, if she ever told anyone about the abuse. This threat affected Lorna so that as an adult she was very anxious. She was unable to talk about the abuse because she believed she could actually see her abuser in the room with her and could hear him threatening her. Many survivors hallucinate their abusers; that is, they see, hear, smell, taste or feel the abuser when the abuser is not actually there. These experiences are often associated with the Survivor feeling very fearful, especially about the abuser's threats.

Adult fears that may seem to be irrational can often be traced to an association with the abuser, the abuse situation or to the threats that accompanied the abuse. Many things can trigger these fears in everyday life.

Obsessional problems

Some anxious people suffer from obsessional problems. They may feel they have to clean their house for hours every day, count things, do something a particular number of times, or check that the doors are locked over and over again. There are usually repetitive thoughts that go along with these actions; for example, "If I don't check the doors six times, my son will have a terrible accident," or "If I don't clean the kitchen floor again, everyone will know how dirty I am." Some people have repetitive thoughts but do not engage in repetitive action.

Survivors may cope with their anxiety and memories of the abuse by repeatedly doing something. While they are busy cleaning, counting or checking, they are distracted from thinking about their past and tend to feel less anxious. Cleaning is a common obsession for Survivors. When Survivors feel dirty inside, they often try to make up for it by trying to keep their homes immaculately clean. They may spend many hours every day cleaning the house and be unable to leave a cup unwashed or a speck of dirt on the carpet.

> I have huge fights with my husband if he leaves anything on the floor. I always take my vacuum cleaner to bed with me and sometimes I have to vacuum the whole house at four in the morning. Pam

Some Survivors also wash their bodies over and over in an attempt to feel clean. Fiona was sexually and physically abused as a child. She felt dirty and was often nervous and afraid; she coped with these feelings by cleaning her bedroom.

> When I was a child, I used to scrub my bedroom at all times of the day. I felt dirty, so I'd roll back the carpet and scrub the floorboards and the walls. I was always cleaning. I'd even get up in the night and start sweeping my bedroom. Fiona

This way of dealing with her feelings continued when she was an adult.

> When I grew up and got my own house, I was obsessed with cleaning. I'd start at seven in the morning and still be at it at midnight. If I didn't half-kill myself cleaning, I felt bad and dirty so it was like a ritual, I cleaned to make myself feel better. Fiona

The more anxious a person with an obsessional problem feels, the more he or she cleans, counts or checks. Doing these things brings temporary relief from anxiety, followed by a feeling of even greater anxiety. When a Survivor is anxious because she feels out of control or in danger, repetitive thoughts and actions can be reassuring. They may also be a superstitious or childlike way of trying to ward off danger.

Fiona was in danger of sexual and physical violence throughout her childhood. As an adult, she still saw danger around her all the time and believed any happiness she had would be taken from her just as in her childhood. When she was under stress, Fiona had obsessional thoughts about her daughter and husband being killed. She tried to ward off her fears by cleaning her house until it was spotless.

> I feel as if Amy and Andrew are going to be taken away from me.
> Every minute I'm with them seems like the last. I can't enjoy them.
> I get flashes of them gone. The thoughts are different every day.
> One day it's Amy getting killed on her bike or being knocked down,
> the next it's that they are both going to get killed in the car, and
> another day I am sure the house is going to burn down. Everything
> around me feels dangerous. My obsession with cleaning the house
> is back and it has taken over this last week. Fiona

Coping with anxiety and fears

Feeling afraid increases your feelings of powerlessness; overcoming your fears will help you feel more in control of your life. If you experienced a great deal of fear in your childhood, you may still feel tense and anxious as an adult. Trying not to think about your abuse can increase your anxiety. Working through your feelings about your childhood abuse can help reduce your anxiety. Fears a Survivor experiences as an adult are often related to her fears as a child and to the situations in which she was abused. If you have a phobia or intense fear of certain situations, objects, people or animals, think about whether there is a link between the phobia and your abuse. Is there a connection between whatever frightens you now and your abuser, where the abuse occurred, what happened during the abuse or the threats the abuser used?

Understanding the link between your specific fear and where it originates can help you reduce the fear. You may realize that you are afraid of bathrooms because you were abused in one, or that you are phobic about knives because you were threatened with knives as a child. Some fears may have no obvious link with the abuse, yet the stress caused by the abuse probably played an important part in creating and maintaining the fear.

After attending a Survivors group and working through her problems, Kate realized that her fear of men was linked to her abuse.

> I can handle men much better now. So much so that I recently took driving lessons with a male instructor and really enjoyed learning to drive. Kate

You have *learned* to feel anxious and afraid through your bad experiences. You can also learn how to reduce the bad feelings and live a normal life without all the fears. Anxious people are often afraid they are going to lose control. You can overcome this fear by learning to gain self-control in situations that are usually frightening. The suggestions in the rest of this chapter can help you reduce your symptoms of anxiety. It may also help you to read one of the books suggested at the end of this chapter or to go to an anxiety-management or relaxation class. Learning to control your general anxiety will help reduce your fears and obsessions. If you are very anxious or have a phobia or obsession that is disrupting your life, ask your doctor to refer you for expert help. You do not need to tell your doctor about the sexual abuse.

Look at the list of anxiety symptoms in Table 5 and check any that you experience. In the following section, we suggest ways in which you can learn to deal with the three parts of anxiety.

Physical symptoms

Begin to control the physical symptoms of anxiety by learning how to relax, learning how to breathe correctly and by exercising.

When people are afraid, they tend to tense their muscles. This can cause headaches, chest pains, stiffness or pain in almost any part of the body. If you are anxious, you are probably getting more and more tense as the day goes on. You need to find a way of relaxing your muscles. It will help to learn a relaxation exercise like the kind taught in prenatal classes or at the end of a yoga class. Your doctor might know of a relaxation class near you, and some doctors' offices and adult-education centers run classes.

Remember, you have learned to be tense, so you need to learn how to relax and let go of your tension. Practice a relaxation exercise every day at first. When you feel generally less tense, you only need to do the relaxation exercise three or four times a week and when you are feeling particularly stressed. When people have been tense for a long time, they sometimes feel strange when they begin to relax. Persevere and you will eventually become familiar and comfortable with the feeling of being relaxed.

For some people gardening, running, knitting, yoga, meditation or cooking can be relaxing. Breathing exercises are also good ways of relaxing. It is important that you choose a way of relaxing that you like and that you try to relax completely every day. When you can relax, you can learn to notice the first signs of tension. At that point you can let go and relax right away, before the tension builds up. Learning to relax will also help you sleep better.

Controlling your breathing

When we are afraid, a natural reaction is to breathe very fast or to gulp air (hyperventilation). We breathe in oxygen and breathe out carbon dioxide, and the bloodstream usually contains a balance of carbon dioxide and oxygen. Hyperventilation occurs when someone breathes too fast and therefore breathes out too much carbon dioxide. This creates an imbalance of oxygen and carbon dioxide in the blood. Many of the physical symptoms of anxiety are due to hyperventilation. Unfortunately, hyperventilation also makes you feel short of breath, so you try to breathe even faster, creating a greater imbalance in your blood.

When you feel yourself becoming afraid, try to breathe very slowly and smoothly. Try closing your mouth and breathing through your nose. It's hard to breathe fast through your nose. Some people find it helps to breathe in and out of a paper bag. Hold the bag tightly round your mouth and nose, breathe out into the bag and then breathe the same air back in. By doing this, you inhale the carbon dioxide you have just exhaled, thus correcting the balance of oxygen and carbon dioxide in your blood.

Overbreathing like this can become a habit, causing some people to breathe too fast, or sigh a lot, even when they are not afraid. Practice breathing slowly and gently and become more aware of your breathing.

Exercising

Your body increases the production of stress hormones when you are afraid. Residues of these stress hormones left in your body can leave you feeling restless and unable to sleep; exercise can help eliminate them from your bloodstream. Exercise has also been shown to change people's mood and help them feel better.

Challenging negative thoughts

Feeling afraid usually begins with negative thoughts about what is happening, what is about to happen, or what other people are thinking. A vicious circle begins, with negative thoughts producing physical symptoms of fear. These physical symptoms lead to more negative thoughts, and so on. The fear may build up until you feel out of control. You can break this vicious circle if you learn to talk yourself through your fear by challenging your usual negative thoughts with more realistic thoughts.

Here is an example of the thoughts one Survivor has who feels nervous about going into a local store alone. On the left are her usual negative thoughts and on the right are more realistic ways of thinking.

Negative thoughts make you feel more afraid. You may not realize you are having negative thoughts and believe that the fear just descends upon you. By becoming aware of your negative thoughts and arguing against them, you can reduce your fear.

Negative thoughts	*Realistic thoughts*
Everyone is staring at me. They know there's something wrong with me. They think I'm dirty. My heart's going funny. Oh no, it's starting again. I'm going to have one of my episodes. I have get out of here before I pass out.	People are not staring at me, they are just looking around. No one can see what I'm feeling. My heart is not going funny; it's only beating faster because I'm nervous. It won't hurt me. I've had these funny feelings before and they always pass. If anyone did notice what was happening to me, they would just think I felt sick or something. No one knows I've been abused. I'm not going to pass out—I haven't before. I'll just breathe slowly to calm myself down and I'll be fine. I'll buy the bread and go home for a cup of herbal tea.

Write down the thoughts you have when you feel afraid and then try to challenge these thoughts by writing down more realistic ones. This won't be easy at first, but it is a skill you can learn. With practice, you will reduce your negative thoughts and your anxiety. (Chapter 10, *Depression and Low Self-Esteem*, contains more examples of how to challenge negative thoughts.)

Changing what you do

No escape

A common response to fear is to run away, or to want to run away. Escaping from frightening situations may make you feel better immediately, but it can make you more anxious in the long run. Fear and panic die down in time, but if you escape you do not learn that your fear would have died down anyway. You begin to believe that you are afraid of the situation itself—when in fact, it is your negative thoughts in that situation that trigger the fear. When you go into that situation again, you are more likely to run away because you escaped last time and felt better. This may happen in more and more places until eventually there are few places where you feel comfortable. This is how agoraphobia develops. Other phobias develop in a similar way.

The key rule is DO NOT ESCAPE when you are feeling afraid or are having a panic attack. Try to stay in the situation until your fear dies down. Find a quiet corner or sit down somewhere, but try to stick it out. If you do feel you have to leave, then do so slowly, wait until you feel calmer, and then return to the situation you left. Leave if you want to *after* your fear has died down. Remember, panic attacks are very unpleasant but they are not harmful. *Note:* These instructions only apply to situations where you are afraid but you are not in any real danger; for example, if you are in a situation where you may be attacked, then you must leave for your own safety.

Facing your fears

Once you have been frightened in a situation, you may avoid getting into that situation again, and this will cause your fear to get worse. The next important rule is DO NOT AVOID. To defeat your fears, you have to face up to them. You can devise and work through a program to help you overcome your fears.

The first step is to find out exactly what situations trigger your fears. Be as specific as possible. Going out alone may be what frightens you. Maybe only supermarkets frighten you, or only supermarkets when they are very busy. Try to define exactly which situations increase your fear, including where it happens, when it happens and what people are around (or not around) when it happens.

Draw up a list of situations where you become frightened, starting with a situation where you experience only a little fear (for example, going into a local store when it's empty) and finishing with your most feared situation (for example, going into a crowded supermarket alone on a busy Saturday afternoon). You may find it is easier to work through your program on your own, or you may want to have someone with you when you first start practicing, but make it a goal to try it on your own when you can. Try to include as many steps as possible between the least and most frightening situations.

Start by attempting the situation on your list that frightens you the least. Learn to control your fear by not escaping, trying to relax, slowing your breathing and talking yourself through it by challenging your negative thoughts. You need to practice this every day. When you can cope with the least difficult situation, then move down your list and try the next task. Relax, breathe slowly, control your negative thoughts and, step by step, face your feared situations.

However, sometimes anxiety attacks are triggered by things that you can easily avoid without it interfering with your life too much. You may be able to avoid some triggers easily in the long term, while you could avoid other triggers in the short term as a means of stabilizing your feelings and experiences and gaining a sense of control. For example, you may find that watching programs about child abuse or listening to certain types of music trigger flashbacks or anxiety attacks. These kinds of triggers usually can be avoided fairly easily (turn the TV or radio off; leave the room) until you feel better able to cope with them. You will find more about dealing with triggers in the *Breaking Free Workbook*.

Taking control of panic attacks

> I have to be strict with myself and know that even when I panic now it doesn't mean it's the end of the world. I try to stay where I am, breathe slowly and concentrate on telling myself, "I can do it, I will succeed." It helps me. Polly

Panic attacks are intense waves of anxiety. To control them, you need to deal with the three parts of anxiety in the ways described above:

+ Physical symptoms. *Try to relax, breathe slowly and smoothly.*

+ Behaviors. *Stay where you are. Do not escape.*

+ Negative thoughts. *Think realistic thoughts; for example, "It's only a panic attack, it will pass soon, I won't pass out or go crazy. I've had them before and they aren't pleasant, but nothing terrible happened."*

When you have a panic attack, you may also experience a feeling of dread as if something awful is going to happen. In fact the panic attack itself is the awful thing—nothing worse is going to happen. Just try to let the panic attack wash over you, don't fight it.

Coping with nightmares

Whenever I had a flashback or a nightmare I would write it down, and that really helped. Polly

Nightmares are a way for your subconscious fears and memories to come to the surface. The best way to deal with them is to write them down in detail after you wake up so they cannot stay at the back of your mind as a subconscious fear. Processing your memories about the abuse and working on your feelings about it will help you conquer your fears, and the nightmares will subside. Remember that nightmares are not necessarily accurate memories of events.

A note on medication

You may be taking tranquilizers or antidepressants to help you with your anxiety. These drugs can help in the short term by suppressing your symptoms, but in the long term you will probably need to face your fears to defeat them. The techniques described here may help you control your anxiety symptoms without taking pills. DO NOT STOP TAKING ANY PILLS ABRUPTLY—this can be very dangerous. If you want to reduce your medications, discuss it with your doctor.

Summary

The experience of childhood sexual abuse and the associated feelings of fear and dread often result in the adult Survivor feeling anxious and sometimes also suffering from specific fears, phobias or obsessions. You probably will find your anxiety decreases as you work through your feelings about the abuse. You may also need to work on the symptoms themselves. To overcome your anxiety, you have to face your fears and work on your physical symptoms, negative thoughts and behaviors. You have learned to be anxious and fearful because of your childhood experiences. You can learn to overcome your fears and take control of your own life again.

Suggestions

+ If your symptoms of fear or anxiety are disrupting your life, see your primary-care physician and discuss the problem with him or her. Ask for a referral to someone who can help with anxiety management or relaxation.
+ Try following the steps that were outlined in the *Coping with Anxiety* section.
+ Practice some form of relaxation every day.

Further reading

Beckfield, Denise. *Master Your Panic, 2nd Edition*. San Luis Obispo, CA: Impact Publishers, 1998.

Benson, Herbert, M.D. *The Relaxation Response*. New York: Avon Books, 2000.

Charlesworth, Edward, and Ronald Nathan. *Stress Management: A Comprehensive Guide to Wellness*. New York: Ballantine Books, 1991.

Marks, Isaac. *Living with Fear*. New York: McGraw-Hill, 1978.

Wilson, R. Ried. *Don't Panic: Taking Control of Anxiety Attacks*. HarperCollins, 1996.

Resource groups

A.I.M. (Agoraphobics in Motion) 1729 Crooks, Royal Oaks, MI 48067. (313) 547-0400.

Phobics Anonymous P.O. Box 1180, Palm Springs, CA 92263. (619) 322-COPE.

Anxiety Disorders Association of America 11900 Parklawn Drive, Suite 200, Rockville, MD 20852-2624. (301) 231-9350 or (900) 737-3400.

10

Depression and Low Self-Esteem

How I wish I had sought help long before I did! I can remember feeling isolated, guilty and having little self-esteem from as far back as I can remember. I had no idea that my grim view of life and low opinion of myself were linked to my sexual abuse. Joanne

Survivors often have a low opinion of themselves and lack self-confidence and self-esteem. They may feel worthless, useless and unlovable. Many Survivors put on a "front" and present themselves as capable, cheerful and confident, while feeling wretched inside. Survivors may be so overwhelmed by their low opinion of themselves and lack of confidence that they suffer bouts of depression. Depression immobilizes people, making them unable to act positively or find pleasure in things. This in turn further undermines self-confidence and starts a vicious circle of decreasing self-esteem and increasing depression. This chapter looks at low self-esteem and depression, the links between them and what can be done to overcome them.

Low self-esteem

If children have a loving and supportive environment, they develop self-confidence and self-esteem as they grow up. They learn

+ to trust their own judgment
+ to feel "safe" in the world

+ that they can be liked for themselves
+ that they can make their own decisions
+ that they are valuable
+ that they deserve to be treated with love and respect

Children learn these things if they are around others who love and protect them and yet allow them the freedom to develop in their own way and to make mistakes. When these children become adults, they are less likely to become depressed because their happy childhoods have given them confidence and made them feel positive about themselves. What happens to a child who has been sexually abused? She might learn

+ not to trust her own judgment (the person she trusted betrayed her)
+ to feel the world is a dangerous place where trusted people take advantage of her and use her for their own ends
+ that she is only liked when she does what the abuser wants her to do
+ that she is not accepted for herself
+ that she is controlled by other people and cannot decide for herself who can touch her body
+ that she is not valued for herself and that she is treated as if her feelings don't matter
+ that she deserves to be abused and to have her wishes disregarded

Such experiences have the effect of undermining the child's self-confidence and self-esteem, making her more likely to feel bad about herself and suffer from depression as an adult. Lucy and Jocelyn describe how they felt about themselves as children:

After the nightmare of being raped and sexually attacked by my uncle and father, I lost my self-esteem. I felt shy and had no self-confidence. I was frightened and I hated myself. I felt I could never please my mom and dad and always felt I was second-best. Lucy

My self-confidence was very low. I thought everyone was better than me. I couldn't think of anything I was good at. I could think of lots of things I was bad at. I was nervous, frightened, always tense and I always had a stomachache. I never said what I wanted, what I would like. I didn't think anyone was interested or really wanted

*to know. I didn't know who I was, what I wanted, and I felt I had
no voice. I was letting events and other people carry me along. I
was not in control. I was on a conveyor belt and I couldn't get off.*
Jocelyn

Like Lucy and Jocelyn, many Survivors grow up feeling inferior
and lacking self-confidence. They may feel so worthless and
unacceptable that they put on a "front" to other people and never
let on to their real feelings and thoughts.

*When I left school, I had no confidence in myself, and I found it
very hard to make relationships because of what had happened
to me. I thought I was some kind of pervert. I am still very shy
when I meet people for the first time, and I seem to put a barrier
around myself.* Anthony

Survivors may strive for the approval and love they feel unworthy
of by always looking after and trying to please others. Many
Survivors seek approval in order to feel acceptable and think any
form of rejection is devastating proof that they are unacceptable
and unlovable.

Lack of self-confidence and self-esteem can lead to problems
such as

- not being able to say "no" to people
- not being able to ask for things
- always putting other people's needs first
- not being spontaneous
- not being able to make decisions
- waiting to see what happens rather than making a choice
- acting passively
- staying in bad relationships
- letting people take advantage
- feeling guilty
- feeling obliged to do things
- a feeling of having no choice or control
- hiding real feelings
- not being able to express opinions
- feeling let down by people
- compulsively caring for other people at one's own expense

When children are sexually abused, they usually cannot fight back or stop the abuse. They are powerless and learn to accept the abuse passively, remain silent, and keep their feelings to themselves. The child learns that the abuser's feelings and needs are more important than her own. Her opinions and feelings don't count; she has no rights. She learns to be passive. Many Survivors grow up continuing to keep their feelings of anger and distress inside and passively accepting abuse from other people.

> I was so used to being used. I didn't know I had a right to free will and choice about how I wanted to live my life, so I married an abusive man when I was 17. In many ways he was like my brother (the abuser)—he abused me verbally, battered me and intimidated me by smashing the furniture. His threats to kill me became almost a routine. I accepted my fate without rebellion for many years. I did not like my husband, yet if I had to describe my feelings during all those abusive years, the only word that comes to my mind is "numb." I was certainly passive. Ingrid

Survivors who always put other people's feelings and needs before their own and never stand up for themselves are likely to be used and abused again as adults. They may also be prone to occasional aggressive outbursts when the bottled up feelings can no longer be held back and often then hate themselves and feel guilty, frightened and out of control. Passive behavior can make people feel more helpless and worthless and makes them more likely to become depressed.

Depression

Depression can be a disturbing, frightening experience. People often feel that depression descends upon them from nowhere. They feel powerless to understand or change how they are feeling. It can cause physical changes, such as tiredness and loss of appetite, but depression is not primarily a physical problem. Depression is rooted in a person's past experiences; her thoughts and feelings about herself and the world; and the ways she has learned to cope.

Depression can be broken into three parts: depressed feelings, depressed thoughts and depressed behavior (see Table 6, page 120).

Table 6: Depressed Thoughts, Feelings and Behavior

Depressed thoughts include thoughts about being

- punished
- useless
- unable to control situations or alter them
- disliked
- worthless and unlovable
- a failure
- a destructive person
- always used and abused

- ugly and repulsive
- fat

and about:

- death
- illness
- accidents
- catastrophes
- life being pointless

Depressed feelings include feelings of

- sadness
- failure
- guilt
- shame
- self-hatred
- anger

- dissatisfaction
- worry
- being out of control
- being overwhelmed
- helplessness
- numbness

Depressed behavior includes

- crying a lot or being unable to cry
- withdrawing and avoiding people
- eating less than usual
- drinking alcohol, overeating or taking drugs

- staying in bed
- doing very little
- not being able to sleep or waking up early
- being unable to make decisions or do simple tasks

Depressed thoughts and feelings

Children who have been sexually abused often believe that they are worthless, inferior, unacceptable or unlovable. They believe these things because of the way they have been treated and sometimes because the abuser, or someone else, has told them so directly. By the time these children become adults they have already had years of practice in thinking negatively about themselves and often about the world in general.

*I didn't care about myself. I hated everything about myself and
there wasn't one good thing I could say about myself. I blamed
myself for everything.* Rhys

These negative or depressed thoughts become habits, automatic
ways of thinking that Survivors may not even be aware of, and
which lead directly to depressed feelings.

Some Survivors have suffered from episodes of depression
since childhood. Others may become depressed as adults because
an upset, such as not getting promoted, reactivates their negative
thoughts about themselves.

Depressed behavior

Depressed thoughts and feelings cause physical changes in
people's bodies and affect their behavior. Some people feel tired or
lethargic constantly when they are depressed. Others feel agitated
and unable to sleep or eat. Some people are unable to cry when
they are depressed and others become very tearful.

People also change their behavior when they are depressed in
order to cope with their bad feelings. Drinking, overeating,
sleeping, taking drugs and self-injury are all ways of trying to blot
out negative feelings and thoughts.

*I turned to alcohol to try and blot out the past but it just made
the flashbacks worse. Then I started suffering from depression.
That's when I started to hurt myself, because I didn't feel clean
and I felt I had betrayed my body. I would be hostile and abusive
to others. I didn't mean anything by it, because I can't say I'm
violent, but I am short-tempered and sometimes I do feel isolated
from people who just can't seem to understand me.* Anthony

Depressed people tend to withdraw and avoid other people
because they feel so worthless and unacceptable. They may
attempt suicide in order to escape from their painful feelings or
because they feel so helpless and hopeless about the future.

These types of behavior tend to make negative thoughts and
feelings worse. A drinking or eating binge temporarily blocks bad
feelings but then leads to feelings of guilt, self-hatred and
hopelessness. Depressed behavior makes people more likely to
have negative thoughts and feelings. In turn this makes them more
likely to behave in a depressed way. Unless the vicious circle is
broken, the depression becomes worse.

Overcoming depression and low self-esteem

Reading through this book and working on your thoughts and feelings about your abuse will help you build your self-esteem and feel less depressed. You will begin to feel more self-confident and worthwhile when you start to feel less guilty and ashamed, and you will stop blaming yourself for being abused. As you begin to feel better about yourself, your depression will be easier to overcome. Talking to other people, especially other Survivors, or seeing a therapist can also be helpful.

> I have felt lonely and isolated. Being able to discuss how I feel with people and being more open about myself is helps a lot. Anthony

When you feel depressed, it is often extremely difficult to believe that you will ever feel any different. Nothing seems to help. Other people's suggestions can seem impossible to carry out. Feeling hopeless and beyond help is part of being depressed. Fiona has now overcome her depression, but can remember how hopeless she used to feel.

> I can't express how much I hurt. The darkness, the emptiness and the feeling of hopelessness were unbearable. I never thought I'd get through it, and even when it did start to lift, I was afraid of getting depressed again. As I write this and remember the pain I can't stop the tears, but there is no fear because I know now I'll never be like that again. Fiona

Try to remember that people can and do overcome depression.

Below we suggest ways of tackling your depressed behavior and thoughts and becoming more assertive. Don't expect too much too soon. Try to be pleased and reward yourself for any positive changes you make, however small. Don't be hard on yourself if you don't change as quickly as you would like to.

Changing depressed behavior

Depressed behavior is not only a reaction to depression, it also worsens the depression. You can start to break the vicious circle of depression by making small changes in your behavior. It may be hard to get started if you're feeling hopeless. Take it one step at a time. Set yourself easy tasks you can achieve and feel good about. See if you can work on some of the points below.

✦ Get up at a reasonable time rather than staying in bed and then feeling guilty. Reward yourself for getting up. Start the day with positive thoughts (see the section below on affirmations).

✦ Get some exercise. Exercise helps people feel better both physically and mentally. Try walking, gardening, yoga or swimming.

✦ Try to eat regular meals even if you have little appetite. Choose good, healthful food to give you energy to tackle your problems. If you are overeating, read chapter 11, *Eating Problems and Body Image*, and do the suggested exercises. Overeating is often a way of hiding bad feelings and seeking comfort.

✦ Do one thing every day that you enjoy; for example, have a bath, listen to music. If you can't think of anything that you find enjoyable at the moment, do something you used to enjoy.

✦ Try to make some contact with people again. Avoiding people only increases thoughts that you are lonely and unlovable. Being with friends can help you begin to think and feel more positively—there are things to enjoy in life; people do like you; you are not alone.

Changing your behavior is only the first step toward overcoming depression. It is also important to work on changing your negative thoughts.

Challenging negative thoughts

Depression may seem to come out of the blue, but it is brought on and maintained by negative thoughts. Negative thoughts affect your mood. Trying to recognize your negative thoughts and then challenging them by questioning whether the thoughts are realistic helps you reduce your feelings of depression. Negative thoughts happen automatically and can be difficult to identify, so you will need to persevere with the exercise below. Before starting this exercise, read through the instructions and the examples.

Exercise

Draw a line down the middle of a piece of paper and head one side "negative thoughts" and the other side "realistic thoughts." Notice what negative thoughts are running through your head, particularly if you suddenly begin to feel worse. Write down these thoughts under the heading "negative thoughts." Write them down exactly as they go through your head in the first person and present tense (for example, "I'm stupid"). Remember that it is the thoughts, not the feelings, that you are trying to recognize. For example, don't write: "I was sitting feeling depressed and thinking about the future." Write the exact thoughts; for example: "I'll never feel better. I'm going to be miserable for the rest of my life. There's no point in living."

Next ask yourself, are these thoughts really true? Is there another way of seeing the situation, or of explaining what has happened, or of seeing yourself? Write down these alternative, more realistic, thoughts on the other side of the sheet of paper. The negative thoughts may seem realistic to you at the moment because you are depressed. Try to be objective and look at the evidence for and against your negative thoughts. If you cannot think of any more realistic thoughts, ask someone to help you think of some.

Keep pen and paper handy and write down your negative thoughts whenever they occur. Be sure to write down the thoughts rather than trying to do this exercise in your head. This exercise needs to be done regularly over a period of time. Negative thinking builds up over years. It takes time to break the habit completely but you may begin to feel a bit better pretty soon.

Attempt to write down your negative thoughts in simple statements, as shown in the example below.

Example

Negative thoughts	Realistic thoughts
I deserve to be abused.	No one deserves to be abused. I deserve to be treated with love and respect like any other human being.
I am a complete failure.	I am not a complete failure. I have survived being abused and brought up my children.
I am useless.	I am not useless. I sometimes make mistakes like everyone else.
I will never feel any better.	Feeling better takes time and effort. I took the first step by reading this book and facing my problems. Survivors in this book have helped themselves; so can I.

Every time Fiona felt depressed, she stayed in bed. This gave her more opportunity to slip into thinking negatively about herself and her future. These thoughts happened automatically. She wasn't even aware of all the negative thoughts that were running through her head and making her feel even worse. Fiona decided to challenge her negative thoughts to help lift her depression. For the first time, Fiona began to see that there were alternative ways of seeing herself and her situation.

Negative thoughts	Realistic thoughts
I'm not as good as other people.	I'm just as good as the next person, if not better. I'm a caring person who loves her family. I haven't done a bad job in raising Amy, keeping a home and getting educated even though I've had a hard life and suffered abuse. I am going to try to like myself.

continued . . .

I caused my parents and others to treat me the way they did by being disruptive. It was all my fault.	No, it wasn't my fault. I learned to behave like that. I wasn't born disruptive. Circumstances and situations made me like that. I was crying out for help. I had bottled up my anger, frustration, fear and disgust about my neglect and abuse. I don't have to fear anything. I will handle whatever life dishes out. I am going to enjoy life now and get stronger so I can use my experience to help others, which I know I can do.
I'm dirty and my house always looks dirty.	I am not dirty. I am as good as anyone else. My house is not perfectly clean the way I wish it could be, like the ones on the TV. No one can be that clean if there are people and pets living in it comfortably. My house is clean and tidy, a lot cleaner than some and not as spotless as others, but then it is not a showcase house. It is a home where people live and are comfortable.

Over the weeks Fiona began to see that her negative thoughts weren't realistic. She had got into the habit of thinking badly about herself because of how she'd been treated as a child. Fiona began to see that there were many good things about herself. She had survived abuse and had made a new life for herself and was trying to overcome her problems. She began to accept herself and feel more powerful.

Affirmations

Affirmations are positive statements about yourself. They help remind you that you have good points and so they increase your feelings of self-confidence and self-esteem. They also help by counteracting negative thoughts. Affirmations can help in overcoming depression and in stopping depression from developing.

Exercise

Write down three positive things about yourself. They could be things you like about yourself, or are good at, or are getting better at. If you can't think of anything yourself, ask a friend to help you.

Examples

I am good at my job

I am courageous in facing my problems by reading this book.

I am getting to like and accept myself more every day.

I am a good listener.

I am a good gardener.

I like the way I keep trying.

Say your positive statements every day before you get up.

Assertion

Assertion training is a powerful way to increase your self esteem and can help in overcoming depression. It teaches that everyone has rights and that they can learn to think, feel and act positively by respecting their own rights and those of other people. Assertion training distinguishes among four different types of behavior:

✦ *Assertive*. Expressing feelings openly and honestly. Not allowing yourself to be used and put down, and not using or putting down anyone else.

✦ *Passive*. Not saying how you feel. Putting other people's feelings and rights before your own. Putting yourself down ("I am stupid") and allowing other people to use you.

✦ *Aggressive*. Putting your own feelings before anyone else's feelings. Using and putting down other people ("You are stupid"). Shouting and being physically aggressive.

✦ *Indirect*. Trying to get your way without appearing to do so. Putting down other people while appearing to be friendly on the surface. Lying, being sarcastic, "guilt-tripping" others, making excuses and being manipulative.

Most people behave in all these different ways at some point but they usually have one style of behavior that is more common than the others. Many survivors behave passively most of the time, indirectly some of the time, and have occasional aggressive outbursts. Few Survivors have learned to be assertive.

There are numerous assertion-training all over the country and some good books with exercises you can use to become more assertive: See the end of this chapter for details. Assertion training is usually more useful for Survivors in the later stages of recovery. In the following account, Katarina shows how assertion has helped her.

> Since I went to an assertion class, I have stopped accepting the blame and apologizing for everything that goes wrong in the lives of my family and other people. Before, I truly believed that everything was somehow my fault. Even if I was not directly involved, somehow I found a connection, a link that printed GUILT, BLAME, SHAME in capital letters in my mind. Now I realize I am not responsible for my family's happiness. I can love them and care for them, but ultimately they must create their own happiness. I cannot keep all unhappy experiences or problems away from them.
>
> Because I refused to feel guilty any more, I understood that assertion is about how you value yourself. It is not right for me to treat other people better than I treat myself. I became more understanding, more forgiving and accepting of myself. I can see my faults and shortcomings but because I can accept them in others, I don't need to be perfect, either.
>
> Assertion has done something else for me. It has finally released me from this terrible need to put up the front of being "superwoman," the one who can cope with everything and anything without getting tired or stressed.
>
> Too many people and things were eating away at my time and energy. There was not enough left for myself. So I decided to change my life. I ignored the rooms with no wallpaper on their walls and I sat down in a chair and did nothing for an hour. It was the first time that I'd sat still without feeling guilty because there were other things to do. Then I made a list of my priorities and decided only to do the things that were really necessary or important to me.
>
> The conscious decision to say, "I don't have time for this," or "I feel tired," lifted enormous stress off me. I relaxed and found

peace again. I have now gone back to doing some things that I gave up for a little while. But now I do them because I want to and not because I have to. This is the big difference in my life. Katarina

Fiona's coping methods

After suffering from depression most of my childhood and adult life, at 29 years of age I am now living. I know I have a long way to go but I no longer suffer depression the way I used to. I still get a little down, but who doesn't? I see life differently now. I'm interested in lots of things, whereas before I used to think, "What's the point?" Now I am trying to make up for those lost years, enjoying life and getting as much out of it as I can. I am now able to love my family dearly and to accept love. Fiona

Fiona tackled her depression by changing her behavior (she made herself get up earlier, eat regularly and start seeing people again) and by challenging her negative thoughts. She realized she had gotten into the habit of thinking badly of herself and this made her feel depressed. Fiona also went to an assertiveness group and began to express her feelings and change her behavior. As she began to respect her own rights and feelings and those of other people, her self-respect and self-confidence grew. At the same time, Fiona was working on her memories and feelings about being sexually abused. As she began to see the abuse wasn't her fault, she stopped feeling guilty and ashamed, understood more about her past behavior and began to feel more acceptable and worthwhile.

Fiona had felt helpless, and hopeless about ever feeling any better, but she overcame her depression. She started to feel better about herself, more hopeful about the future, and had renewed interest in life. Fiona regained her own strength and power, and you can, too.

Suggestions

+ Begin to change your depressed thoughts, feelings and behaviors by following the suggestions and exercises in this chapter.
+ Read a book about assertiveness (See Further Reading, below). Attend a class on assertiveness or confidence-building or form your own group with friends.

Further reading

Assertiveness and self-esteem

Alberti, Robert, and Michael Emmons. *Your Perfect Right: A Guide to Assertive Living—25th Anniversary Edition.* San Luis Obispo, CA: Impact Publishers, 1995

Dickson, Anne. *A Woman in Your Own Right.* Quartet Books, 1983.

Klein, Donald F., and Paul H. Wender. *Understanding Depression: A Complete Guide to Its Diagnosis and Treatment.* New York: Oxford University Press, 1994.

Lindenfield, Gael. *Super Confidence.* London: Thorsons, 2000.

Phelps, Stanlee, and Nancy Austin. *The Assertive Woman: Third Edition.* San Luis Obispo, CA: Impact Publishers, 1997.

Smith, Manuel. *When I Say No, I Feel Guilty.* New York: Bantam Books, 1975.

Depression

Hauck, Paul. *Overcoming Depression.* Louisville, KY: Westminster John Knox Press, 1973.

Greenberger, Dennis, and Christine A. Padesky. *Mind Over Mood: Change How You Feel by Changing the Way You Think.* New York: Guilford Press, 1995.

O'Connor, Richard. *Undoing Depression: What Therapy Doesn't Teach You and Medication Can't Give You.* New York: Berkeley Publishing Group,1999.

Papolos, Demitri, and Janice Papalos. *Overcoming Depression: The Definitive Resource for Patients and Families Who Live with Depression and Manic Depression, 3rd Edition.* New York: HarperCollins Publishers, 1997.

Preston, John. *You Can Beat Depression: A Guide to Prevention and Recovery, 2nd Edition.* San Luis Obispo, CA: Impact Publishers, 1996.

Rowe, Dorothy. *Depression: The Way Out of Your Prison, 2nd Edition.* New York: Routledge, 1996.

Sanford, Linda, and Mary Ellen Donovan. *Women and Self-Esteem: Understanding and Improving the Way We Think and Feel about Ourselves.* New York: Viking Press, 1985.

Resource groups

National Depressive & Manic Depressive Association
730 N. Franklin, #501, Chicago, IL 60610.
(800) 82-NDMDA or (312) 642-0049.
http://www.ndmda.org

Depressed Anonymous
P.O. Box 17414, Louisville, KY 40217.
http://www.depressedanon.com

NOSAD (National Organization for Seasonal Affective Disorder)
P.O. Box 40190, Washington, DC 20016.

11

Eating Problems and Body Image

When I became a teenager, I wanted to look pretty. I lost some weight, I looked like all the other girls. Yet when I looked in the mirror I only saw a fat girl, so ugly that I felt like apologizing every time someone had to look at me. I only saw myself with my brother's eyes. Katarina

The difficulty was, how to get thin? I couldn't diet because I ate for comfort. I ate to stop myself thinking, to keep the fears at bay. So I kept eating and just vomited the food back up. I ate when I felt bad about myself, then vomited. I gave in to sexual demands because I needed affection and reassurance. Then I'd feel bad about being promiscuous, so I'd eat. As the bulimia spiraled out of control, I learned to feel guilty about that, too. When I was sexually assaulted as an adult, I ate as a way of coping. I ate because I felt angry about the abuse. I hated myself because I couldn't stop it from happening. I ate because I had no control over my body. I ate because I felt angry that other people felt they had a right to hit me, to abuse me. But most of all I ate because I was afraid I deserved the abuse. I vomited because I could not hold so much pain, so much fear, so much hate and so much anger within myself and I could find no other way of letting it out. Shirley

In Western society, the pressures on women to remain slim and their responsibilities to provide food mean women are more likely to have problems with body image and eating than men. Many women have a poor body image and are concerned about their weight; some develop eating disorders. In the past it was believed that women experienced eating disorders almost exclusively. There is now a growing number of young men who have difficulties with eating and with their body image. Approximately 10% of people with eating disorders are male.

Survivors of sexual abuse are even more likely than the general population to have problems with their body image and eating. Survivors are often left with a dislike or even a hatred of their own bodies, which usually focuses on their weight, size or shape. They may dislike all of their bodies or just certain parts, such as their stomachs, genitals, chests or hips. Many Survivors do not like to get undressed in public changing rooms, do not like their partners to see them with no clothes on and often even avoid looking at their own bodies. It is not surprising that Survivors feel particularly bad about their bodies because during sexual abuse the body is invaded and treated without respect.

This dislike of the body often leads to attempts to change it by repeated dieting, usually interspersed with periods of breaking the diet and overeating. Survivors frequently turn to eating when they are upset or angry and find it difficult to eat "normally." Dieting and overeating can develop into a way of coping with bad feelings about themselves and what has happened to them. Some of these Survivors end up with a much more serious problem by developing anorexia nervosa, bulimia or compulsive eating. Research studies of women with clinical eating disorders have found at least half had been sexually abused as children.

What is an eating problem?

Many women, and a growing number of men, have problems with food and eating. People with eating problems are over-concerned or preoccupied with their body size, weight and shape. Women are often self-conscious about feeling overweight. They may weigh themselves every day and feel their mood change according to what the scales tell them. They may not leave the house if their weight has increased of if they feel fat. Men are more likely to worry about being too small or thin or about their lack of muscles. Both men and women with eating problems can feel that life would be a lot better if they were a different size or shape. These feelings often lead to constant attempts to diet, to body build or to use other ways of trying to control and transform their bodies.

Unfortunately when people try to follow a strict diet they often end up breaking the diet and overeating when they are under stress. Instead of eating when they are hungry, eating becomes a response to stress, bad feelings or difficult events in their lives. Eating can temporarily ease uncomfortable feelings.

If people eat according to their own strict rules about what and when they can eat, instead of in response to their body signals, they can end up no longer knowing whether they are hungry or not. At times everyone eats in response to how they feel (agitated, lonely, upset) rather than because they are hungry, but for most people eating does not become their main way of dealing with bad feelings. For some people, though, the problem develops into an eating disorder that can take over their lives and prevent them from dealing with the underlying causes of the problem. The main eating disorders are:

+ *Compulsive eating.* Compulsive eaters are people who feel out of control around food and who eat in response to bad feelings or to avoid feeling anything at all. They may no longer even know when they are hungry or full. Compulsive eaters are often, but not always, overweight. They frequently eat between meals and usually feel out of control when they do so. They have low self-esteem and are preoccupied with their body size. They don't like to eat, or to eat much, in public, and regularly try to diet. They are often afraid of being hungry and so eat when they aren't hungry to make sure they never experience the feeling of hunger. When inevitably they fail at dieting, they feel even more worthless—so they eat more to cope with this feeling. Many women, whether they have been sexually abused or not, are compulsive eaters.

+ *Anorexia nervosa.* At the other end of the scale, the woman with anorexia nervosa generally eats very little at all. Anorexia nervosa is diagnosed when someone deliberately loses a quarter of her normal body weight, has a morbid fear of becoming fat and has hormonal changes, which can include the loss of menstrual periods. Half of women with anorexia nervosa regularly lose control of their strict dieting and binge—eat large quantities of food. They then feel a need to get rid of the calories by self-induced vomiting, exercising, fasting or by taking laxatives, diuretics or diet pills. Many young women go through a phase of restricting their food and losing weight, but true anorexia nervosa is still rare. Boys and men also diet and restrict their food intake at times and can be diagnosed with anorexia nervosa, but this is very rare.

✦ *Bulimia and bulimia nervosa.* A much more common problem is bulimia (binge-eating) or bulimia nervosa. Bulimia is common but it is a secret problem. Most people who binge-eat are normal weight so, unlike anorexia nervosa, the problem is not visible to other people. Perhaps 10% of young women in their late teens or early twenties binge-eat, although for many it will be a passing phase. The majority of people who binge-eat are women, but a growing number of men also have this problem.

Bulimia is a disorder that includes phases of dieting, followed by episodes of binge-eating very large quantities of food in a short amount of time. During a binge the food is not usually chewed or tasted but is gulped quickly. This is accompanied by a feeling of being out of control. The foods most commonly eaten in a binge are those that people usually try to avoid eating when they are dieting, such as chocolate, bread and other high-calorie foods. Binge-eating may temporarily lift the person's mood but afterward she feels depressed and guilty about overeating and terrified of becoming fat, and so she attempts to diet again.

Some people who diet and binge-eat use more drastic ways of preventing any weight gain after a binge. They may immediately make themselves vomit all the food, take large amounts of laxatives, diet pills and diuretics or exercise excessively. These are all attempts to eliminate the extra calories and keep the weight down. For many this purging is also a self-punishment for losing control and overeating. This dieting/bingeing/purging cycle is called *bulimia nervosa.*

Even if you do not have a serious eating disorder, you may feel uncomfortable with your own body and the way you eat. If you are unhappy about your eating habits, the ideas and exercises in this chapter may help you understand more about why you eat or why you restrict your eating. Over time they may help you develop a more "normal" relationship with your body and your food intake. If your eating problem is disrupting your life or you feel unable to take control of your eating (or noneating), then seek some outside help (see Resources at the end of this chapter).

Eating problems—the background context

As a teenager I learned that being thin, looking acceptable on the outside, gained me approval and praise, it gave me some self-esteem, although not enough to rid me of the fear that I was a "bad" or "unworthy" person, so I had to try harder, get thinner, achieve more. Shirley

Western society holds different stereotypes of the ideal body image for men and for women. The media is influential in the setting up of an image of the ideal woman as young, slim and sexually attractive.

I was afraid of being regarded as fat, because I felt that fat women have little status in our society, are viewed as "failures," are the butt of jokes and are not seen as individuals. Shirley

Women in our society are expected to take daily responsibility for providing food—planning meals, shopping, preparing, cooking and presenting meals. The pressure on women to be slim, dynamic, sexually attractive and to be a plump, motherly homemaker lead to conflicts about their body image and their role in life. As a result, most women feel dissatisfied with their bodies and regularly put themselves on diets regardless of whether they are overweight or not. Dieting is rarely successful in the long term and certainly doesn't change the size and shape of the particular body parts that cause concern. Dieting can leave women feeling like failures—they can't even take control of their own eating and body size. This leads them to dislike themselves and their bodies even more. Some of the books suggested under *Further reading* at the end of this chapter will help you to look more closely at why women develop this preoccupation with food, body shape and dieting.

More recently, teenage boys have come under pressure from their peers to take care of their appearance and spend more time and money on clothes and grooming. They have become more concerned with their body image. Unlike women, men often want to increase their body size, by eating more or working out at the gym, to help them conform to the masculine stereotype and feel more acceptable and more powerful.

> *I'd love to be bigger, I look too skinny. I'm embarrassed about my body but I can't get myself to eat enough to put weight back on. You expect men to be gladiator-like musclemen. Being thin isn't socially acceptable for men; being big and muscle-bound is.* Rhys

Women usually want to be thinner than they are but cannot stop overeating, whereas men often want to be bigger than they are but some, like Rhys, cannot get themselves to eat. Men are not expected to be fat, but they are under pressure to be big, powerful and muscular.

The pressures to conform to the masculine and feminine stereotypes result in many women dieting, on and off, throughout their lives and to some men trying to build up their bodies. However, only some people go on to develop eating problems. Whether a person develops an eating problem is the result of additional individual pressures, such as the eating habits of their families, their own weight history and history of dieting, pressures to diet or bodybuild from peers and how they have learned to cope with their emotions. Women have low status in our society and often feel powerless in the outside world. When they have problems, they are more likely than men to turn inward and try to control their bodies instead of dealing with the outside world.

Childhood abuse leaves victims feeling very bad about themselves and their bodies. Many Survivors blot out their feelings about themselves and memories of the abuse by becoming preoccupied with their body size and their eating habits, and thus develop an eating problem. In the next section we look at why Survivors in particular are prone to developing eating problems.

Sexual abuse and eating problems— issues in common

At least half of women who have eating disorders have been sexually abused as children. What are the links between sexual abuse and the development of eating problems?

Body image

Eating problems usually develop in people who already have a poor body image and a history of dieting. When people are sexually abused they learn to detest their own bodies.

Survivors associate their bodies with the physical and/or emotional pain and the shame of what has been done to them. The poor body image of Survivors makes them more likely to begin dieting or overeating and so to develop an eating problem.

Swallowing feelings

> After I became aware of the connection of my eating problem and the fact that I had been sexually abused as a child, I realized that at all the times in my life when I was under stress and felt unsafe and unsure of the future I ate more and put on weight. This fact became especially clear to me after my daughter told me she had been sexually abused by a neighbor a few years earlier. During that first week, while I was trying to get help for her and also trying to cope with the memories of my own abuse and the pain I felt, I reached for food almost nonstop. I was very frightened, fearing that she would grow up with the same problems I had, and also fearing that I could not cope. I felt threatened. I so much wanted to be protected from all the pain, I wanted to feel safe. So I ate and put on three or four pounds in that one week. Katarina

Survivors are left with many traumatic memories and bad feelings about themselves. We all know how easy it is to reach for food when we feel bad. It doesn't take away the bad feelings but it does push them away—we swallow our bad feelings and may, briefly, feel better. Overeating can be useful at first by blocking off bad feelings and bringing a sense of relief. The bad feelings about the abuse are still there, but they become buried deep inside. Instead, Survivors feel bad about breaking their diets. They feel out of control, stupid, guilty and fat. They are therefore left with bad feelings about themselves instead of anger at their abusers or sadness about their childhood. They often feel so bad about themselves that they reach out for more food to help them swallow their feelings. Eating to avoid bad feelings can become such a habit that people start to binge in response to any bad feeling or minor difficulty. Many people with eating disorders end up feeling completely numb and out of touch with their feelings. On the other hand, some Survivors have feelings of guilt and shame but cannot remember anything about the abuse.

People who suffer from bulimia cannot cope with having unfilled time ahead of them. They often binge-eat to distract themselves and fill the time to keep away unwanted memories, thoughts and feelings.

Guilt

Although the responsibility for sexual abuse always lies with the abuser, the victims nearly always feel guilty and blame themselves. Survivors sometimes harm themselves as a form of self-punishment for being so "bad." The physical pain may also help by blocking off the emotional distress. Dieting itself can be a form of self-deprivation and self-punishment. People who are dieting feel greedy and guilty when they overeat because they have broken their diet. It may be easier to cope with the guilt about overeating rather than the guilt about the abuse. Unfortunately this leaves Survivors feeling worse about themselves while the real problem goes unresolved. People who deliberately vomit, take laxatives, diuretics or diet pills are attempting to lose weight by getting rid of the calories, but these are also powerful ways of punishing themselves to help cope with the feelings of guilt.

Shame

> The abuse changed my life from a very early age. I was ashamed of my body and frightened that people would be able to tell what was happening just by looking at my body. Kate

Many Survivors feel great shame because of what has happened to them, whether they feel guilty or not. For some, dieting is a way of purifying the body and attempting to make the body perfect rather than dirty or shameful. In its extreme form, we call it anorexia nervosa, where women are often striving to be perfect in body and mind.

People who suffer from bulimia nervosa and deliberately vomit after eating feel much shame and disgust at their behavior. Vomiting and feeling this self-disgust may be safer ways for Survivors to express their feelings of disgust about the abuse. It may be that vomiting after overeating is repeating what happened to some Survivors as children when they vomited, or wanted to vomit, after oral sex.

Secrecy

Common to all the eating problems we've described is the need to eat in secret. People with eating problems will not eat in public or will eat very little in front of other people. Their eating is mostly done in secret and may involve secret episodes of vomiting. People with bulimia nervosa are usually so ashamed of their bingeing and vomiting that they go to great lengths to make sure no one finds out about it. Bulimia has been called the "secret disorder." Sexual abuse and eating behaviors share this theme of secrecy. Sexual abuse always occurs in secret and may be kept secret for many years.

Feelings of loss of control

Sexual abuse is forced on children by the power and authority an adult or older child has over them. Children may also feel powerless to resist because of threats or actual physical violence from the abuser or because they feel very confused about what is happening to them. When people feel powerless and out of control, the one thing they can control is their own body. Small children who are being abused often overeat, refuse to eat, or wet or soil themselves (see chapter 6). These are body functions they alone can control and which adults cannot take control of. If feelings of powerlessness and loss of control develop as the child grows up, the body may again become a means of regaining some control. Some people try to control and change their bodies by dieting and exercising. While dieting is an attempt to feel in control, the feelings of powerlessness are also expressed through losing control in bingeing and overeating. Unfortunately the feelings of powerlessness increase when their dieting doesn't work or when they lose control and binge.

Eating for protection

Women who overeat often experience conflict in their feelings about being overweight. On a conscious level they usually hate the idea of being fat and want to become slim. However, when they explore the underlying feelings they often find, to their great surprise, that they are actually terrified of being *thin*. Some Survivors believe that being fat makes them unattractive to others and therefore prevents unwanted sexual advances. For others being fat makes them feel physically stronger while being thin makes them feel vulnerable. Men may find it especially difficult to deal with feeling vulnerable and may consciously want to get bigger and fatter to feel more powerful and able to protect themselves. A woman may feel that when she is overweight she has more presence, power and identity because she is seen as a person rather than as a woman. Being overweight can therefore be useful for a Survivor who does not want to be seen as sexually attractive or who feels vulnerable and powerless because of the sexual abuse.

The underlying reasons for overeating vary for each individual, but being fat often has a protective function. This is why some people find they can lose weight fairly easily at first but then as they lose weight, their hidden fears begin to surface and they start overeating again.

Concern about their bodies and eating becomes an obvious and initially useful way for Survivors to deal with bad feelings. Through dieting, bingeing and purging, Survivors can express many of their feelings relating to their body image, guilt and shame. Usually, though, they end up with bad feelings about themselves instead of about the underlying problem (the sexual abuse). To overcome an eating problem, you need to start uncovering these bad feelings, accepting and expressing them.

Overcoming the problem

During the last few months, I have had a few times again when I was under great stress, but I have learned so much. I have learned there is a lot more strength in me than I thought, and that no matter how difficult a situation may seem, somehow time dilutes the pain, and solutions can and will be found. Instead of running away from my problems and feelings by eating I have to face them and deal with them.

I had a few days lately that were really difficult to cope with. But suddenly, as the problems were solved, I realized that I had eaten normally during those times. No more eating nonstop, no more putting on weight. I don't need that protection anymore. I can only figure this is because I feel strong enough to cope with anything the future will bring and don't want to run away anymore. Nowadays I eat anything I want to and I am gradually losing weight. The irony of the situation is that now I like my body and losing weight is totally unimportant to me. Katarina

To overcome an eating problem, you have to find ways of letting the emotional issues surface again and find more useful ways of coping with them. It is also important to look at eating and dieting behavior, because bad habits of weight control can also lead to the development and maintenance of eating problems. If you have an established eating problem or have difficulty in regaining control of your eating, you would benefit from getting some professional help.

Dieting

An eating problem rarely develops without a history of dieting. People put themselves on diets in order to lose weight (often when they are not even overweight to start with), but strict dieting rarely helps anyone lose weight in the long run. In fact repeated dieting slows down the metabolic rate (the speed at which the body burns up calories). After a return to normal eating, weight gain can therefore be a lot quicker, so people who diet often end up fatter than before. *Dieting Makes You Fat*, by Geoffrey Cannon and Hetty Einzig (see *Further reading* at the end of the chapter) argues strongly that strict dieting does not lead to permanent weight-loss.

When people are dieting, they are trying to control their bodies. They try to ignore the signals telling them they are hungry and that their bodies need food. This self-starvation makes them preoccupied with food and leaves them feeling deprived. If they break their diet by eating something "bad" (for example, high-calorie food) they feel they have lost control. This usually leads to binge-eating or overeating.

Strict dieting not only makes people fatter but also can lead to binge-eating or overeating. The first step in overcoming an eating problem is to *stop dieting forever.* This doesn't mean you cannot try to lose weight. A more practical way of losing weight is described later in the chapter.

Exploring your feelings about your body size

People with eating problems use eating and concern about their body shape as a way of coping with their feelings. To stabilize your weight at a reasonable level and develop a healthy relationship with your body and food you need to find out what feelings you are hiding under your fat and find more useful ways of coping with them. *Fat is a Feminist Issue*, by Susie Orbach, is an excellent book for women that explores these ideas and makes practical suggestions. In this and the follow-up book, *Fat is a Feminist Issue II*, the author provides exercises designed to help women to explore the feelings they have associated with their own body, food and eating. Most women fear becoming fat or fatter. Exploring your feelings about your weight often helps you see that being fat may also be useful to you in some way. It may make you feel protected and safe, sexually unattractive, or more powerful. Clearly it is very difficult for anyone to regain control of their eating or to lose weight if they have underlying fears about becoming slim.

Binge-eating

Binge-eating is usually triggered by an unpleasant event, stress, bad feelings or memories.

> My weight fluctuates between 147 to 190 pounds. I don't eat very often. Sometimes I don't eat for a week, I just drink coffee. Then something makes me feel bad and I binge on candy bars and chocolate cookies. Rhys

Often the person is feeling deprived of love, safety or comfort. They want or feel "something" but don't know what this "something" is. They are invariably dieting or restricting their food intake, feel hungry and reach out for food. You can use your binge-eating, or eating when you are not hungry, as a way of finding out what you really want or what feelings you are avoiding.

Exercise

Next time you feel you are going to binge, try delaying the binge for 10 minutes. If this is hard to do, try 5 minutes or 1 minute. Do something for yourself in this 10 minutes instead of bingeing; for example, have a bath, read a magazine, phone a friend, go for a run. Think of things you enjoy doing that are free or cheap, last 10 to 20 minutes, and have nothing to do with food. Write down these rewards. Instead of bingeing give yourself one of your treats. Binge afterward if you have to. The first step is to learn to delay the binge. Learning that you can delay a binge may also help you feel more in control.

Once you can delay your binges, the next step is to use this delay to sit quietly, relax and think, "What do I really want? What am I really feeling?" This exercise is a way for you to find out what triggers a binge and to discover what you really want and feel. If feelings like guilt, shame, and so on surface, you can work on them by using the ideas from the other chapters in this book. If you feel sad because you cannot get what you want immediately you may want to express this by crying. It is better to cry because you are sad than to eat because you are sad.

Learn to eat whatever you want to if *you really want it*. Don't eat if you find that you are really feeling sad, angry or hurt rather than hungry.

When you stop bingeing you may feel more depressed initially as your buried problems begin to surface but now you have the opportunity to deal with them directly instead of thinking about food and worrying about your weight. You may need to get professional help.

Purging

After bingeing, many people learn to purge themselves by making themselves vomit all the food they have eaten or by taking large quantities of laxatives, diuretics or diet pills. These are all attempts to get rid of the calories just consumed and therefore avoid becoming fat. All these ways of purging are physically very dangerous. There are many unpleasant and medically dangerous side effects of purging, including damage to the teeth and gums, throat hemorrhages and electrolyte disturbances (which can lead to epilepsy, kidney failure and other serious problems). None of these methods of purging eliminate all the calories. Laxatives only stop a very small proportion of the calories from being absorbed. However often you vomit, you will still only prevent a portion of the calories from being absorbed. Some people with eating problems exercise excessively instead of purging—the ideas below can help you understand and control the level of exercise you engage in.

Use the same technique to control your purging as you do to understand your bingeing; that is, delay for a little while and use that time to find out why you have the urge to do it. Perhaps you will discover that painful and dangerous purging is a way of punishing yourself or of indirectly expressing your anger or other bad feelings.

Controlling my weight by vomiting was a way of coping with the hatred I felt toward myself, and it was a secret expression of the anger I felt inside myself but was too afraid to direct at the real causes of my anger. I could literally swallow my anger and pain by eating, then purge myself of it. Shirley

Most people who stop bingeing also stop purging. If you do not stop purging, try to use the technique described above or seek professional help.

How to lose weight

If you feel that you've explored and worked through your feelings about your weight and you are overweight, you may next want to try to lose some weight. It's obviously very difficult to lose weight before you've dealt with any fears about being slim. The method below will not work unless you have overcome these fears. If you have been dieting on and off for years, you may find it difficult to lose weight because your metabolism may have slowed.

+ Stop dieting. Try to eat three meals a day, however small.

+ Aim to lose one or two pounds a week maximum. If you lose more than this, you will only lose water, not fat.

+ One pound of fat is equivalent to 3,500 calories, so to lose one pound of fat per week you need to lose 3,500 calories per week (or 500 calories per day) from your usual calorie intake.

+ Plan to cut 250 calories a day *only* from your normal eating by cutting down on your fat intake. Try to replace fatty food and junk food with wholesome, unprocessed foods, such as fresh fruit. Junk food contains many calories but does not provide the nutrients your body needs so you quickly become hungry again. Eating healthful foods will make you feel better as well as help you control your weight.

+ Burn off the other 250 calories a day by doing some exercise. Exercise not only burns off calories but can increase your metabolic rate so you burn off *more*

calories whatever you are doing. If you try to lose
weight without doing exercise then you will lose
water and lean tissue (muscle) instead of the fat that
you want to lose.

Remember that strict dieting is unlikely to help you lose weight
and keep off the weight. You actually may end up heavier, feel
more deprived and find yourself thinking about food much more.
You will also be more likely to overeat when you do break your
diet.

Body image

*Most of my problems have disappeared. What has taken me
longer is to accept that it is possible for a man to look at me
without feeling repulsion. My poor body image and my eating
problem have been with me for so long that they will take longer
to leave me.* Katarina

Disliking your body can distort your perception of your body so
that it appears to you to be bigger and fatter than it actually is. You
really see yourself as fat when objectively you may be normal
weight or even thin. Men may see their bodies as too thin and not
masculine or "normal" enough.

*I think I was so busy trying to look normal so no one would
discover my secret. I did get obsessed about my body and went to
the gym excessively.* Luke

It is possible to change your perception of your own body, but it
takes a lot of practice over a period of time. You've spent many
years building up a distorted image, so it will take time to see your
body accurately again. Try reading one of the recommended books
and try the exercises they suggest.

Exercise

When most women look in a full-length mirror, they focus
on the part of their bodies that they dislike the most, their
stomachs, hips, breasts, and so on. This critical focus distorts
the way they see themselves. Men may also focus on the
parts of their bodies they dislike—their chests, legs, arms,
stomach, and so forth. Try looking in a full-length mirror

naked. What parts do you focus on? If you hate your thighs because you think they are too big, then focusing on them makes them appear even bigger to you. If you feel your chest is narrow and puny, focusing on it will make it appear even smaller to you. Try to look at your body as a whole. Try not to judge it—just look at it. Try to accept and like yourself: "This is my body." Do this exercise twice a day, when you are getting dressed and undressed.

Summary

Many women in our society dislike their own bodies and are preoccupied with food and their body image. Dieting is a way of trying to transform the body but it rarely leads to permanent weight loss and usually leaves people fatter than before and feeling even less in control of their lives. Some then go on to develop more serious problems, such as compulsive eating, anorexia nervosa and bulimia.

At least 50% of women with eating problems have been sexually abused as children. Many Survivors develop difficulties with eating as a way of coping with their emotional problems. Both people with eating problems and Survivors of sexual abuse have feelings of dislike or disgust toward their own bodies. They also share feelings of guilt, shame, low self-worth and loss of control. Problems around eating may result in Survivors experiencing a temporary relief from their distress about the abuse because they are able to bury their memories and bad feelings through eating. In the long run, these patterns lead to physical problems and lower self-esteem.

To overcome an eating problem, allow the underlying memories and feelings to surface so that they can be processed and dealt with. One way of doing this is to explore what you are thinking and feeling when you reach for food. It is equally important to change your behaviors around food, such as restrained eating, binge-eating or purging. To do this, you have to stop dieting. As you grow to understand and accept yourself, you will probably find you can also learn to respect and accept your own body.

> Sharing the pain with other women helped me to find better ways of coping. As the wounds caused by the abuse began to heal, as I began to see myself as a whole person—when the good in me

began to feel as real as the bad things I had found in myself—I no longer saw myself as being fat. I am free of the bulimia because I am free of the abuse, free of the guilt, free of the hate, and I am free to find in myself the person that I want to be, not the person I am afraid to be. Shirley

Exercises

1. Follow the suggestions and exercises described to help you stop dieting and to overcome your eating and body-image problems.

2. Seek professional help if you have a serious eating problem or have difficulty gaining control of your eating.

3. Read *Dieting Makes You Fat*, by Geoffrey Cannon and Hetty Einzig, to help you understand the physical basis of losing weight. Read *Fat Is a Feminist Issue*, by Susie Orbach, to help you understand the psychological issues involved in eating problems. The Orbach books are written primarily for women who are compulsive eaters, but the ideas are useful for any women concerned with their eating and body size.

4. Try not to deprive yourself by dieting or ignoring your negative feelings. Spend time on yourself and your own needs.

Further reading

Eating

Claude-Pierre, Peggy. *The Secret Language of Eating Disorders*. New York: Vintage Books, 1999.

Fairburn, Chris. *Overcoming Binge Eating*. New York: Guilford Press, 1995.

Hall, Lindsey, and Leigh Cohn. *Bulimia: A Guide to Recovery, 5th Edition*. Gurze Designs & Books, 1999.

Orbach, Susie. *Fat Is a Feminist Issue*. New York: Budget Book Service, 1997.
—*Fat Is a Feminist Issue II: The Anti-Diet Guide to Permanent Weight Loss*. New York: Berkley Publishing Group, 1987.

Roth, Geneen. *Feeding the Hungry Heart: The Experience of Compulsive Eating*. New York: Plume Books, 1993.
—*Appetites: On the Search for True Nourishment*. New York: Plume Books, 1997.

Body Image

Dickson, Anne. *The Mirror Within*. London: Books Britain, 1986.

Freedman, Rita. *Bodylove: Learning to Like Our Looks & Ourselves*. New York: HarperCollins, 1990.

Ussher, Jane. *The Psychology of the Female Body*. New York: Routledge, 1989.

Chernin, Kim. *The Obsession: Reflections on the Tyranny of Slenderness*. New York: HarperPerennial Library, 1994.

Resource groups

Your doctor can refer you for professional help for an eating problem.

American Anorexia/Bulimia Association, Inc.
165 W. 46 Street, Suite 1108, New York, NY 10036.
(212) 575-6200
http://www.aabainc.org/

ANAD
(National Association of Anorexia Nervosa & Associated Disorders, Inc.)
P.O. Box 7, Highland Park, IL 60035
(847) 831-3438
http://www.anad.org

ANRED (Anorexia Nervosa and Related Eating Disorders)
P.O. Box 5102, Eugene, OR 97405
(503) 344-1144
http://www.anred.com

B.A.S.H. (Bulimia Anorexia Self-Help)
P.O. Box 39903, St. Louis, MO 63138

National Eating Disorders Organization
6655 South Yale Ave., Tulsa, OK 74136
(918) 481-4044
http://www.kidsource.com/nedo/

12

Sex and Sexuality

M any Survivors of childhood sexual abuse experience difficulties with sex and relationships as a result of their inappropriate and usually disturbing introduction to sexual matters. For children who are not sexually abused, sexuality is a developing process. Children gradually become aware of, and explore, their own bodies, their own sexuality and their relationships with other people. Knowledge and experience develops slowly, giving the child time to adjust. Sexual experiences should be associated with good feelings and with pleasure and relaxation. Even though teenagers often pressurize each other about relationships, they can still make their own choices about whom they want to develop sexual relationships with and how far to go. The child who is sexually abused has no control over this process and is thus prevented from developing her knowledge and sexual experience at her own pace.

We discussed the process of "traumatic sexualization" in chapter 3. When children are sexually abused they are introduced to sexual acts which are not appropriate to their age or level of development. This can be very confusing for them.

> When I got out of the bath, my uncle took the towel and started rubbing me all over my body. He began touching my penis and he kept asking me if I liked what he was doing. The next thing I was on the floor and I felt something wet on my backside, which I now know was petroleum jelly. He penetrated me and I cried out, telling him to stop it, it was hurting me that much. When he

> *stopped I was crying my eyes out. He told me every little boy and*
> *girl cry the first time, but now I wasn't a virgin because he had*
> *broken me in. He said when you grow up you will know how to do*
> *sex. I just couldn't understand what was happening.* Anthony

They may feel forced into submitting to sexual acts or doing things they don't want to do. Abusers often punish children who try to object to the abuse and give presents, money or affection for submission to sex. Children learn that sex can be exchanged for rewards and may continue to use sex in this way in adult life. The sexual abuse is often confusing, frightening or physically painful, so sex becomes associated with negative feelings: fear, shame, tensions and dirtiness. The abuse may also be associated with good feelings, with affection, physical pleasure and orgasms. This can leave the child feeling even more confused.

> *He rubbed my clitoris with his finger until I had an orgasm. It was*
> *very confusing, because while I liked the feelings it produced, I*
> *hated it because it was him who made it happen. My own body*
> *had now betrayed me.* Sandra

Even if the abuse involves some good feelings, children are still subjected to sexual experiences they haven't chosen or that are too advanced for their age and with inappropriate people, such as family members, adults or older children. Children do not have any control over the situation. They are not able to make choices about their sexual experiences, nor to develop sexually at their own pace with their peers. Their experiences are very different from children who have not been sexually abused.

This process of traumatic sexualization leads to a variety of sexual problems in the adult Survivor. Not all Survivors experience sexual problems, but many women with sexual problems have been sexually abused. One study of a group of women seeking help for sexual difficulties found that 90% had been sexually abused as children.

This chapter looks at some of the sexual problems Survivors experience and suggests ways of understanding and overcoming these difficulties. The chapter is for people who are heterosexual or homosexual, and people with or without partners. It is for anyone who is interested in understanding more about their sexual feelings and learning to be more comfortable about sexual matters, as well as for people with specific sexual difficulties.

Ingrid, in her story below, describes the sexual difficulties she experienced as a result of being abused as a child.

Ingrid's story

I was sexually abused from around 1953, when I was four years old. In the years that followed, as I grew into the age of harmless dates with boys, I guessed that my feelings and attitudes were not the same as those of my friends. I had no way of relating to boys. My mother wanted to protect me and did not allow me to talk to or play with the boys in our neighborhood. The only boy I knew was my brother and he abused me. When my friends started to go out with boys and in giggles and whispers talked about kissing in doorways, I did not understand them. As they talked, I could almost feel my brother forcing his tongue down my throat and felt repulsion and disgust. My friends all seemed happy and excited. I felt like an outsider.

By the time I was sexually involved with a man at sixteen, I knew that my emotions were crippled, my feelings distorted. I looked at other girls and wondered why I could not be like them. I fell in love as totally as my friends, but when it came to kissing, touching and finally sex, I froze and lost all feelings. I felt numb, paralyzed, trapped. I agreed to sex more out of gratitude than desire and because I didn't know how to say "No." He was the first man who wanted me, the first who did not get bored with me after two or three weeks because I was so quiet, and he really seemed to like me. So when I became pregnant when I was seventeen, we got married.

At first I thought I was too young to like sex. I knew something was not right with the way I hated any physical contact. Maybe the problems would not have gotten as large if he had been a more patient and understanding man. He knew about the abuse but did not care much. But sex was very important to him. It was never love-making, only sex. There was never any love-play involved. As I was cooking dinner, he pulled me away into the bedroom, with a wide grin pulled down my pants and had intercourse. At other times he came from behind when I was busy with something and suddenly masturbated all over me. But when I had time I was expected to be always ready and always willing to satisfy him. He wanted me to have an insatiable sexual appetite and initiate sex several times a day. To please him, I tried to be like that but sometimes the disgust with my own behavior, the repulsion with the way he wanted sex was so great I would rather let him beat me. I felt sexually abused all through my marriage. The disgust I felt against my own abuser and what he did to me turned inward and I felt disgust with myself.

I hated it. I felt as if I was degrading myself. I felt dirty. I felt humiliated, especially when I tried my hardest to please him in bed and during intercourse he told me that all my friends and my brother's wife were better in bed than I was. I never learned what a loving touch could be like. He never stroked me, never caressed me, never tried to arouse me. My husband was abusive, unfaithful and humiliated me. Finally when he tried to persuade me to become a prostitute, I had enough and left him. Maybe it was the sexual abuse that led me to get involved with him in the first place. Maybe it was because of the abuse that I stayed with him for seven years.

After my divorce, I always had problems saying "No." I did not want sex but I had been programmed from early childhood right through the years of marriage to be submissive so I just could not refuse. I did not think anybody could like me for what I was. I imagined my only value was to be used. I went through a period of sleeping with a number of men. I couldn't say "No" and I was searching, without success, for some good feelings in sex, the way my friends felt, and the way it was portrayed, in gentle love-making scenes in movies and books. I did not find it.

For years during my first marriage and after the divorce I kept wishing I could be a lesbian or nun so I would never have to be touched by a man again. They seemed like the only acceptable reasons to refuse sexual advances.

I met my second husband when I was 27. He was friendly to me and did not ask for sex. I was sure he would not physically or sexually abuse me. During my fourteen years of marriage to him, we rarely had sex and when we did I blocked off any feelings of pleasure. Sometimes a touch felt nice, but as soon as I recognized it was pleasure I felt, it was like running into a brick wall. I consciously refused to enjoy any touch. Most of the time I could cope with the physical side of my marriage. But at times he behaved in a way that made me once again see myself as dirty. At times like those I could feel myself choking with disgust, as if somebody was strangling me and I could not breathe. All I wanted to do then was to run away, but I had not learned to say "No" or to express dislike for certain behavior. And so all too often, as soon as my husband turned toward me, I froze and inside me the abused child that was still present screamed with sheer terror. After a few years I learned to develop an asthma attack as soon as my husband followed me into the bedroom or as soon as I thought he wanted sex. I knew I was bringing on the attack myself through my own will. A whole range of sudden symptoms like hives and hot flushes, and other things, gave me time to delay and often stopped any attempt at intimacy

At first we used to joke that I was allergic to him, although I knew why I felt ill. Until I married my second husband I had felt disgust with sex; in later years, it turned into indifference. During therapy I gradually began to realize that I could allow myself to feel sexual pleasure without feeling disgusted and dirty. Now my sexual problems have gone and I regret bitterly the wasted years of being unable to enjoy intimacy when it was offered.

Sexual problems

Table 7 (page 154) shows some of the physical and sexual difficulties that are often experienced by teenage and adult Survivors of sexual abuse. Survivors may experience different types of sexual problems at different times in their lives. Some of them are discussed below.

Avoiding physical contact and relationships

Some Survivors dislike all forms of physical contact and avoid any touch or closeness, such as friendly hugs, handshakes or sitting next to someone. Many Survivors find the idea of sexual contact especially unpleasant, frightening or disturbing and may therefore avoid relationships. This often happens when the Survivor is a teenager:

> When my girlfriends at school were experimenting with boys, I shied away. Jocelyn

> I didn't like boyfriends or being on my own with men. I used to spend a lot of time in my bedroom on my own. Polly

Avoiding relationships often adds to a teenage Survivor's feelings of isolation and of being different from other people. Anita recalls being teased at school for not having boyfriends and being

Table 7: Sexual Difficulties and Responses to Sexual Abuse

- dislike of touching or looking at oneself
- dislike or avoidance of relationships
- dislike or avoidance of physical contact
- dislike or avoidance of sexual contact
- dislike or avoidance of certain sexual activities
- lack of physical pleasure in sex
- dissociating or blocking off during sex
- flashbacks
- inability to have an orgasm
- vaginismus (tightening spasms of the vaginal muscles)
- not being able to say "No" to sex
- having sex indiscriminately
- prostitution
- aggressive sexual behavior
- sexual pleasure linked to pain
- feeling guilty about sex feeling
- sex is dirty or disgusting
- confusion about sexual identity (male/female)
- confusion about sexual orientation (heterosexual/homosexual)
- lack of sexual knowledge
- sexualizing relationships and situations
- obsession with sex
- obsession with masturbating

sexually inexperienced. These problems may gradually disappear as a teenage Survivor reaches adulthood and manages to form relationships and deal with physical contact. Some Survivors choose to avoid men and develop sexual relationships with women. However, some Survivors carry the fear of physical contact into adulthood and avoid relationships altogether.

Indiscriminate sex

In contrast, many Survivors report that they have gone through a phase of having indiscriminate sex with many different people. This may start at an early age or follow a period of avoiding relationships and physical contact.

Jocelyn shied away from boys as a young teenager but went through a period of indiscriminate sexual activity with many men in her late teens and early twenties.

> When I did eventually sleep with someone I became promiscuous. Sex didn't really mean anything. My feelings didn't enter into it. I was living a role. Jocelyn

Like Jocelyn, many Survivors have learned as children to separate their feelings from their sexual activities. As adults sex may become a meaningless activity. Many Survivors feel that it doesn't matter what happens to them or their bodies any more. As a teenager finding someone to have sex with and staying out at night may also be a way of avoiding going home to the abuser.

Many Survivors feel unable to say "No" to sex or feel that they have no choice and no control over their bodies.

> I'm afraid of saying "No" to sexual advances. Often I initiate them in order to be in control of the situation and then end up getting a bad reputation. Paula

Sexually abused children learn that they cannot say "No" to sex; they have no choice. Children often also believe that they were responsible for the sexual abuse because they think they caused the abuser to become sexually excited. As adults, Survivors may still believe that they are responsible for other people becoming sexually aroused and therefore feel they must satisfy them.

> I have been in situations where, when I look back, I could have said "No" to sex but I have felt unable to say "No." I often felt I led the other person on in some way. I did not realize that men should be in control of their own bodies. I did not want to be a "cock teaser." My stepfather called me a "bitch in heat" when I was thirteen because I was out with a few friends who just happened to be boys. Maybe I believed him. Jane

Survivors who find little pleasure in sex or experience sexual problems may try to find a solution to these problems by having sex with many different people. For some Survivors sex is an attempt to get close to someone and receive some comfort, although they often end up feeling dissatisfied or even more lonely, disgusted and ashamed.

> I was desperate for someone to like me, desperate for some feeling of tenderness, caring, comfort and closeness. I remember days when I stood at the window, alone in my apartment, looking out and waiting. I was so lonely that I would have taken anybody, and I mean anybody, as lover or friend, just to know someone cared. I would have sold my soul to the devil for somebody to put his arms around me with genuine feelings of liking me. There were a few men I only knew one evening before we had sex. I searched for love and closeness, but the morning after, when I woke up, the

only feeling I had was of desperation, shame, guilt and a terrible emptiness. After a few months of searching for friendship and love, I withdrew. I did not go out any more and so did not get into contact with men anymore who were interested only in satisfying their sexual desire. The few moments of tenderness and holding was not worth the loneliness and the bad feelings afterward.
Katarina

For some Survivors, indiscriminate and unsatisfactory sex becomes a pattern they continue throughout their adult life. Many Survivors, however, opt for one-to-one relationships or revert back to avoiding relationships. They often feel ashamed of what they describe as their "promiscuous phase." Fiona has come to understand that picking up men was a reaction to her loneliness and fear and is now able to accept herself without judgment:

I felt lonely most of my childhood, but when I reached seventeen and my mother left home, I was extremely lonely. I'd go with men at night whom I met in bars and nightclubs. I never intended to have sex with them, I just wanted to be with someone. I hated going home alone. The house was so empty, everywhere was so empty. I was looking desperately for someone to care. When I did find the odd man who cared for me, I rejected him. I couldn't accept love, so I just got hurt time after time with the ones who just wanted one thing. I'd sleep most of the day till it was time go to out. Some nights I'd sit at the bottom of our street hoping to find someone to talk to. The feelings as I sat there was as if I was chained to that place and I was crying out for someone to come and take me away. It was a big, empty, dark world out there, but I'd pray every night that someone (Mr. Right) would come for me and I could love him and he'd love me. Some nights if I'd been to a nightclub and hadn't met anybody, I'd walk home alone feeling so desperate. Then my desperation would turn to anger. I would want to cry but couldn't. My throat would feel so tight, I could hardly swallow, so I would get angrier, and try harder to cry, but couldn't. I would think of throwing myself under a car but I didn't have the guts. I'd finally get home, pig out with food, smoke a cigarette and sleep for 24 hours.

On the other hand, if I did meet somebody, it usually ended up with them having sex with me. To them I was just another screw. I'd go home, usually the next day, feeling more depressed, and cry and feel ashamed. I'd usually fall in love with that kind

*(well, I thought it was love) and end up feeling hurt and used
when they didn't speak to me the next time I saw them. There
seemed to be no hope for me.*

*I'm free now, and with writing this for the first time I've
realized that. I realize how bad I felt growing up and I can see
how I've carried a lot of emotions and hurt into my adult life. I also
know now that I wasn't a whore at seventeen years old. I was an
empty, lonely, frightened young girl who had never loved or been
loved. The nearest to love I got was being sexually abused time
and time again, but now I'm learning to love.* Fiona

Survivors who go through periods of having sex with many people
may see sex as a meaningless activity or be desperately trying to
seek some affection and closeness, or feel unable to say "No" to
sex.

Avoiding or disliking sex

Many Survivors dislike sex or find it disgusting or boring.
Survivors who have chosen homosexual relationships may feel the
same way. Survivors often marry or live with someone as adults
but they may still dislike sex and try to avoid it whenever possible.
Some Survivors marry but do not consummate their marriages.
Others marry people who aren't particularly interested in sex and
make few sexual demands. Ingrid chose a sexually undemanding
man as her second husband. Many Survivors find excuses for not
having sex or bring on physical symptoms to avoid sex: Anita
avoided sex throughout her pregnancy; Ingrid developed rashes
and had asthma attacks.

However, many Survivors do have sex, even though they
dislike it or don't get pleasure from it. Sometimes this is done for
their partner's sake or because they feel they have no choice.
Women, especially married women, may feel it is their duty to
have sex, however much they dislike it. Men can also feel under
pressure to perform and that they "should" want to have sex
whenever there is an opportunity.

*My first husband didn't understand why I had never played the
field, so to speak. My first sexual experience, besides my father,
was my first husband and then I never relaxed. I was always
uptight and ended up crying most times. That marriage ended in
divorce.* Pam

Some Survivors lie passively and let their partner have sex with them without participating. Often this pattern repeats their behavior when they were being abused. Some Survivors realize they can still dissociate or switch off during sex, just as they did when they were children. They may dislike sex or have no interest in it, but they switch off and have sex, perhaps because they feel they have no choice or they want to please their partners.

Dislike of sex is usually a result of the bad feelings the Survivor has associated with sex. Feelings of fear, tension, guilt and shame can prevent Survivors from experiencing any sexual pleasure. Guilt about having sex or getting pleasure from it can cause Survivors to block out good feelings during sex or touching, leaving them feeling dissatisfied or disgusted.

Some Survivors find no pleasure in sex, while for others the pleasurable feelings may come and go.

Turn-offs

During sexual activity Survivors may suddenly "turn off" sexually or feel frightened, angry or disgusted. This happens because something (a word, a smell, a certain type of touch, or sexual position) has triggered memories of the abuse. This is not always a conscious process; they may simply feel bad without realizing why. Survivors often dislike certain sexual activities that happened during the abuse (for example, oral sex) and may feel that kind of behavior is perverted and disgusting. Some Survivors recognize that their feelings are connected with the abuse and that they are being reminded of the past.

> A lot of the things my husband does to me would be considered natural behavior but to me they are sickening memories of my childhood abuse. Gail

Others may not yet have made the link between their childhood abuse and adult feelings.

Triggers that can cause Survivors to turn off or start to feel bad include:

+ words; for example, breasts, father, dick
+ phrases; for example, "I love you," "You like this, don't you"
+ smells; for example, tobacco, alcohol, aftershave, perfume, engine oil
+ touches; for example, stroking the face, grabbing the legs

✦ positions; for example, woman on top, man on top
✦ behaviors; for example, oral sex, masturbation
✦ clothes; for example, denim jeans, robe
✦ other things; for example, pubic hair, false teeth, glazed eyes

Turn-ons

Some Survivors are concerned about the kind of things that "turn them on" or increase their sexual arousal. They may be turned on by memories of the abuse or by objects or situations associated with the abuse. They may fantasize about the abuse or the abuser while masturbating. Other people are aroused by behaviors that occurred during the abuse and feel driven to reenact aspects of the abuse either alone or with a partner. Some Survivors may be horrified to find they are sexually aroused by children, even though they know they would never act on it. Survivors who respond sexually to people or things associated with the abuse usually feel very ashamed and guilty about this. Although it can be disturbing to become aroused by associations with the abuse, it is common and does not mean that you were responsible for the abuse or wanted it. It can be difficult to control what we are sexually aroused by, but we can learn to control how we act on these feelings. If you are disturbed by the things you are sexually aroused by, you might find it helpful to see a therapist.

Get some help if you are sexually aroused by children and planning, or fantasizing about, making sexual contact with a child (even if you believe you would not act on it). You should definitely seek help if you are acting out, or have acted out, abuse with a child. Contact one of the agencies in the Preventing Abuse section of the Resources section at the back of this book.

Flashbacks

During flashbacks, the Survivor experiences a vivid memory of the abuse, so vivid that she feels she is reliving the abuse. She may feel she is a child again and see her partner as the abuser. This can be a terrifying experience. Some Survivors lash out at their partners during flashbacks because they believe their partner is the abuser. Flashbacks commonly occur during sex but they can occur in any situation that reminds the Survivor of the abuse.

The kind of triggers listed above that cause Survivors to turn off or feel bad during sex can also cause flashbacks to occur. Smells in particular are powerful triggers for flashbacks. However, anything can trigger a flashback. What causes a flashback for an individual Survivor depends on her experiences and her memories of the abuse.

> I have flashbacks. My husband once said he liked something I was doing to him and to continue. I felt sick. The words triggered something—the abuser was making me do something to him because he enjoyed it. Jocelyn

Partners may have no idea what is happening during a flashback. They may also have little understanding of why Survivors suddenly turn off during sex or start to feel bad. This can cause major difficulties in relationships and leave both the Survivor and her partner feeling confused, frightened, upset, angry or rejected.

Sexual orientation

A major issue for boys abused by men is the impact on their sexuality and how that manifests itself in adult sexual relationships.

> I'm not gay but I hate myself because I was forced to perform gay acts. It makes it even worse that I had an erection when it was happening. I won't ever trust another man as long as I live. Graham

Survivors of sexual abuse may feel confused about their sexual orientation. It is natural for children to respond to stimulation of their genitals, whatever the sex of the abuser. Some Survivors who were abused by a person of the same sex may continue to respond sexually to people of the same sex and may or may not feel comfortable about this. Some Survivors are confused about whether or not they are homosexual:

> My sexuality was deeply affected. For many years I thought I was homosexual and that it was just a matter of time before I "came out." What 11-year-old boy wouldn't react the way I did when his penis was touched? I thought that made me homosexual. Yet this didn't feel right, it wasn't what I wanted, although I would fantasize about men. My mother taught me that homosexuality was a crime but now I know it doesn't matter at all what my sexuality is. Luke

Luke now believes he is heterosexual but had felt confused because he had responded sexually to his male abuser's touch and had had sexual fantasies about men. Some male Survivors who were abused by men have sex with as many women as possible in an attempt to cover up worries about their own sexual orientation. They may make anti-gay comments or even go "gay-bashing" to try to "prove" to themselves and others that they are not gay.

Some men who had a same-sex abuser may live an outwardly "heterosexual" lifestyle but struggle with internal conflicts about their sexuality or feel compelled to go out and reenact the abuse during homosexual encounters.

Being abused by someone of the opposite sex can also affect a Survivor's sexual orientation; for example, some women Survivors abused by men avoid sexual relationships with men and choose female sexual partners.

Some Survivors, both male and female, are homosexual as adults but wonder if they would have been if they had not been abused. There is no way of knowing the answer to this question. There is nothing wrong or unnatural about being attracted to same-sex partners, although some people still find this difficult to accept in themselves and others. The most important thing is feeling comfortable with your choice of partner and with yourself.

Lack of knowledge

Survivors may have had many sexual experiences from a very early age but still have little sexual knowledge or understanding. They may have been too young to understand what was happening during the abuse or they may have closed their minds to what was happening. Children who have been abused sexually often do not show the usual curiosity about sexual matters or experiment like other children and teenagers. They may avoid sex education lessons, and books, articles, TV programs or teenage talk about sex.

> When my teenage friends talked about sex, I either pretended I was in a hurry, or I deliberately concentrated on something else, so I wouldn't hear anything they said. As an adult woman, I didn't want to know about sex. It was disgusting, repulsive, humiliating. I knew all I needed to know for my purposes, which was how to bring the man to a climax as quickly as possible to get it over and done with. I wanted no further knowledge of sex. Katarina

Subjects that are met with embarrassed giggles by many children can be traumatic reminders of abuse for an abused child. This situation leaves many Survivors in ignorance of basic knowledge about the makeup of men's and women's bodies, sexual behavior, contraception, pregnancy and childbirth.

Many adult Survivors continue to avoid matters concerning sex or bodies and may avoid looking at their own bodies.

> *I was in my early twenties when I looked at my vagina for the first time. I did not know what it was supposed to look like, but felt sure it was deformed somehow. I immediately made an appointment with my gynecologist, who assured me I was perfectly normal.* Katarina

Lack of knowledge about sex means that Survivors often do not know what would be considered "normal" or "abnormal" sexual behavior and do not know how to tackle problems that may arise.

Preoccupation with sex or with particular sex practices

Some Survivors appear to be preoccupied with sex. They tell sexual jokes, bring sex into every conversation and see sex in all sorts of situations. For some Survivors this is a conscious "front" put up in order to hide their own ignorance, insecurity and anxiety about sexual matters. Others become preoccupied by sex because so much of their childhood experience has been connected with sexual matters, and this is how they have learned to view the world.

Some Survivors feel compelled to keep having sex or to masturbate again and again. This may be a sign of distress or a way of distracting themselves from thoughts and feelings about the abuse. Survivors may find themselves only able to gain pleasure from particular sexual practices; for example, using certain objects, being tied up, having pain inflicted on them or inflicting pain. This usually reflects what has happened during their abuse. In this way adult Survivors "act out" their abuse through their own sexual behavior.

Prostitution

Sexual abuse can leave Survivors feeling that it doesn't matter what happens to their bodies and seeing sex as something that can be exchanged for money or goods. Survivors may therefore see prostitution as a means of supporting themselves. Research studies have found that many prostitutes were sexually abused as children. Prostitution may be one of the few ways to get money for teenagers who have run away from home to escape the abuse or for Survivors who have lost out on their education, have small children to support or are in abusive relationships. Some Survivors, both male and female, feel that prostitution is a way of taking back control and getting even by making men pay for services they were forced to give as a child.

Overcoming the problems

You may find yourself becoming less negative about sex as you work your way through this book and begin to feel less guilty and ashamed about what has happened. Try to keep in mind that it isn't sex that's painful and frightening, but being abused. Your body was assaulted and your feelings were disregarded. Sexual feelings can be pleasurable, and sexual experiences alone, or with a partner, can be loving and enjoyable.

> As I begin to love myself and my body, I have also discovered that to have sex with someone I love deeply is the highest expression of joy, a celebration of being alive. My hunger for knowledge about my own body and that of my partner is insatiable. A whole new world is opening up for me. Now a kiss can move the earth and a touch takes away all gravity and makes me feel as if I can fly.
> Ingrid

Sexual problems cannot be dealt with in isolation. Sexual problems are closely bound up with people's physical and emotional state of health, their relationship with their partner, feelings of self-worth, body image, sexual knowledge, and the ideas they have about what sex should and shouldn't involve.

Physical and emotional health

When people are anxious and depressed, they often lose their interest and enjoyment in sex. If you're feeling distressed, it may be better to work through some of the other chapters in this book or seek help with your emotional problems before tackling your sexual problems directly. It's difficult to enjoy sex if you are depressed, anxious, angry or tense. Give yourself time to feel better emotionally before dealing with this area.

The same applies to physical health. Physical injury, illness, poor health or tiredness can all lead to disinterest in, or aversion to, sex. Taking medication could also affect your interest in sex. Wait until you feel more physically healthy before tackling sexual difficulties.

Relationships

Sexual problems are often associated with tension, anger, misunderstanding and lack of communication between partners. There is little hope of having a good sexual relationship with a partner if your relationship in general is not very good. It may be that you are angry with your partner for something he or she has done or not done. Maybe you feel hurt, neglected or just bored. These problems need to be dealt with first before you can deal with the sexual problems.

Talking about how you are feeling with your partner instead of bottling up bad feelings is a useful start. Assertiveness training can help you with this (see chapter 10). Change becomes possible once you start to communicate more openly.

You may have chosen a partner whom you do not feel sexually attracted to because he or she seemed "safe" and undemanding or because you accepted the first person who wanted you. You may feel so indebted to your partner for being with you that you feel you need to pay him or her back with sex. Sex can become a focus for many other problems. Sometimes sex turns into a power struggle between partners: not having sex or having sex can become a way of punishing the other person or a way of taking control.

You may need to get outside help or sort out problems in your relationship. A third party often can see more clearly what is going on than partners themselves can. Counseling can help partners understand each other better and strengthen their relationship. It can also give people the courage to leave relationships that aren't good for them. Survivors may be more likely to become involved in abusive relationships as adults as we discussed in chapter 3, and as some of the Survivors' stories in this book have already illustrated.

No partner

You may not have a partner at the moment or have never had a partner. Don't be put off by our references to relationships or partners; these exercises are for you, too. Having time and space free from a relationship can be useful for exploring your sexuality, expanding your knowledge and understanding, and feeling more comfortable with your body. If you wish to form a relationship but have been held back by fear, anxiety or anger, working through these exercises can help you begin to understand these feelings and become more relaxed and open to other people.

Exercise

Write down all the things you feel are holding you back from having a relationship with someone else. Include any fears and anxieties about being close to someone and trusting them, and about the sexual side of a relationship.

Myths and messages

The first step in exploring your own sexuality and overcoming sexual problems is to understand what ideas you have learned about sexual feelings and behavior and where these ideas have come from. We learn about sex directly from what other people say to us or from what we read and see. We also learn about sex indirectly through the "messages" we receive in what people say or don't say, or in what they do or don't do. For example, a child who has her hand slapped when she is touching her genitals might feel she is doing something wrong and shameful. This is one message she has received about her sexual behavior.

The exercise below helps you to find out the messages you received about sex and to discover the thoughts and feelings about sex and your own sexuality that you have grown up with. Before doing this exercise, read through all the instructions and the example.

Exercise: Messages about sex

Relax and let your mind reflect back over your childhood and teenage years. Think about the messages you received about sex. Write down the name of the first person that comes to mind who gave you a message about sex. Then write down what that message was. Next, write down the name of another person and the message they gave you. Continue doing this until you can't think of any more. You might name an individual person or a group of people. You will have received some message about sex from your abuser. Put this message on your list if you can. If you find it too distressing to think about, leave out the abuser from this exercise for the moment.

Example: Polly's messages about sex

Person	*Message*
MOTHER	Never spoke about sex, turned off the TV when bed scenes came on. The message I got was sex is shameful and embarrassing.
SCHOOLTEACHER	In sex education lessons we learned about rabbits, sperm, eggs and conception. The message I got was that sex was a cold and clinical subject that had more to do with biology than feelings.
ABUSER	Raped me. The message I got was that sex is something that's done to me. I have no control or right to refuse it. How I feel sexually doesn't matter.
BOYFRIEND	Said I was cold and not very romantic. I got the message that I was sexually inadequate, that there was something wrong with me.

Exercise:
Challenging the myths and negative messages

Look at your list of messages about sex. Challenge any negative messages or thoughts about sex by writing down the negative thoughts on one side of a piece of paper and more reasonable or positive responses to these thoughts on the other.

Notice which negative messages are influencing your feelings, thoughts and behavior now. Learning to challenge these negative thoughts is the first step toward a more positive attitude.

Negative thoughts	Reasonable thoughts
I have no control over sex or right to refuse it.	It's my body. I have a right to say "No" to sex.
Sex is embarrassing and shameful.	Sex is natural. Some people are embarrassed by it but it doesn't have to be that way. I can learn to feel more relaxed about the subject.
Sex is dirty	What's dirty about it? It's natural.

Learning about your body and sex

Having knowledge about how your body works and about sex is important in overcoming sexual difficulties. Fear thrives on ignorance. Fight your fear with knowledge and by learning to love and accept your body.

+ Do the body image exercises recommended in chapter 11. Learn to accept your body in its entirety, including the parts you may have avoided looking at and especially the sexual parts.
+ Find books or leaflets to read with good, clear information about your body and sexuality. Challenge the myths you have learned with facts. Challenge the negative messages with positive information. Your local Family Planning Clinic probably stock useful free leaflets. We also particularly recommend a woman's handbook called *Our Bodies, Ourselves* (see *Further reading* below).

The Survivors' group has also changed me. Now I can't learn enough about the way it feels in body and mind when making love with someone special, so I have read a few books on sex. To say they were an eye-opener is an understatement. The effect they had on me was huge. I always thought there was me, the one who doesn't really know how to behave or what to feel—the mystery, the enigma. The first book I read, Making Love, *turned out to be a book for men with sexual problems. In my ignorance, I thought a man was always ready, willing and able to have sex and orgasm after orgasm. As I read, I understood that men are not all that different from women. They worry about the size of their penis as we do about the size or shape of our breasts. I had put men and sex on a pedestal to look up to and be in awe of. Now I understand that they have the same fears, worries and insecurities about their bodies and performance during sex. How could I ever hope to enjoy the relaxation needed for good sex if I pull in my stomach to make it look flatter? Or worry whether he has noticed a stretchmark or would he notice my thighs are too fat when he gives me oral sex? How many men worried about whether they were good enough for me when we had sex while I was nervous about whether I was touching and moving in the right way? The books I read made me feel an equal to the man. I realize how important communication is in lovemaking and how essential it is to feel relaxed in body and mind.* Katarina

Learning to communicate

Learning to communicate more openly about sex and your feelings is essential in resolving sexual difficulties. Many people do not know what words to use for the sexual parts of men's and women's bodies and for sexual activities, and this makes it hard to talk about sex. Some words may seem too crude and others too clinical.

Exercise

Write down all the words you can think of to describe the female genitals (for example, vagina, pussy, cunt); the male genitals (for example, penis, cock) and sexual intercourse (for example, fuck, make love, screw). Choose the words you want to use and say the words out loud until you feel comfortable with them. If you have a partner, say the words out loud with your partner until it becomes easy. It's hard to talk about sex if you don't have any words to use.

Follow your feelings

You have a right to say "Yes" or "No" to being touched by another person or to having sex with them. It is your body and your choice. As a child, you may have been unable to say "No" to being touched or to sex, and you may still feel that you do not have a choice. Many Survivors think that they must touch or have sex with another person even when they don't want to because

+ the other person wants to
+ the other person is sexually excited
+ it's their duty (for example, to a husband or wife)
+ they've already responded to the kisses and cuddles
+ other people's feelings are more important than their own
+ the other person has been nice to them
+ the other person will be bad-tempered/upset/aggressive if they don't

These thoughts may have been learned from being abused. Jane learned to give in to sex to avoid her stepfather's anger. You don't have to have sex, touch someone else or be touched unless you want to and choose to. This is your right whatever the circumstances. However, you may not feel able to exercise this right if you are afraid of the consequences, feel guilty or are being threatened or overpowered.

Many Survivors feel anxious about sex because they begin to feel powerless, out of control and physically invaded again. Ultimately it can only be damaging to your own sexual feelings or relationship to have sex with someone when you don't want to. Learning to make a choice about what you do, and do not do, based on your feelings is a way of treating yourself and the other person with respect. It also helps you feel more in control of your own body and your own life.

While you are trying to deal with your feelings about being sexually abused, you may not want to have sex or any physical contact at all. Follow what you are feeling. Listen to your body. If you feel uncomfortable with someone, then probably you do not want any physical or sexual contact. This is your right. If you have a partner, explain how you feel and ask him or her to respect your wishes. These feelings do not have to last forever. Reassure your partner that this is part of the healing process. Many sexual problems arise because people do not talk about what they really feel, or act on those feelings; instead they pretend to their partner, or do what they think their partner wants them to do.

Learning to relax

Learning to relax is essential for dealing with sexual difficulties. Tension prevents the experience of sexual feelings and pleasure. You may have learned from the abuse to tense your body automatically when you are in any sexual situation and when you begin to have sexual feelings. Learn to relax in nonsexual situations to begin with. Learn to notice the difference between feeling relaxed and feeling tense. Notice where you hold tension in your body and what causes that tension to start. Next, start to apply these techniques to sexual situations. Try to relax, notice where in your body you are holding any tension and what caused the tension to start. Many Survivors discover that they automatically tense their bodies as soon as their partner hugs or kisses them, or as soon as they begin to feel aroused.

Touching yourself

Survivors often feel uncomfortable about their own bodies and try to avoid thinking about them, looking at them, or touching them. They may have negative feelings about their bodies because this was the focus of the abuse. Learning to touch yourself is a way of exploring and overcoming these negative feelings and learning to love and accept your own body. Read through the exercise below before attempting it. Be aware that it might bring up negative feelings; recognize and accept these feelings. Discovering what sorts of touches bring up bad feelings can be helpful.

Exercise

This exercise does not have to be done in one sitting. Do it a little at a time and stop when you want to or if you feel too distressed. Come back to the exercise when you feel ready.

Make some time when you can be on your own and feel relaxed. Find somewhere comfortable to lie or sit and then slowly begin to explore your own body by touching and stroking it or maybe gently massaging it with oil. Start with a part of your body that feels safe; maybe your face, feet or hands. Try different types of touching; gentle, firm, tickling, slow and fast. Notice your feelings as you are doing this and what feels good and what doesn't feel good.

Move to another "safe" part of your body and repeat the process. Gradually work through all the parts of your body in this way. Leave your breasts and genitals, or any areas that you feel anxious about, until last. Only attempt these areas when you feel ready and when you can relax and feel comfortable and safe.

As you are doing this exercise, be aware of what gives you pleasure. Notice if you begin to feel tense or anxious with any type of touching or any part of your body. Does this remind you of anything that happened when you were abused? Notice any disturbing thoughts, images, feelings or memories that come up and write them down as soon as you can.

This exercise can help you learn about your own body and feelings and understand and appreciate your own sexuality. This is a basic foundation for learning to feel comfortable with masturbation or a sexual relationship with another person.

Giving and receiving touch

When you have completed the exercise on touching yourself, you can then go on to repeat a similar exercise with your partner, if you have one. The exercise is aimed to help you feel safe and comfortable with touching your partner and being touched. It also helps partners to communicate about what feels good or bad.

Exercise

The exercise below is in two parts and may take a number of sessions over a few weeks or months to complete. Go at your own pace and not try to rush through the exercise.

Before beginning this exercise, make a pact with your partner that you will not have sexual intercourse or genital contact during the exercise sessions. You may feel safer and more relaxed when you know that touching will not lead to sex.

Find a time when you and your partner won't be disturbed, and choose a warm, comfortable place to do this exercise. Find a way to relax together, perhaps by doing a relaxation exercise or listening to music, but avoid using alcohol or drugs. Ask your partner to touch the part of your body that feels the most comfortable and safe to you (for example, your hands, arms, feet). Relax and simply accept the touches. Ask your partner to vary the speed and firmness of the touches and tell him or her what feels good and what doesn't. Repeat this exercise for different parts of your body. Take your time and gradually work toward the parts of your body that you have felt less comfortable with your partner touching. Only ask your partner to touch these parts of your body when you feel safe and ready for this.

Reverse the roles and become the person who gives the touches while your partner relaxes. Start with the part of your partner's body that you feel most safe and comfortable with. Tell your partner how you feel as you are touching him or her. Repeat this exercise for different parts of your partner's body, gradually working toward the parts you feel most uneasy about. In this part of the exercise, look at your thoughts and feelings about touching someone else. Some Survivors have more difficulty touching their partner than being touched themselves. However, you might also want to ask your partner to tell you how she or he feels about the different types of touch you are giving.

Throughout these exercises, notice how you are feeling. If you begin to feel anxious, tense or uncomfortable, stop or ask your partner to stop. Relax and let any feelings, thoughts or memories come to the surface. Write them down and discuss as much as you want to with your partner. Go back to that area of the body or that type of touch only when you feel more comfortable with it.

This exercise enables Survivors gradually to work through any negative feelings about being touched or touching in a safe and relaxed atmosphere. It also helps partners to start to communicate about what feels pleasurable and what doesn't. Often partners have never done this and may have guessed incorrectly what the other person likes or dislikes. Learning to communicate openly in this way can help to break down anger, resentment and hurt that may have built up in the relationship.

Dealing with flashbacks

Flashbacks can be very distressing and frightening to Survivors and confusing to a partner when they happen during sex. If your partner doesn't already know what happens when you get a flashback, explain it to him or her as soon as possible. When a flashback happens, stop whatever you are doing and tell your partner that you are having a flashback. Then ask your partner to help you follow the four steps below. You can also follow these steps when you have a flashback and are on your own.

+ Remind yourself how old you are, where you are and who is with you. Look around the room and name the objects in the room. Keep reminding yourself that you aren't a child with the abuser, but an adult who is safe (for example, "I am 27; I have my own home in Clinton; I am with my husband, Mike; I can see my closet, my hairbrush, my shoes; the abuser is not here; I am safe").

+ Find out what triggered the flashback: a word, a phrase, a smell, a touch, a certain type of sex or a certain sexual position. Tell your partner.

+ If you were having sex and want to continue, do so. If you feel bad, and don't want to, don't.

+ Write down the memory you had in the flashbacks as soon as you feel able. Flashbacks have the power to frighten you when you try to push the memories away. Keep writing down your flashbacks. They will stop eventually.

Summary

Many Survivors of sexual abuse experience sexual difficulties as teenagers and adults. This is a result of the process of "traumatic sexualization" that the Survivor has experienced as a child. The sexual difficulties and responses range from a preoccupation with sex and sexual matters to fear and avoidance of sex and relationships. Some Survivors feel confused or fearful about their sexual orientation. Survivors often find that their sexual difficulties and responses vary at different times of their life. Overcoming sexual difficulties begins with working on feelings of guilt and shame about the sexual abuse. It also involves allowing yourself time to understand, explore, and develop your sexual knowledge and experience in a way that was denied to you as a child. Difficulties with sex and sexuality are part of a bigger problem and cannot be tackled in isolation.

Dealing with sexual difficulties involves looking at emotional and physical health; relationship problems; myths and negative attitudes about sex; knowledge and understanding about bodies and sexual matters; and ways of communicating about sex. You can learn to understand and feel more positive about your body and about physical and sexual closeness. You can learn to feel in control, to relax and to enjoy sexual experiences on your own or with a partner.

Suggestions

+ To explore your sexual feelings and overcome related problems, follow the suggestions and do the exercises described in the chapter.
+ Read some of the books listed under *Further reading.*

Resources

See your doctor for a referral for help.

Further reading

Barbach, Lonnie G. *For Each Other: Sharing Sexual Intimacy.* New York: Anchor Books, 1983.

Boston Women's Health Collective. *Our Bodies, Ourselves for the New Century: A Book by and for Women.* New York: Touchstone Books, 1998.

Carnes, Patrick J. *Don't Call It Love: Recovery from Sexual Addiction.* New York: Bantam Books, 1992.

Castleman, Michael. *Making Love.* New York: Penguin Books, 1988.
A book for men on making love but interesting and informative for women to read.

Comfort, Alex. *The New Joy of Sex.* New York: Pocket Books, 1992.

Covington, Stephanie. *Awakening Your Sexuality: A Guide for Recovering Women.* Center City, MN: Hazelden Information Education, 2000.

Dickson, Anne. *The Mirror Within: A New Look at Sexuality.* London: Quartet Books, 1986.

Haines, Staci. *The Survivor's Guide to Sex: How to Have a Great Sex Life—Even If You've Been Abused.* San Francisco, CA: Cleis Press, 1999.

Maltz, Wendy. *Sexual Healing Journey: A Guide for Survivors of Sexual Abuse.* New York: HarperPerennial Library, 1992.

Stanway, Dr. Andrew. *The Loving Touch.* New York: Carroll & Graf, 1994.

Resource groups

Sex Addicts Anonymous
P.O. Box 70949, Houston, TX 77270
(800) 477-8191
http://www.sexaa.org/

National Council on Sexual Addiction and Compulsivity
1090 Northchase Pkwy., Suite 200, South Marietta, GA 30067
(770) 989-9754
http://www.ncsac.org/main.html

Codependents of Sex Addicts (COSA)
9337-B Katy Freeway, Suite 142, Houston, TX 77024
(612) 537-6904
http://www.shore.net/~cosa

Center for On-Line Addiction
http://netaddiction.com/resources/referral_links.htm

PART FOUR

Feelings Toward Others

13

Children

Survivors sometimes have difficulties in relating to children. They may find they have no feelings for their children, cannot touch them, or they feel angry and hostile toward them. Other Survivors feel anxious and fearful for children and overprotect them or feel out of control and unable to cope. This chapter discusses the links between being sexually abused as a child and having problems with children as an adult, then looks at some of the problems in more detail and suggests ways of overcoming them.

Fiona's story

As I carried my baby, I was afraid I would not be able to love it. When Amy was born, I overprotected her. I wouldn't let her out of my sight nor let anyone do anything for her. She was mine, the first human I could love. I had a terrible fear of losing her and this made me depressed. I worried about her all the time and I was afraid to leave her with people in case she was abused.

I decided she wasn't going to be like me. She had to be perfectly clean and tidy and so had the house she lived in. This became an obsession with me. Even her hair had to be perfect. I'd blow it dry every morning. I'd buy clothes for her and then wouldn't let her wear them in case they got dirty. I washed her if she got the least bit dirty.

I cared too much about what other people thought about me and Amy. I reprimanded her when I thought other people would think that was the right thing to do. It got to the point where I didn't know what was wrong and what was right. If I spanked her in front of others for doing something naughty, then afterward I felt that they thought I was a bad mother. If I didn't spank her, I felt they would talk about her and wouldn't like her.

I wanted so much for everyone to like her, but often I convinced myself they didn't, so I would push her away. My moods were always changing. I used to explode at her then feel that I was a bad parent. I would get so depressed. Even though I have never physically abused her, I was always afraid: "What if I explode next time and hurt her?" So I would avoid rebuking her and she would only have to cry to get her own way. I tried so hard to be a perfect mother but the pressure would become too much, and I would erupt again and then sink into a depression.

I'd have wrapped her up in cotton balls if I could. If other children teased her, it would really hurt. I'd imagine Amy to be feeling the way I did as a child, "No one likes me." I used to get mixed up and confuse my own emotions with Amy's. It was hard to cuddle my child, because I never knew what was wrong or right. I'd feel guilty and was afraid people might think I was abusing her. Because of all these obsessions, my daughter became very clingy. Again I imagined she felt like I did as a child, so I wouldn't want to leave her. I believed she couldn't bear to be without me. I'd get irritable and angry when she'd cry for me.

I dreaded her starting school even when she was a baby. What would I do without her? I was always living in the future. I avoided playing with her and was afraid to enjoy her company because I knew she would go off to school one day.

I was tormented with the thought that she was lonely the way I had been. I thought of having another child as company for her but I knew I couldn't cope with another one. I felt guilty about this and so sorry for her that I spoiled her to make up for it.

As time goes on, I am beginning to get better and my obsessions are slowly going away. I no longer chastise her for other people's sake, but for what I think is right or wrong. I cuddle my daughter without fear. I know I would never hurt her. Now she is seven and I can explain my outbursts to her, telling her that it isn't her fault. I am working on all the other problems, which are smaller now. She has been affected by all this, but with time and care I know I can make it up to her. We have a special relationship. She isn't clingy. I know she can survive without me being there to protect her all the time. I enjoy the freedom when she is at school, and she enjoys school. I am learning to be assertive with her and to realize she is not me. She never will suffer abuse and pain the way I did. She is a happy little girl.

Fiona's story illustrates many of the difficulties that Survivors experience with children.

Sexual abuse and problems with children: Making the connection

Below we discuss three consequences of being sexually abused that can lead to problems with children: being reminded of the abuse, feeling needy, and the lack of a good parenting model. Making the links between their present problems with children and their own past sexual abuse is the first step for Survivors in trying to understand and change their relationships with children.

Being reminded of the abuse

> Something surprising happened to me a few days ago. I went to buy my daughter some shoes and while she looked through the shelves, I sat on a low seat. A man came in with a little girl holding his hand. She was about two years old. They stood next to me and I was at eye-level with the child. We looked at each other, holding each other's eyes. Her eyes looked old, knowing. I wondered if she was being abused, and thought, "maybe not now, maybe in two years." I was four when I was abused. I saw myself in the child. I looked at her eyes and cried. I did not sob, but my tears flowed relentlessly. Katarina

Survivors often try to bury their painful memories and feelings about their abuse. When Survivors are with children, this way of coping can break down because they are reminded of their own childhood and abuse. This causes Survivors to have difficulties with children.

Forgotten memories and feelings about sexual abuse are brought back particularly by children who in some way remind the Survivor of herself as a child: children of the same age the Survivor was when the abuse started; children who look and act like the Survivor as a child; or children who have been sexually abused. Survivors who give birth to baby girls are often reminded of their own vulnerability as a child and of their own abuse. Giving birth to a boy can also be a reminder of the abuse, a reminder that some boys grow up to be abusers. Survivors may be disturbed and reminded of their abuse by seeing a baby boy's erection, a small child playing with her genitals, or signs of a child's developing sexuality.

Ingrid was reminded of her abuse and experienced intense feelings of fear when her son reached the age her abuser was when the abuse started.

> *Although I could feel love for my daughters, I felt mainly indifference toward my son. But when he grew into a teenager, the age my abuser was when he abused me and threatened me, I began to fear him.* Ingrid

Survivors' neediness

Survivors were often needy children because they weren't protected or understood and no one paid attention to their feelings. Adult Survivors, who are still very needy themselves, often are unable to meet their children's needs, or they attempt to compensate for their own neediness by trying to give the children everything they didn't have themselves. Both reactions can cause problems in relating to children.

Survivors often find that they do not have the emotional or physical energy to meet their children's demands and to give the care and attention that is needed. For Survivors who have to cope with their own feelings and difficulties, a child's demands can feel overwhelming. They may emotionally withdraw from their children or be unable to provide a happy and stimulating atmosphere. Some Survivors find even the physical demands of feeding, dressing and washing a child are more than they can cope with.

Problems are also caused by Survivors trying to compensate for their own neediness through their children. Fiona had never been clean as a child, so she tried to keep Amy absolutely clean all the time. Fiona often had felt lonely as a child, so she spoiled Amy when she thought Amy felt lonely. Fiona's "compensation" didn't help Amy because Fiona wasn't responding to Amy's feelings or needs but to her own childhood feelings. She was trying, through Amy, to put right what had been wrong for her as a child.

Lack of a good parenting model

People usually learn the basic ideas of parenting from their own parents' behavior. Survivors who have been sexually abused by parents, and sometimes physically and emotionally abused as well, may find they have difficulty parenting because they have never learned basic skills that others take for granted.

Survivors may feel so anxious about how to be a good parent that they feel paralyzed by uncertainty or try to copy others. Survivors may sometimes repeat their parents' poor behavior (for example, by not listening to a child or threatening the child with being taken into foster care) without realizing the effect they are having on the child. More commonly Survivors are so desperate not to repeat the abusive parenting they suffered that they go to the opposite extreme—allowing children to do anything they want to, avoiding physical contact with them and never saying "No" to the children.

Problems with children

Table 8 (below) lists some of the problems Survivors experience with children. Below we discuss some of the main problems in more detail.

Table 8: **Difficulties with Children**

+ excessive fear for children's safety
+ overprotecting children
+ inappropriately protecting children
+ rejecting children
+ anger and hostility toward children
+ not being able to show love and affection to children
+ not being able to touch children
+ overcontrolling children
+ having difficulties with children of a particular age
+ physically abusing children
+ emotionally abusing children
+ verbally abusing children
+ sexually abusing children

continued ...

- over-indulging children
- not being able to assert your own needs with children
- not being able to say "No" to children
- feeling helpless and out of control with children
- not feeling love for your own children
- not being able to bath children
- excessively washing children
- unable to cope with the child being upset/hurt/angry
- confusing own feelings with the child's

No feelings

Some Survivors find that they do not feel love for their children or are unable to give the emotional care and support a child needs. Below Ingrid describes her lack of feeling for her son.

My son was born and when I saw him for the first time I felt nothing. No joy, but no resentment either. "Well," I thought, "maybe mother-love comes later." I tried to be the kind of mother I had seen others be, but the mother-love never came. I did like him most of the time, but also felt no need to have him close to me. I had no understanding of the child's needs. I fed him, clothed him and gave him material things, but I did not nurture him emotionally. I had nothing to guide me and no emotions to give. I never hit him, but I never showed him love, either. I was glad when my son stopped coming to me looking for love and affection.

Sometimes I felt sorry for him and tried to pull myself together and play with him or read him a story. But within minutes I felt as if something inside me was screaming to get away. I felt imprisoned and crowded. I knew I had to share myself with him, give him part of myself, but there was so little left. So much had been taken away from me by abuse, humiliation and hurt. There was a small part of me that I had made my little haven of peace by blocking out emotions and feelings. I felt this little place would now be invaded by this child, and I would be forced to acknowledge feelings of some kind. Ingrid

Ingrid was unable to love her son because she had tried to forget about her abuse and had buried her feelings. In burying her bad feelings, she had also buried her ability to love and feel happy and close to someone. Ingrid felt threatened by her son. She felt if she opened herself up and started loving him, she might also awaken feelings about her abuse. She was also very needy and felt she had so little left of herself that her son might take it all. Ingrid had not been given the emotional care she had needed as a child and didn't have the parenting skills to cope with her son.

Like Ingrid, Survivors may be unable to give anything for their children or simply not know how to give emotional care and love if they have never experienced this themselves. The child who does not receive the love he or she needs may become over-anxious and clingy, angry and badly behaved, or cut off and emotionally withdrawn.

Avoiding touch

> I still remember the relief I felt when my 6-year-old son asked me not to hold his hand in the street any more, because he was a "big boy" now. From that day on, I used that excuse not to touch him physically. I think the last time I kissed him was when he was about five or six years old. Ingrid

Some Survivors avoid physical contact with their children. They avoid hugging, kissing or holding hands with the child and may refuse to bathe the child or have the child sit on their knee. When Survivors are very needy themselves, or are emotionally distressed, a child wanting to be hugged and kissed can feel like another demand that they are unable to meet. Survivors who are withdrawn or depressed may find it hard to express physical affection and Survivors who have no feelings for their children or feel hostile toward them may not want to.

Physical contact between a Survivor, as an adult, and a child may bring back memories and feelings about the abuse. In pushing away the child, the Survivor pushes away these memories and feelings. Survivors who sometimes physically reject children may at other times be able to show love and affection and overcompensate at these times by pulling the child toward them and hugging and loving them profusely. This see-saw between physical rejection and compensating "over-loving" can confuse and emotionally hurt a child.

Survivors may also be unsure about what kind of touching is right for a parent or adult to give a child. Is it normal to hug, kiss or stroke a child, or is it abuse? Is it normal to bathe a child, or be in bed with a child, or hold a child when the parent is naked, or is it abuse? Survivors who have been abused by their own parents are more likely to have these worries and may feel so frightened of abusing that they stop touching their children altogether.

> It is natural to play with your baby, but it felt wrong to me, like I was interfering with her. I couldn't cuddle her without feeling bad about it. I loved Lynn very much and she needed to know that, but I just couldn't show her. So Lynn was isolated in her own little world. She was also always putting her arms around strangers. Now I find Lynn either won't leave me alone or doesn't come near me at all. Sally

As a child, Graham had no father and was sexually abused by his mother. He never learned what a parent-child relationship should be like, but he did learn that physical contact with his mother always resulted in sexual abuse. This has affected his relationship with his own children:

> It's hard for me to talk to my children or play with them, and I can't cuddle them or show love and affection. Graham

An unfortunate consequence of the growth in awareness of child sexual abuse is that many fathers, whether Survivors or not, avoid bathing and cuddling their children because they are scared of being seen as abusers. Survivors are particularly concerned that they will be seen as abusers and so may avoid physical contact with children. The myth that all Survivors become abusers makes some Survivors fear they will start abusing their children.

Most Survivors, however, feel strongly about wanting to protect children and do not want sexual contact with them.

Children can be distressed when their parents avoid touching, cuddling and kissing. They may feel anxious or angry or become clingy or withdrawn.

Anger and rejection

> There I was, finally I had a baby. All mine, all I'd ever wanted, a baby. "Congratulations, it's a boy!" Why was I crying? My wish had come true but I wanted a girl.
>
> I was just so happy at first to have a baby that I quickly got over it being a boy. Two years later, I was in the middle of a nervous breakdown. I hated my 2-year-old son. I couldn't stand the

sight of him. I hated men of all descriptions. I felt that they were full of demands, especially my son, because he couldn't do anything himself. "I want my breakfast now, mom, please," is a pretty normal request in anybody's eyes, but the "I want" syndrome grated on my brain. Everybody always seemed to be wanting, but nobody said, "What do you want? How do you feel? What do you want to do?" or even, "Thank you."

As I became more depressed, I couldn't bring myself to do anything but the minimum, like give my son breakfast, dinner, a snack, etc. I couldn't love him, cuddle him, play with him, be interested in any way in him or spend time with him. I didn't even want to be in the same room with him for any length of time. This lasted until my husband pointed out that I was being a rotten mother to my son and he would grow up hating me.

One day, my son had done something wrong (hardly surprising since he spent all day, every day, playing alone in his bedroom, out of my sight) and I went to town on him and couldn't stop spanking him. If my husband hadn't come home when he did, I would have probably spanked my son so much that it would have been classed as physical abuse. I sat on the landing in my husband's arms shouting and screaming, "I swore I'd never beat my kids like my father beat me."

My husband at that point made me realize I needed help. I went to a group for adults who were sexually abused as children. Talking to other women and mothers, I found out I wasn't the only one who felt this way or treated her children this way. I realized the reason I hated my son so much was the fact that he was a boy, and I was afraid of him becoming an abuser. I'd just never understood that before. Pam

Pam was trying to meet the demands of a 2-year-old child when she had not sorted out her feelings about her sexual abuse and was in great need of care and support herself. As with Ingrid, Pam's own neediness interfered with her ability to meet her child's needs and she felt angry and resentful about his demands. Pam saw her son as a potential abuser and was angry at him for reminding her of her abuse.

Underneath her depression, Pam hid a huge well of anger about her own childhood, her abuse and the abuser. These feelings buried anger were beginning to surface and Pam was directing them at her son. Children are always easy targets for anger and hostility. They are smaller and less powerful than an adult and usually forgive their parents' outbursts. Survivors may vent feelings on children that they are too frightened to express elsewhere—anger is expressed at a small son but not at the abuser. Some Survivors are angry and hostile toward their children because they do not know how else to maintain control. This may have been the only form of discipline they saw from their own parents. Many Survivors want to love and care for their children but don't know how to overcome their bad feelings or change their behavior.

Anger and rejection toward a child can lead to problems in the child, such as bed-wetting, temper tantrums, running away, sullen or clingy behavior. The Survivors may find herself unable to cope with these problems and feel even more anger and resentment toward the child.

Overprotecting

> I'm always worried about my children and I overprotect them.
> Graham

Many Survivors find themselves overprotecting their children because they are afraid that their children will also be sexually abused. This may involve keeping the child in the house, not allowing him or her to do normal childhood things, shouting at the child for showing physical affection, making sure the child keeps his or her body well covered at all times, not allowing the child to play with other children or to go on trips. A Survivor may not react in the same way with all her children. Some Survivors overprotect girls but not boys. Survivors are particularly likely to overprotect any child who reminds them of themselves as children.

Sally's eldest daughter, Lynn, looks and acts very much as Sally did as a child. Sally feels Lynn is a vulnerable child who is destined to be abused.

> I was very protective with Lynn and still am at times. No one is
> allowed to come near her. I am always so afraid that she is in
> danger from others. Sally

She acts much more strictly with Lynn than with her younger daughter and gets extremely angry if Lynn hugs or kisses Sally's male friends.

Ingrid had been abused by her brother and because of this tried to protect her daughters from males in the family.

> I have to be very careful not to destroy my family life. The suspicion I have against my son and my husband whenever they get close to my daughters tears me apart. If my son suggests a game of chess in his room with his sister, I have to force myself not to interfere because I see the abuser getting me into the bedroom under pretence. Because of my abuse, I have destroyed any beginnings of a normal brother/sister relationship because I try to separate them whenever possible. For the first years I did not realize what I was doing. When I did realize, I forced myself to stop, not always with success. If one of my daughters sits on my husband's lap, I have to keep my eyes away because I cannot bear to watch what it might lead to (or would have led to had it been me and my abuser). Often I have to go out of the room.
>
> While I was watching and worrying about my own family, my youngest daughter was sexually abused by a neighbor. She did not tell me until three years after the abuse. Ingrid

Ingrid was reminded of her own abuse. She was responding to her own feelings of vulnerability and fear about being abused, rather than usefully and realistically protecting her children. She didn't concern herself with the danger from people outside the family, because this hadn't been her experience. This kind of protection—seeing danger for specific children only or from a specific type of person—is inappropriate and does not guarantee children's safety.

Louise was enraged when her daughter Rebecca showed her underpants while doing a somersault at a party. Rebecca was spanked and sent home. Louise still blamed herself for being abused and felt she provoked it by not keeping her body covered. She was frightened by Rebecca's behavior and spanked her because she did not want her to be abused and did not know how else to protect her.

> I know children have always done somersaults and that my reaction to Rebecca showing her underpants was extreme. I try to hide it, but I live in constant fear of her exposing herself and perhaps creating the conditions that caused me to be abused as a child. Louise

Louise's attempt to protect Rebecca was inappropriate. Rebecca wasn't putting herself at danger by showing her underpants;

people don't suddenly abuse because they see a child's underwear.

Children are vulnerable and need to be protected in appropriate ways. Survivors, however, often overprotect their children in ways that are restrictive and stifling and which can cause problems for and with the child. Inappropriate protection may leave children feeling confused or ashamed and it doesn't help to keep them safe from abuse.

No control

Roxanne didn't like to say "No" to her children and spoil their fun. She let them do whatever they wanted. They were always climbing on her, pulling at her, demanding her attention and asking for candy and presents. Roxanne became worn out and her children became more and more unruly. Every so often, Roxanne's patience snapped and she shouted and screamed at her children and then felt guilty. She'd cry and tell her children she was sorry over and over again, and buy them candy to make up. Roxanne felt helpless and out of control.

Roxanne had been physically and sexually abused as a child by her father. She had grown up feeling frightened and without self-confidence and did not want her own children to be like this. She was so frightened of treating her own children badly that she didn't put any restrictions on them at all. Roxanne was trying to make up for the abuse she had suffered as a child through her own children. She also had never experienced parents treating children firmly but fairly, and she didn't know how to be assertive. Like Roxanne, many Survivors are so anxious to make their children's childhoods different from their own that they allow their own feelings and needs to be trampled on.

As children, Survivors were deprived of their rights when they were being abused. As adults, Survivors may not know how to assert themselves or may feel they have no right to do so.

> I was totally unable to assert myself with my children. It was difficult for me to ask them to help with any housework. Sometimes I forced myself to ask meekly if one of them would be kind enough to wash the dishes or vacuum the rug. It was very, very difficult for me, and I could only do it after apologizing profusely. If they refused, I gave up and ended up doing it myself, fighting back the tears of humiliation about being treated like a maid. Katarina

Survivors often find it hard to trust other people and lack friendships and close relationships. Survivors sometimes feel that the only people they can trust and love completely are their own children and are very anxious not to jeopardize these relationships. They may be fearful of making demands on their children, saying "No" to them, or putting any limits on what they can do, in case they lose their children's love.

Like Roxanne and Katarina, many Survivors feel out of control with their children or worn down by continually meeting their demands. Problems will arise between Survivors and their children if Survivors do not teach their children the difference between acceptable and unacceptable behavior.

Deprived of children

Sexual abuse can result in some women being unable to have children because they have been physically damaged by sexually transmitted diseases, forced sexual intercourse, sexual torture or insertion of objects in their vaginas. This can leave them infertile, prone to miscarriages or in need of hysterectomies.

Sexual abuse also causes emotional damage which may make Survivors decide not to have children because they think they won't be able to cope, or because they fear "passing on" their problems to their own children. At one time Rhys thought he would not be able to have children because he was concerned about the effect his own childhood abuse would have on his relationships with children:

> I never wanted children. Now I have a son and I love him so much. I live for him. Rhys

Rhys overcame his fears and has a very good relationship with his son. Luke did want children, but also had to work on concerns arising from his own abuse before he could become a father.

> I always wanted children, but I had anxieties and worries about having children. I was able to discuss my worries openly and freely with my partner. Now I have children and I love it. Luke

Some Survivors are deprived of having children because of their fears of relationships or sexual intercourse. Being deprived of children in these ways can be a further cause of grief and anger to Survivors and can cause feelings of resentment and jealousy toward parents and their children.

Some Survivors who do have children are unable to cope with looking after them because of the emotional problems they are suffering themselves or because of difficulties with the child. They may have to allow other people to take over care of the child temporarily or permanently, or have the child put into foster care. Survivors may miss out on stages of their children's lives, and feel guilty for not being able to cope or not being a good enough parent. Having children put into foster care or losing custody of children can feel like additional punishment or abuse.

Sexually abused children

Ingrid had been sexually abused as a child and recently discovered that her daughter Rosie, aged eight, had also been abused a few years previously.

> When my youngest daughter told me she had been sexually abused, I developed eczema on both my legs within hours. I scratched it until it bled, and in the days that followed opened the wounds again and again. I did not know if I could cope. Would I be strong enough, not only for myself but also for her? I felt ashamed of myself and my lack of self-control. I realized what I was doing but I could not stop. Scratching my eczema had been my only way of coping with my suffering as a child. I was coping in the same way again. Ingrid

Rosie's abuse brought back disturbing memories and feelings for Ingrid but because Ingrid had attended a Survivors' group she could cope and was able to support Rosie without blaming her. Fiona also discovered that her daughter Amy had been sexually abused by two neighborhood boys.

> The day I found out what had been happening must have been the worst day of my life. At the time I was still in therapy myself and I was very sensitive to it all. I kept calm although I wanted to scream at her. I was loving and supportive, although at that time I disliked her, and my overwhelming instinct and desire was to run away, to get away from her. The whole situation brought up things I didn't want to cope with. I saw my daughter the way I saw myself all those years ago. She was dirty, ruined and no good. She was like a damaged toy. I couldn't handle this. I'd protected her and worked hard all those years to make sure my daughter wouldn't be like me. Fiona

Fiona felt the same disgust for Amy that she felt for herself, but she was at least able to outwardly support and accept Amy. In therapy Fiona worked through her own feelings about herself and stopped blaming Amy when she stopped blaming herself.

> Now, 18 months later, Amy and I talk openly about all of it. I now trust her and know she would tell me if anything ever happened again. I am learning that what happened to me wasn't my fault just like it wasn't Amy's fault. Many years ago, it seemed like the end of the world when Amy told me. I never believed I could love her or that things would be normal between us again. Now I have dealt with my worst fear and the whole situation has helped bring up things about myself and by dealing with them I am a stronger person. Fiona

Survivors who discover their own child has been abused have to deal with their feelings about both their child's abuse and their memories and feelings about their own abuse. Survivors who are teachers, doctors or nurses, social workers or work with children in any way are also likely to come in contact with sexually abused children, and may have difficulties in dealing with this situation.

The Survivor may feel angry and hostile toward sexually abused children for reminding her of her own abuse or for disclosing the abuse when the Survivor herself has kept silent. The Survivor may also remain detached about the child's abuse, or feel powerless to protect the child and consequently do nothing. Survivors who still blame themselves for being abused may also blame abused children.

A Survivors' reaction to an abused child is often mixed up with her feelings about her own abuse. Dealing with a sexually abused child can be traumatic for a Survivor who has not worked through her own sexual abuse. A Survivor who has helped and healed herself is in a position to help and support an abused child with strength and confidence.

Overcoming the problems

Working through this book, getting therapy and talking to other people about your sexual abuse will generally help you feel better and improve your relationships with children. Below we discuss ways in which you can work on overcoming your problems with children by remembering the abuse, dealing with your own neediness and learning to be a more confident parent.

Remembering the abuse

Trying to forget the abuse is a coping strategy that doesn't always work and makes you vulnerable to being suddenly reminded of your abuse and childhood feelings. Children may remind you of your own abuse and this can cause problems unless you are willing to face your memories and feelings by allowing them to surface and dealing with them.

Exercise

When you are with children, try to observe your own thoughts and feelings. Notice if they remind you of yourself or of your abuse. Take note of any strong feelings (anger, distress, fear) that you have when you are with children. As soon as you can, write down your observations and any childhood memories and feelings that have surfaced.

Observing your own feelings, memories and behavior, and writing them down, will help you sort out which feelings are about your own childhood and abuse and which are about the children you are with. Getting therapy for yourself individually or in a group, or talking to other Survivors can also help this process.

Survivors' neediness

Many Survivors hate who they were as children. Try to understand and accept the child that you were at the time when you were being sexually abused. You cannot change what happened to her but it is possible to find this needy child within yourself and to understand and care for her in the same way that you might care for any child who is feeling frightened, vulnerable or distressed. With this care, the needy child can mature into a strong and independent adult. Without this care, part of you will remain frozen as a needy child who feels frightened and alone. Penny Parkes' book, *Rescuing the "Inner Child"* (see *Further reading*), explains these ideas in detail and is well worth reading. Below we suggest two exercises to help you contact and accept your inner child.

Exercise 1: Photograph

Find a photograph of yourself at the age you were being abused. Try to recall what you were like and what you did and felt. Try to remember feelings you had that you weren't able to express, and the times you were misunderstood and not cared for. What kind of love and care did you want that you weren't getting? Keep this photograph with you and every time you look at it, try to accept the child you were.

Exercise 2: Letter to and from the inner child

Write a letter to this inner child from the adult you are now, allowing yourself to express all the feelings you have toward her, both good and bad. Write your letter in simple language, the sort of language a child could understand. Next write a reply from this child to yourself as you are now. Write about how you felt and what you needed that you didn't get. Continue writing letters to and from the inner child until the adult part of yourself is able to support and accept the inner child, and the inner child feels comforted.

This exercise may be much harder to do than it appears, especially for Survivors who hate or fear their inner child. You may find yourself feeling upset or disturbed as you begin to experience the pain of your childhood. Take your time. You may need to write a series of letters over a number of weeks or months.

Extracts from Luke's letters to and from himself as a child:

> Hi,
>
> I want to talk to you about rights. The rights of every person, man, woman or child, black or white, old or young, rich or poor. We have the right to breathe, chat, sleep, play or even go to the toilet. Children especially have the right to be safe, yet sometimes their rights are taken away. The right to be safe includes what happens to your body. If someone tries to touch you in a way you don't like, you have the right to tell them to stop. It doesn't matter if they are young or old, or if they are family members. If you need help, then I am always there. LOVE BIG LUKE

Hi,

Thanks for the letter, no one has ever talked to me like that before, like I matter. You talked about rights, I don't think mom and dad think kids have rights. When the abuser touched my penis, he wouldn't stop and I couldn't tell him to stop. He was older and I was the youngest and no one listened to me. When he touched me and I enjoyed it I thought it was my fault. LUKE

Hi,

Thanks for writing back. You made me feel proud, it takes a lot of courage to talk about the things that happened to you. I respect you and I respect the trust you put in me. I want to tell you that you do matter and you are worth something.

When the abuser touched your penis, he violated your rights. Enjoying the touch was normal. Yet you had nothing to feel ashamed about—he was responsible. I want to talk to you about "good touch" and "bad touch." Good touch is when you get a hug or a kiss that makes you feel safe and loved. Bad touch is when you don't feel safe and feel awkward and uncomfortable. When someone touches you and you don't like it you are allowed to say "no," even if it is someone you love, or ask for help. It is your body and your right. LOVE BIG LUKE

Hi,

I don't feel so alone now. It's like I've got a friend, someone who loves me for me. Thank you. LUKE

Ingrid's letter was written at a time when she had begun to love and support her inner child.

Ingrid's letter

My dearest Ingrid,

I am sorry you had to wait such a long time on your own, confused and lonely. I did not know you were there and when I first saw you in my mind a few weeks ago, still waiting, still crying, I was frightened and needed to think for a while before making contact with you. Please don't feel sad anymore. I am here now, strong enough for both of us. Let me explain to you about what happened. I can still sense your confusion.

As I write now I am looking at a photo of you. You are in a park with mother and your brother, Hans. I picked this photo out because it showed me clearly the difference in size, and consequently power, between you and Hans. It is obvious that you couldn't have stopped him abusing you. Try to remember this. It will help you to stop blaming yourself.

Sometimes you cried during the abuse. You were so young then that you did not know what he was doing but you felt disgusted. What he tried to do with you was something too advanced for your age, something adults do and then it is OK; it is not disgusting when it happens between loving adults. Please, don't be ashamed that you allowed him to touch you and kiss you. You were so eager to be liked by everyone that you were willing to do just about anything in return. Please don't feel bad about it. You did nothing wrong. Maybe it will help if you understand why your need to please was so great.

Mother tried to kill herself when you were two years old. Father wanted to divorce her. She refused and he stayed but hardly talked to any of the family after that. Mother was so involved in her own problems that she could not see your problems and only looked after your physical needs. Every member of the family was so wrapped up in their own problems that they couldn't give you the love and attention you so desperately needed. It was not because you were not nice enough, it was simply because they needed all their strength to cope with themselves. You thought if you were nicer, more giving and the best at school, they would love you and notice you. You obeyed every wish they had and tried your hardest to please them.

Dearest child, I am on your side, and I will always be standing by you. Nobody has the right to abuse another person, no matter what has happened to them. Hans had no right to do that to you. What you must understand is that the abuse happened because of something in him that made him want to abuse you, not because of anything you did or said. It was his fault the abuse started, his fault it continued and his responsibility alone. You were only abused because you had to share his bedroom. If another child had been sleeping in that room, that other child would have been abused.

I have learned that it is never too late to change. Just because you have been alone and lonely for almost 40 years, does not mean you have to stay that way. When I first saw you as the distressed child still within me, I saw you with your arms outstretched, tears streaming down your face and so much in *need of love that I cried. I felt bad because you were so unhappy, and because I had neglected you. All we can do now is make a new beginning.*

Promise me that you will tell me whenever something frightens or worries you, and I promise to listen. I will be there for you whenever you need me. You are safe now, and I will make sure that nobody ever hurts you again. Put your hand in mind and come with me. I am your best friend and the one person that will never leave you. I love you, my child. You will never be alone again.
Ingrid

Writing the letters to and from the inner child and keeping the photograph of yourself as a child with you, will help you accept and care for yourself as a child. Once your own inner child feels supported and cared, for you will be better prepared to offer the same support and care to children you are with.

Confident parenting

You may already have good parenting skills but lack self-confidence. No parent or child is perfect. Tantrums, bed-wetting and arguments about eating or bedtime are common at certain ages and don't necessarily mean you lack skills as a parent. Survivors often begin to feel more confident about their parenting skills once they start to talk with other parents and share their anxieties, problems and different coping methods.

Reading a book on childcare (see *Further reading*), attending a parenting-skills class or talking to someone who is skilled with children such as a nurse or teacher can also be useful. Don't be afraid to ask for help or to share your anxieties with others. Only concerned parents do this. You can also build up your parenting skills and become more confident by learning to be assertive with your children and discovering useful ways to protect them. We discuss this below.

Assertion

Building up self-esteem and self-confidence and learning to behave more assertively can help you feel stronger and more in control of yourself and your children. It can also help you deal more fairly and equally with children. What children feel and want is important, but what you feel and want is important too. Children need to be taught to respect other people's rights as well as their own. Look back at the section on assertion in chapter 10.

Children are always trying to test the limits of what they are allowed to do. If you never say "No" or you allow children to do anything and then suddenly become very angry and restrictive, they feel confused. Try using a five-stage system (see box, below) to signal to a child that they are pushing the limits with their behavior. Start with a simple request and if the child does not do as you ask, "turn up the gas" and become firmer at each stage.

Example of five-stage system

1. *(Firm voice at normal level)* "Please don't touch that. It could break. Come over and look at this." *(Offer an alternative toy.)*
2. *(Firm voice, frown and point at the object)* "I have told you before, don't touch that. Come over here."
3. *(Raising voice)* "No! Don't touch." *(Softer voice, smiling)* "Come and look at this."
4. *(Keeping voice raised)* "No! Don't touch that. If you try to do that again, you will have to go to your bedroom for five minutes." (Or "I will take you home," "You will not go swimming this afternoon," etc.)
5. Carry out what you said you would do at stage 4.

At stage 4, make sure that what you say you will do is not too harsh or out of proportion to the child's bad behavior, and that you are prepared to carry it out. Your child will begin to learn when she is going too far and stop before stage 5. This system also helps you know what to do next. You can use this method to ask the child to do something or to stop doing something. If the child is endangering herself, you will need to take immediate action.

Not being firm and never saying "No" is exhausting. It will not help children learn how to deal with other people, nor will it make them love and respect you. Adults and children respect and like other people who behave assertively rather than allowing themselves to be walked on. Finding the right balance between what you need and the child needs benefits both of you. Children are likely to grow up feeling self-confident and cared for it they are treated fairly, consistently and with love.

Protecting children appropriately

Feeling constantly fearful that your children might be abused comes from feelings of fear and vulnerability resulting from your own abuse. It is therefore important to sort out your own feelings first and then work together with your children to help protect them from abuse. However, do take immediate action to keep children away from anyone who has abused a child. Chapter 17 looks at how to protect children from sexual abuse and suggests a number of guidelines. Many books deal with protecting children that you might find helpful to read (see the *Further reading* list in chapter 17).

Survivors may have heard that people who have been sexually abused become abusers. This is sometimes said but it is not correct. It is true that some abusers have been sexually abused themselves as children, but most people who have been sexually abused never abuse children.

Hugging, kissing, stroking and bathing a child are all normal expressions of love and care if they are given and received in that spirit. The same actions can be abusive if they are done for the adult's benefit and are inappropriate or unwanted by the child. People who are touching children in this way or are having sexual fantasies about children need to get help now by talking to a counselor or phoning a helpline (see the *Hotlines* section in the Resources section).

Learning new and more appropriate ways to protect children can help increase your confidence and remind you that it is not the child's behavior, dress or words that "provoke" abuse. It can also help you to feel better about giving your children the affection and love they need.

Getting help for your children

I got a social worker and Sarah started a day care full time. The staff often remarked that she just sat in a corner playing with a doll. How did I feel about that? I had created this baby and I could not give her what she needed. I felt so bad about it. Now Sarah is a lot better. She is able to mix with children and play. With the help we have received, Sarah and I now have a pretty good mother-daughter relationship. Sally

If your problems with your children have been going on for a long time, especially if you have been angry and rejecting toward them, your children may have developed their own problems and require help. If your child is showing signs of disturbed behavior or is withdrawn and unhappy, get help for her or him now. This does not mean you have failed as a parent. It is an acknowledgement of your own problems and a responsible and caring way to help your child.

Summary

Adult Survivors often have problems with children because of the ways they have been affected by being sexually abused. As Fiona's story shows, these problems can be overcome with the right help. Working on your memories and feelings about your own sexual abuse, and on your neediness, will help you begin to relate to children in their own right rather than as reminders of yourself as a child. Learning new parenting skills will also help you become a better and more confident parent. After attending a Survivors' group, Pam had a very different attitude toward her son.

> I am now aware that my son is a person in his own right and is influenced by his parents, including me. Now I can love my son for the first time, and it's wonderful. The things I've missed out on are unbelievable. I wish I'd sought help earlier. It's wonderful to be able to cuddle him, climb into bed with him, to read him a bedtime story, and to do these things because I love him, not out of a sense of duty. The only thing I can't do yet, because he is a boy, is bathe him, but this is a small problem compared to how I was before. At least he knows I love him and he loves me. Pam

It is possible to make things better for you and your children. Keep working on it and don't give up hope.

Suggestions

+ Being sexually abused can affect the way you relate to your own children. Write down any ways in which you think your abuse may have affected the way you feel about, or behave toward, your children. Look at Table 8 (page 180) and check any of the difficulties with children that apply to you.

+ You can help yourself to overcome your difficulties with children by learning to become a more confident parent, and by dealing with your memories and feelings about the abuse and your own neediness. Follow the suggestions and do the exercises described in the chapter.

+ Read one of the books on protecting children from sexual abuse, listed under *Further reading* in chapter 17. Talk to your children about how to keep themselves safe.

Further reading

Parks, Penny. *Rescuing the "Inner Child": Therapy for Adults Sexually Abused as Children*. New York: Souvenir Press, 1993.

Green, Christopher. *Toddler Taming: A Survival Guide for Parents*. New York: Fawcett Books, 1998.

Guhl, Beverly. *Purrfect Parenting*. Tucson, AZ: Fisher Books, 2000.

Bayard, Robert T. *How to Deal with Your Acting-up Teenager*. New York: M. Evans & Co., 1986.

14

Mothers

S urvivors of sexual abuse often have difficult relationships with their mothers. Mothers are supposed to love, support and protect their children. They are expected to prevent bad things from happening to their children and always be there to listen and to make things better. The child who has been sexually abused did not have this help and protection. She may not have been listened to and her mother may not have been there when she needed her. Mothers do sometimes sexually abuse their children; if this happened to you, work on your relationship with her using chapter 15, *Abusers*. More often, however, the mother is not abusing and is potentially in a position to help and support the abused child. In this chapter, we look at the way in which sexual abuse can affect a Survivor's relationship with her mother or person in a similar caregiving role.

Difficulties between mothers and Survivors are not inevitable. The mother may realize that her child is being sexually abused and support and protect her. The mother-child relationship can be strengthened if the child can share her feelings with her mother and feel loved and supported.

> *My mother found out about the abuse when she heard me cry out from my bedroom and came to investigate. I told her everything that had been going on and her reaction was very positive. She told my father and brother and they got my abuser to leave the house immediately.* Anthony

Unfortunately this rarely happens. Mothers usually do not know that their children are being sexually abused because sexual abuse happens in secret and is kept secret. Sometimes mothers do know or suspect that their child is being sexually abused but do not stop the abuse or protect the child. Mothers may be unable to cope with their own feelings of anger or distress about the abuse of their child. There are many ways in which sexual abuse can damage the relationship between the child or adult Survivor and her mother. Survivors' feelings toward their mother are often a confused mixture of anger, love, hatred, pity, resentment and a desire to protect them. Some difficulties Survivors experience in their relationships with their mothers are discussed in more detail below. Exercises are suggested to help understand and come to terms with the feelings and overcome these difficulties.

Difficulties with mothers

Feeling protective

> As a child I felt that telling would make my mom more unhappy and she'd feel guilty. I felt very protective toward my mom. Jane

Few children tell their mothers that they are being sexually abused. They are frightened of the consequences of telling—of being blamed, disbelieved or punished. Many sexually abused children also fear the distress and pain their mothers might feel if they knew what was happening. Abusers often keep children silent by telling them that their mothers would be upset if they knew. Children therefore tolerate great pain themselves in order to protect their mothers from suffering. The child finds herself protecting her mother rather than being protected by her.

> As I got older, I didn't want to upset my mother. How could I hurt her by telling her what had happened? I feel really sorry for her because her life has been so unhappy. I wouldn't want her to feel upset because she didn't protect me. I love her and wish I could change her life for her. Kate

The child may feel especially protective if the abuser is her mother's partner.

The secrecy can create a barrier between mother and child and this causes relationship difficulties. The mother cannot understand why her child is distressed or why she is behaving differently and the child cannot tell. Many Survivors describe having a close relationship with their mother until the abuse started. New stepfathers are sometimes jealous of the mother's relationship with her child; abusing the child can have the added "benefit" for him of destroying this close relationship.

The secrecy frequently continues into adulthood. Survivors who have overcome many of their difficulties and speak openly about their abuse may still feel strongly that their mothers must never know. They find it hard to break the habit of protecting their mothers and may look out for her feelings at their own expense. Survivors often try to give their mothers the care and protection they would like to have had themselves as a child. Underlying this caring and giving, however, is often a great well of neediness. Survivors may feel grief and anger that as children they never really experienced the feeling of being mothered and of being dependent and secure, and that now, as adults, they do not have a close, confiding and trusting relationship with their mothers.

Katarina decided it was better to believe that her mother would have protected her if she'd known rather than actually tell her and risk a different reaction.

> I could not tell my mother about the abuse. I was afraid of what her reaction would be. As long as she didn't know, I could cling to the thought she would have protected me. She was a very strong believer in family unity. What if she had not completely separated me from my brother (the abuser)? He would have carried out his threats, without doubt, and she was too gullible to think badly of her own son. I would have lost that last ray of hope—the complete trust in my mother. Katarina

Katarina was not only protecting her mother by not telling, she was also protecting her own hope that if her mother had known she would have given her all the love and protection she needed.

For adult Survivors, protecting their mother can create practical problems and add further strain to the relationship. Survivors may find themselves caught up in a web of lies in an attempt to explain why they are avoiding the abuser or why they are receiving counseling. If the abuser lives with her mother, the Survivor may visit infrequently and keep her children away in order to protect them. Mothers who do not know about the abuse and do not understand why this is happening usually feel hurt and rejected by this behavior.

I finally decided I never wanted to see my abuser again, so if I knew my brother was visiting my mother, I left before he arrived or didn't go in the first place. I stopped going to her birthday parties or for Christmas dinners. She felt hurt by this and often asked me why. I told her it was because I didn't like my brother, but when asked for the reason I remained silent. She asked my brother. He told her he didn't know what I could have against him, he hadn't done anything wrong. She was hurt by my behavior but I thought she would feel even more hurt if she knew the truth. She could blame me for being willful; if she had known the truth she would have blamed herself. Katarina

Survivors may jeopardize their relationships with their mothers in order to protect them from knowing about the abuse.

Feeling neglected

Survivors often feel angry, upset or resentful about their mother's failure to notice that they were being sexually abused. Mothers are expected to be sensitive to their children's feelings and needs and to know what is happening to them. When a child's distress is not noticed, the child may feel let down and neglected even if she has consciously tried to hide the abuse from her mother and put on a cheerful face. Jane felt let down by her mother's failure to make time for her and really listen and find out what was wrong.

I was abused by my stepfather from the age of about seven to seventeen. My mother's marriage to my father had been violent and that's why she divorced him. My mother worked hard studying to become a teacher. When she married my stepfather, we moved to another city. I don't think she suspected that he was abusing me and my sister, Lizzie. If we had nightmares or tantrums, she thought we were disturbed because of the visits with our father.

The more I look back over my childhood, the more I realize how absent she was. I used to think she threw herself into her work (teaching) because she was unhappy at home, in her marriage. I didn't feel that my mother was there for me. With hindsight I can understand why, but at the time it made me feel as though I wasn't worth looking after. Jane

Many Survivors feel angry with their mothers for not noticing the abuse. Katarina feels her mother should have realized that she was being abused.

I was four or five years old when my brother ejaculated between my closed legs. His semen wet my nightclothes and the sheet. I was blamed for wetting the bed. As an adult now I feel a mixture of anger and contempt for my mother for not noticing the difference between semen and urine when she changed my nightclothes and sheet. Katarina

If the abuse remains secret and these feelings from childhood are not resolved, adult Survivors may continue to feel let down and uncared for in the relationships with their mothers, whatever their mothers do. They continue to hope silently that their mothers will notice their distress and voluntarily offer the care and support they crave. When this doesn't happen, Survivors may be overwhelmed with anger and distress and emotionally withdraw from their mothers in an attempt to protect themselves and to punish their mothers.

Feeling abandoned and badly treated

In some cases mothers are aware that abuse is happening and take no action to stop it. They accuse the child of lying, or turn a blind eye to it and allow the child to continue to be abused.

When I finally told my mom about being abused by my dad and by her boyfriend, she said I had made it up. As far back as I can remember my mom would try to convince me that things I knew were true were lies, and in the end I would just believe her. At one point I tried to convince myself that maybe I had dreamed it up. I know she knew about it, though, even before I said anything, because I can remember hearing her and her boyfriend arguing about it. Sally

Some mothers support and stay with abusive partners even if this means losing custody of their child or destroying their relationship with the adult Survivor.

As an adult, Joanne told her mother she had been abused by her stepfather, Ken, and was blamed and abandoned by her. Her mother chose to stay with Ken, even though he had just been released from prison for abusing his natural daughter.

I felt hurt at my mother's decision to side with my stepfather and abandon my family and me for him. Joanne

Even if the mother stops the abuse or leaves the abuser, she may still be angry at the Survivor or blame her for what has happened.

Some mothers are openly hostile and treat the Survivor badly. Others are cold and distant and play on the Survivor's feelings of guilt.

Adult Survivors may feel angry and resentful toward their mothers for abandoning them and treating them badly. They may find ways to get back at their mothers or feel consumed with a rage they can't express. However, Survivors are often devastated by their mother's reactions and feel no anger but instead an overwhelming sense of grief and loss.

> I still feel confused about my mother. Although I am the victim, I am the one who has lost my family. I now don't speak to any members of my family except my auntie. I don't know what hurts most—the abuse or losing my family because of it. I have a husband, three wonderful kids and a nice home but I still wish I had a real mother and a grandmother for my kids. Sally

They may try to gain their mother's love and understanding by doing things for her and always trying to please her.

> I have always had a bad relationship with my mom. I have tried hundreds of times to make it better, but the more I tried and the more I did for her, the more she wanted, and thus the relationship was one-sided. On the few occasions she did anything to help me, I never seemed to be able to show her enough thanks. Sally

Some Survivors continue to accept poor treatment from their mothers or to be abused and disregarded by them in the hope of one day gaining the love and acceptance they crave. Others, like Sally, may stop seeing their mothers but continue to feel abandoned and to grieve for the loss of the relationship.

Dealing with mothers' distress about the abuse

> There are really no words to describe my feeling when I understood that my daughters had been sexually abused. It was like hearing of the death of someone you love—in fact, something did die. There was pain and an overwhelming sense of loss and desperation. When that passed, there was overwhelming anger. Anger against my husband for his treachery and against the girls for what seemed like deceit on their part because they hadn't told me. I was angry with God that such evil had overtaken us. I had a tremendous feeling of failure, which crept into all my activities and

sapped my self-confidence. I swung between thoughts of murder and suicide, but ended up rejecting both. Grace (Jane's mother)

Mothers are often thrown into emotional turmoil when they find out that their daughter or son has been sexually abused. They may be overwhelmed with grief, anger, distress or with feelings of failure and helplessness. They may also suffer financial and practical problems if the disclosure results in a marriage breakup or a breadwinner going to prison.

Survivors can have difficulty coping with their mother's distress about the abuse and this may add to their own feelings of guilt.

> *My sister, Lizzie, and I finally decided to tell my mother about the abuse because we felt that it would help her understand the estranged relationship between her and Lizzie. When we told her, I was sure she believed us but she was very upset, which I had always imagined she would be. I felt responsible for causing her that pain and distress. We didn't discuss our feelings or any details about the abuse with her. I really felt that she couldn't cope with any more.* Jane

Survivors often blame themselves for causing their mother's distress and other people may also blame them for disclosing the abuse.

Some mothers openly express their distress. Mothers may look to their son or daughter for support, especially if the abuse has remained a secret between the two of them, but Survivors may feel unable to cope with their mother's feelings as well as their own emotional pain. Mothers and Survivors thrown together in this situation often cannot help each other and may make each other's problems worse. Survivors may also feel that their mothers are so involved with their own distress that the Survivor's feelings and needs are being overlooked.

> *My mother would not be honest with me in discussions and always turned it around to discussing her own unhappy childhood. Maybe this was her way of coping with her guilt feelings, but I began to feel strongly that I could no longer rationalize or cope with her feelings when I was trying to help myself.* Jane

Survivors may find themselves in the familiar position of trying to protect, support and "mother" their own mothers and feel angry and resentful about this situation.

Alternatively, both mother and son or daughter may avoid mentioning the sexual abuse or the abuser for fear of upsetting the other person. This creates a barrier in the relationship and may lead to misunderstandings and a lack of closeness in the relationship. Melanie thought she had ruined her parents' lives by disclosing the abuse. She didn't talk about the abuse again because she felt guilty and didn't want to hurt her mother.

> Mom never knew exactly what happened to me. I could never really talk about It. I felt I had broken my mom and dad up as a normal husband and wife, because from that time on my mother didn't want anything to do with him on the sexual side of the marriage. What happened to me turned her off. She blamed my dad because he was nearby when it was happening. Melanie

Melanie's mother, however, felt guilty for not protecting her daughter. She thought Melanie blamed her and so she avoided mentioning the abuse. The relationship became more and more strained, and they both became extremely sensitive to any criticism from each other.

Dealing with the problems

Below we look at ways in which you can begin to explore and understand your feelings toward your mother and consider changes you might make in your relationship. Dealing with the general problems caused by your sexual abuse by working through this book and by talking to other Survivors or a counselor can also help. It is useful to read this section and do the exercises even if your mother is dead or if you have no contact with her.

Exploring your feelings

The relationship between you and your mother may involve complex and conflicting feelings. You may not have allowed yourself time to find out what you really feel about your mother.

As an abused child, you may have felt that your feelings didn't matter and that you had no right to express them. It is useful to get in touch with these childhood feelings by doing the letter-writing exercise from the inner child (see chapter 13) before going on to the exercise below.

The exercise below helps you to explore your feelings toward your mother and express them in a safe way. You may be surprised by your feelings. Many Survivors think they feel only anger for their mothers, but discover that underneath they yearn to be loved and accepted. Others find that the love and respect they feel toward their mothers masks strong feelings of anger and resentment.

Exercise: Letter to your mother

Write a letter to your mother (not to send) expressing all the feelings you have toward her and all the things you would never dare say. Below are two examples of letters written by Survivors.

Joanne's letter

Dear Mother, It's sad when you realize a mother and daughter relationship is over, even if it wasn't very good to begin with. I remember the letter you wrote to me after you heard that I was going to the police. "How could you do this to me?" you said. How could I cause you to be by yourself if he were to be convicted once more? I'm afraid I was so full of anger at the time, that that point didn't even occur to me.

I know that the day I brought the abuse out into the open with you was the final straw, and after that we seemed to drift apart forever. You asked why we didn't visit with the children when Ken was in the house. I never said at the time that I could remember the time you came home early to find the doors locked while I was being abused, and the day I was trying to tell you what he was doing to me, only to remember his threats and back down, afraid to finish the sentence. I never said I could remember the time you shoved a newspaper article under his nose on a case of incest and took no further action when he just laughed off the suggestion and said you were being stupid. Why on earth didn't you protect me from his abuse? For that matter, why didn't you protect yourself, me and my brothers from his cruelty and violence? I feel even more hurt that you didn't protect us now that I have children of my own. What kind of a mother were you?

I know you probably cannot understand why I am still so bitter at what Ken did to me. Perhaps you believe that because the abuse has ended I shouldn't be affected by it any more. What a misconception that is! I guess I could excuse you for thinking that, however, because even I had no idea that the abuse was the cause of all my problems until I began meeting with the Survivors' group.

Now I'm really glad that I have had the opportunity to air my feelings with you. They have haunted me for years. It does sound sad but it looks likely that my life will continue without you. How sad it is that we couldn't have a close relationship with one another, which I believe every mother and child should have, but you have made your choice, mother, and decided to stand by the man who sexually abused his daughter and your own daughter. How can I ever come to terms with that!

Polly's letter

Dear Mom,

I am writing this down because I find it hard to say. I want to tell you how I feel and have felt over the years.

When I confronted you about grandad, you said we had to understand that my nanna was a cold person and that my grandad was a sensitive, warm person. This was your excuse for what he did to us. Well, I think that is garbage. If he needed sex that much, then why didn't he find a prostitute or leave nanna, but to abuse us children was wrong. I feel angry at you because you didn't protect us in spite of it happening to you when you were little. You say he put his hands down your pants but you told him not to and he stopped. Well, he did worse things to us. He made us have anal sex, oral sex, made us touch his penis and do other things.

Why is it that none of us could talk to you? You were so strict about anything to do with sex, like turning TV channels, never talking about periods or anything. Yet all those years, you let that happen to all of us and not only from grandad but other men as well. I could scream at you sometimes.

I couldn't understand how you never noticed—or did you just ignore it? You keep going on about how wonderful he is. Well, I don't want you to because it makes me feel sick. He was an old, perverted bastard and I hate him. The way you just overlook everything makes me hate you as well. You have always blamed nanna for it all, but you are blaming the wrong person. You were there and I needed you as much as the others. It seemed that you did not care or you were too busy to notice, I don't know which.

Notice if you are directing all your anger for the abuse toward your mother and excusing the abuser. Mothers are not responsible for abuse committed by another person. Mothers who fail to listen to the child, to take action, or to stop the abuse are responsible for this, but the abuser is always responsible for the abuse. Many Survivors initially blame themselves for the abuse, then blame their mothers for not protecting them and then finally place the responsibility for the abuse with the abuser.

Exercise: Letter from your mother

If you have already written a letter to your mother, you can now write a reply to that letter. Write a letter to yourself as if you were your mother at the time you were being abused.

Seeing the situation through your mother's eyes can help you understand that your mother may not have known about the abuse. Until very recently, most mothers were not aware of the risk to their children of sexual abuse, especially from relatives or friends. If you were behaving badly or strangely, the idea that you were being sexually abused would probably never have occurred to your mother.

Seeing the situation through your mother's eyes can also help you understand that she treated you the way she did because of her own circumstances, not because you were a bad or unlovable child. She may have been too busy to notice your distress or unable to cope with the circumstances she was in. She may have been afraid of losing her partner, her home, her family. She may have been depressed, anxious, angry or resentful about her own life and she may have been sexually abused herself.

Mothers may cope with the suspicion that their child is being sexually abused by pushing it to the back of their minds, blocking it out and pretending it isn't happening. They may remain silent because they fear the consequences of telling.

Whatever your mother's problems or circumstances, she was still responsible if she neglected you, treated you badly or abandoned you. The aim of this letter-writing exercise is not to make excuses for your mother's behavior. It is to help you understand that you did deserve love and protection. She behaved the way she did because this was her way of dealing with life, and not because you were unlovable.

Lorna wondered if she hadn't been protected because her

mother didn't care. However, when she thought about the family circumstances at the time she was being abused, she realized her mother was trying to cope with working night shifts, a husband who was always out drinking, and bringing up six children (one of whom was in the hospital). Lorna then wrote this reply to herself from her mother.

> Dear Lorna,
>
> I could not help you when your Uncle Sam was abusing you because I did not know what he was doing. I knew that you didn't like him, but you would not say why. I asked you lots of times, but you just drew the curtains on me. There were times I tried to talk to you or listen, but you were not having any of it. It's true that I punished you when I thought you had run away, but I did not know what else I could do. You would not, or could not, talk to me. I thought you were making a play for more attention. Your sister was in the hospital and I had four other children at home to look after beside you. There was not always the time that was needed for everyone. All my children had been fairly happy—then you changed, became moody and would not talk to me. It was really difficult. I knew you were unhappy, but I could not help you because I did not know how to. I also had other responsibilities. I thought I had lost you, but I did not know what I had done wrong, or what I could do to help you.

Lorna realized that although her mother had failed to protect her, it was because of the family's circumstances and because her mother did not know how to help—not because Lorna was unlovable.

You may find yourself feeling less angry with your mother as you begin to understand her situation more or cease to blame her for things she wasn't responsible for. You may find yourself feeling angry with her for the first time because you realize you have been protecting your mother when she should have been protecting you.

Making changes

Relationships between mothers and their sons or daughters are never perfect. Many difficulties can arise that have nothing to do with sexual abuse. Mothers are never able to live up to the image of an ideal mother, and children invariably feel hurt in some way by their parents. It's realistic to accept that there may be difficulties now and then. You may never have the totally loving and supportive mother you would really like. Being frequently upset, damaged or abused by your mother, however, is not acceptable.

Many Survivors feel that they cannot assert themselves with their mothers and feel they are victims of their mother's put-downs, constant demands, lack of support or insensitive treatment. Like Sally's mother, your mother may have convinced you that you were always in the wrong. Remember that as an abused child you became accustomed to being treated badly, without respect and as if your feelings and needs didn't matter. You may have learned to put up with this type of behavior and accepted it.

Survivors may also continue to accept bad treatment from their mothers because they feel

+ powerless to do anything else
+ frightened of having an argument
+ frightened of losing the relationship
+ they deserve to be treated badly
+ she's right, they are useless/no good/ to blame for being abused
+ they are in the wrong or being unreasonable
+ they have to respect their mother and do as they are told
+ they have to try to please her
+ they are to blame for upsetting her or making her angry
+ they are to blame for breaking up the family
+ their own feelings are not as important as other people's

No one deserves to be treated badly. Both you and your mother are adults and could have an equal relationship where you respect your own and each other's rights. Accept that there may be difficulties but don't accept being used and abused. Passively accepting bad treatment and trying desperately to please will not gain your mother's love, as Sally discovered. Ask yourself, has this approach worked so far?

Feeling less guilty and responsible for the abuse and for your mother's feelings can help you feel and behave differently. You may be able to make changes in the relationship with your mother by changing your behavior, discussing the problems, and requesting that she makes changes in her behavior. Talking openly and honestly is a good way to encourage someone else to do the same. Behaving assertively encourages other people to behave assertively in return and discourages abusive behavior. Working through the following exercises can be helpful, even if you decide not to confront your mother face-to-face.

Exercise 1

Write a description of the relationship you have with your mother. Think about the way she treats you and the way you treat her. What do you like about the relationship? What do you dislike? Is the relationship with your mother good for you or are you being damaged and abused?

Exercise 2

Make a list of some of the things you would like to change with your mother, starting with the easiest items first.

Example

1. I want to ask her to come to my house once a month instead of me always going to her house.
2. I want to say "No" to going to her house for Sunday dinner every week.
3. I want to ask her not to give the children presents every time she sees them.
4. I want to tell her that I feel hurt and upset when she criticizes my appearance and ask her not to do it.
5. I want to tell her I don't want to hear about what a wonderful man her father (my abuser) was.

Pick out the easiest task from your list and write down how you might approach this assertively with your mother. Decide what you want to say and how you can say it assertively. Write down all the different ways in which your mother might react and how you could respond. Get a friend to pretend to be your mother and practice what you could say. Speak to your mother only if you want to, after you have practiced and feel confident about it.

Talking to your mother about the abuse

You may want to tell your mother about the abuse or, if she already knows, to talk to her about it again. This can help the relationship by breaking the silence, clearing up any misunderstandings and allowing each of you to express your feelings. However, this may not be a helpful step to take. You need to use your own judgment and talk it over with a friend or a counselor. Telling your mother is not an essential part of the healing process, and you may decide you do not want to do this.

If you do decide to disclose to your mother, make sure you only do so after careful preparation and when you are quite sure that you know you are not to blame for what happened. Read the section in chapter 15, *Regaining your power from the abuser.* The preparations you need to make before disclosing to your mother are similar. Prepare yourself for all the different reactions your mother might have; for example, being upset, angry, not believing you. Act out what might happen, with someone else playing the part of your mother so you can rehearse your responses. If possible, arrange for both your mother and you to have someone around to support you afterward. Be prepared for the fact that things won't be better immediately, but it may help in the long term.

If your mother already knows about the abuse, you may have more talking to do. Twenty years after Melanie had first told her mother about the abuse, she brought up the subject again and they were able to clear up their misunderstandings and develop a better relationship.

> Since the abuse, the relationship between my mother and me had been very strained. A while ago I did manage to talk to her about it. It seemed to help us both form a closer knit relationship. It was very hard to talk to her about it, but afterward we seemed to communicate better. Melanie

Melanie realized she wasn't to blame for her mother's upset, nor for the difficulties in her parents' relationship. The Survivor is not responsible for her mother's distress. It is the abuser, by his actions, who is responsible for causing distress to the Survivor and to the Survivor's mother.

> Since I received both one-to-one therapy and group therapy, I don't feel responsible for the abuse any more. My stepfather was

responsible. This has also made me feel less responsible for my mother. Jane

Survivors can encourage their mothers to get help from a therapist or in a group for mothers of children who have been sexually abused. Jane encouraged her mother, Grace, to have individual therapy. Later Jane, her sister Lizzie and Grace went for therapy together to try to sort out the difficulties they had in relating to each other.

By the time my mother, my sister and I met together, my mother had had some one-to-one therapy and had had a chance to talk about her feelings in a more constructive situation. I felt she had had time for reflection. She was less defensive than she had been before about what my sister and I had to say, and I think she really listened. The situation didn't allow her to use diversions as she had done before. The psychologist was objective and could reflect back what each of us was saying and allow us to clarify what we meant. Also, because the psychologist was there, I felt safe. Jane

Not seeing your mother

Sometimes it is not possible for Survivors to change their relationships with their mothers. A mother who supports the abuser or blames the Survivor for the abuse may demand that the Survivor retracts the disclosure or takes the blame for the abuse. Survivors who are presented with these ultimatums or have tried to improve their relationship with their mothers and are still being put down, damaged or abused, may decide that the only thing they can do is stop seeing their mother. This might be a temporary or permanent solution to the problem.

Sally held on to the relationship with her mother for many years, trying to please her and win her love and support. Sally's mother continued to blame and disbelieve her, turned other family members against her, and tried to cause trouble between Sally and her husband. Sally eventually thought that holding on to the relationship, and the small hope that her mother would change, was not worth all the pain and grief it was causing.

I always wanted to be able to talk to my mom and tell her how I felt and even to have a good mother-daughter relationship. I know now that it will never happen. I have not gotten in touch with my

mom for more than a year, and now I feel free to get on with my life with my husband and children. Sally

Although abandoning a relationship with your mother might be extremely painful, it may be the right choice for you. You do not have to maintain a relationship with anyone just because they are a family member. Some Survivors choose to distance themselves from their mothers or stop seeing them while they work through their own problems. They resume the relationship when they feel stronger.

Summary

Survivors often have difficulties with their mothers because of the sexual abuse. They may feel neglected, abandoned or badly treated. They may also have a strong desire to protect their mothers from knowing about the abuse or feel responsible for the distress that the disclosure may cause. Survivors' feelings toward their mothers may be a mixture of love, hate, resentment, pity, anger and disappointment.

Survivors can work on these problems by exploring and expressing their feelings and then trying to make changes in the relationship. In this way, Survivors can sort out their feelings about their mothers, refuse to accept bad treatment, regain their own power and move toward a better relationship.

Suggestion

Follow the suggestions and exercises outlined in the chapter to help you understand your feelings toward your mother and make positive changes.

Further reading

Friday, Nancy. *My Mother, My Self.* New York: Dell Books, 1987.

Gundlach, Julie K. *My Mother before Me: When Daughters Discover Mothers.* New York: Barricade Books, 1992.

Secunda, Victoria. *When You and Your Mother Can't Be Friends.* New York: Delta, 1991.

15

Abusers

There were so many years during which I wanted you to like me and have the relationship of "big brother" that some of my friends had and that I envied so much. I don't think you ever did like me. There were years in which I hated you so much I thought daily of ways to kill you. Katarina

K atarina, like many Survivors, had conflicting feelings about her abuser. She wanted to have a normal, loving, brother sister relationship with him, but she also hated him for what he was doing to her. Children may have negative feelings toward their abusers because of the abuse, but they may also have positive feelings, especially if the abusers are close relatives or friends.

In chapter 4 we looked at how abusers set up situations where they can manipulate and abuse children, and at some of the reasons why they abuse. In this chapter, we will look at the kinds of people who abuse children, the feelings Survivors have toward their abusers and ways in which these feelings can be explored and expressed.

What are abusers like?

What kinds of people abuse children? Here is a list of some of the characteristics Kate saw in her father:

Cunning, deceitful, a liar, gives the impression he's helpful and generous but this is only to cover the abuse that will follow, or because he's afraid someone may tell. Disloyal—uses information told in confidence to suit him. Bad- tempered and violent. Puts others down to elevate himself. Tries to make people feel sorry for him. Thinks his views alone are the right views; he's never wrong. If you disagree or take another point of view, you're wrong and yelled at. Selfish. Kate

To the outside world, however, he was a respected businessman admired by many.

This monster robbed me of the first 30 years of my life. Yet no one outside the family suspected. Social workers liked him, educational-welfare officers liked him, some teachers liked him, policemen liked him. But they didn't know his secret. Kate

Jane's stepfather (her abuser) was cruel and manipulative within the home, but he gave a very different impression of himself to neighbors. An abuser may be seen by outsiders as a good, kind, generous and respected member of the community, the kind of person who looks after others, not the kind of person who would abuse a child. This can be very difficult for children. It can confirm their feelings that they are to blame for the abuse and that no one will believe them if they try to tell. Some abusers, like Joanne's, are violent and cruel.

My stepfather was a violent man and he would drink heavily every night in bars. He'd come home and beat my mother and us if we got in the way. I remember him hitting my mother so badly that she had to stay in the hospital for a week. He was mentally cruel to us too. Looking back, I can see he was very immature and got a lot out of cruelly teasing us. We weren't allowed indoors even when the weather was bad. My brothers and I would stand on the other side of the garden fence and stare into the kitchen window because we were so cold. Joanne

Other abusers are quiet, kind and fun to be with. Few abusers fit the stereotype of a "dirty old man." Abusers may be young or old, male or female, rich or poor, kind or cruel, scruffy or well dressed, strong or frail. Abusers may be dominant men who rule their families with an iron will, weak, ineffectual men, women who keep themselves to themselves, or friendly young men who are well liked in the neighborhood. In fact, they are indistinguishable from any other parent, relative, neighbor or friend. Abusers may be laborers, members of government, professors, unemployed, stockbrokers, housewives, bus drivers, teachers, clergy or from any other occupation.

Although the majority of abusers are men, women also abuse children, both boys and girls. It is difficult for people to accept that women can and do abuse children, especially their own children. It is particularly difficult for victims, both male and female, to accept or disclose that women abused them, especially if it was their mother. A mother is supposed to nurture and protect her children, and those children who are abused by their mother may feel they have suffered the greatest betrayal of all. It is difficult to say what percentage of abusers are female, especially because victims find it so difficult to talk about abuse by women. However, recent studies suggest up to 20% of abusers are women. Women sexually abuse children on their own or with male abusers. Graham's mother sexually abused him and his brother and also allowed other adults to abuse them.

It is not possible to tell abusers from nonabusive people unless you know they are abusing. People of all classes, cultures, ages and personalities abuse.

Feelings toward the abuser

I lie awake at night and I can feel you groping me and I am physically sick. At the memory of your name, I'm sick. I could stab you and not think anything of it. Torture wouldn't be sufficient punishment for you. I hope when you die you go to hell, but even that's too good for you. I will never, ever forgive you for what you've done. You deserve anything evil that comes your way. Pam

Pam's feelings toward her abuser (her father) are straightforward: She hates him. Kate too is angry at her abuser (her father) for the damage he has done to her and to his many other victims.

I feel anger that he robbed me of my childhood, stopped me from developing my skills to their fullest and made me miss opportunities through lack of confidence. I will never, never be able to trust my abuser, even though he may stop abusing. I feel annoyed with him that he's been so disloyal to his wife and family and that he's damaged so many lives. I feel angry that so many people, male and female, have lost years of their lives because of him. Kate

Kate also feels sorry for her abuser.

> I pity the abuser, he now has to live with himself and at some
> stage in his life surely he will have to admit to himself the terrible
> things he's done and the harm he has caused others. I feel sorry
> because he must be a sad and lonely man—being an abuser
> made him miss out on a lot of important relationships in his life.
> Kate

Children are brought up to believe they should love their families
and feel confused when parents, or people taking care of them, also
abuse them. Children may love their fathers, brothers, mothers,
sisters and uncles and find it hard to understand how someone
they love can hurt them so much. When Sheila first came for
therapy she talked about how much she loved her father, even
though he had physically and sexually abused her. She blamed
herself for the abuse and felt no anger toward him. After she
started to understand that he was responsible for the abuse, she
began to feel angry with him, although she still loved him. That is
what she wrote after his death:

> Why did you have to leave me? I wish you knew what sort of a
> mess you have left behind. It's so unfair of you to have escaped
> the way you did. Believe it or not, there were times when I really
> loved you and other times when I hated you. I wish you could see
> the pain I feel inside. Sometimes I sit and think about the past
> and what you did to me, and I feel so hurt and angry. I feel that
> you have destroyed me inside and that you have taken away part
> of my life.
>   When I was young I loved and trusted you, and you just
> used me. How could you do that to me? I will always remember
> when I was young how I followed you everywhere. You were like
> some kind of hero to me. I thought I was very special to you, but
> now when I think of those days, I just want to cry because it hurt
> so much. I felt so guilty when I came up to the hospital to see you
> the first time you tried to commit suicide. I thought it was my fault,
> because the night before I stood up to you and said "No" and ran
> away from you. So when you came home again, I never said
> anything to you, even though you were hurting me and ruining my
> childhood, because I did not want you to leave me.
>   I wish things could have been different because I really did
> love you. Sheila

Abusers can be kind to children and take them on outings, give them treats they wouldn't normally get and pay them a lot of attention. They win the children's trust and affection. A child may therefore love the abuser and enjoy spending time with him or her but feel confused when the abuser behaves sexually.

Moira was abused by her half-brother, Ian, and at times she hated him for the pain she felt because of the abuse. Yet he was her closest friend throughout her childhood and he had loved, protected and comforted her as well as abusing her.

> How can I still love Ian and want to put my arms around him and tell him I still love him and forgive him and yet in the next breath want to tell him I hate him and want to beat the living daylights out of him? I'm so confused. Moira

It can be difficult for a Survivor to feel anger toward an abuser whom she also loves. Abusers can appear to be warm and caring people when they are not abusing. This very confusing notion for the child strengthens the child's belief that she must have done something wrong for the abuser to act this way with her. She feels there must be something bad in her that brings out this uncharacteristic behavior in the abuser. This can make her turn her anger inward so that she hates herself and blames herself for the abuse. By blaming herself for the abuse, she can keep loving the abuser. In adulthood, Survivors may continue to love their abusers despite the pain the abuser inflicted. Some Survivors are so terrified of their abusers that they see them, hear them, smell them or feel their touch when they are not there and even when they are dead.

Survivors experience all sorts of feelings toward their abusers, including hate, love, fear, guilt, concern, disgust, affection, betrayal, pity and anger. Often they have a complex mixture of these feelings that leave them confused. The following exercises may help you understand and work through your feelings toward your abuser.

Working on your feelings about the abuser

Exploring your feelings toward your abuser and finding a way of expressing these feelings can help you break free of confusion and pain. It can help to talk to a counselor or therapist about this. Sometimes it is not helpful to talk to friends and relatives, because they may feel angry about what has happened to you and expect you to feel angry toward your abuser too. Polly feels nothing but hate toward her abuser (her grandfather), whereas her sister (who was also abused by him) still loves him. The sisters are angry with each other because of this difference and cannot share their feelings or talk about the abuse. Polly believes her sister should also hate her grandfather. You cannot change your feelings because you or other people think you should. There is no right or wrong way to feel. It is important to begin by recognizing and accepting your feelings for your abuser, whatever they are, and to start to work from there.

In therapy, Survivors begin to understand that their abusers were responsible for the abuse and that they manipulated the children into the abusive situation. They realize that it is the abuser who is to blame for the abuse and not themselves. For the first time, like Sheila and Moira, they begin to lose their anger at themselves and turn the anger toward their abusers.

As you work through your feelings, you may find that you are also angry at the abuser you believed you loved; or that you love the abuser you thought you only hated; or that under your anger is grief at losing your childhood. The following exercises may help you to discover and release some of your feelings.

About 50% of the Wakefield Survivors have been sexually abused by more than one person. If you have had more than one abuser, apply the suggestions in this chapter to each of them.

Exercise: Talking to a pillow

This exercise can be a useful way for you to explore your own feelings toward your abuser and to express them without having to consider his reaction.

Do this exercise when you are alone and feeling safe and want to work through your feelings about your abuser. Pick a pillow or sofa cushion to represent your abuser. Sit on a chair and place the pillow on another chair opposite you at whatever feels like the most comfortable distance. Imagine the pillow is your abuser and start to talk to him. Begin by telling him how he has damaged your life. You may feel many emotions rising in you, accept them and express them to the abuser. Often talking isn't enough. If you get angry you may want to throw the pillow on the ground and punch it, stomp on it or kick it around the room. This is a useful way for you to let your feelings out without hurting yourself or anyone else. In fact this technique is useful whenever you get angry at someone.

Anger is only one of the feelings that may arise. You may feel upset, afraid, love, hate, pity, distaste, or any mixture of feelings. The aim of the exercise is to allow you to discover what you are feeling and express your feelings outwardly instead of holding them in or harming yourself. The idea of talking to a pillow may seem strange but many people have really benefited from venting their feelings in this way.

Exercise: Letters to the abuser

Writing a letter to your abuser, without sending it, is another way for you to explore and express your feelings. Allow yourself plenty of time and let yourself write whatever comes into your head. You may want to describe all the things the abuser did to you and how it made you feel at the time. You may want to tell him how the abuse affected your life as you grew older and how you feel toward him now. Writing can help you understand the full range of your feelings and give you an opportunity to get them off your chest.

Polly's grandfather had abused her and all her sisters. When she was a young adult, Polly had written and mailed a letter to her grandfather about the abuse, but when her family found out, they forced her to write again and retract what she had said. Polly felt betrayed yet again and was left feeling intensely angry. After she had been in a Survivors' group, Polly wanted to confront her grandfather again, but he had since died. She wrote another letter, this time for herself.

Polly's letter

Dear Bastard,

Yes, Bastard—because you are this and many more names.

I confronted you before in a letter telling you I forgive you for everything you did to me. I was made to deny it for my nanna's sake, in case she might have a heart attack or something.

I now know that you abused all my sisters and my mom. So it was not a matter of any of us leading you on. You were the guilty one and you did whatever you wanted to do to innocent children who could not defend themselves and you made them swear to secrecy.

Well, you dirty old pig, it's time you realized what you have done. We could have had you sent to prison for good because there are too many of us for the courts to say it is our imagination. So how does it make you feel to know you are hated intensely by your own grandchildren? Not once did you show any remorse by saying you were sorry, although you had plenty of opportunities.

Now you're dead, the past has not died with you. I'm so glad you're dead because now I won't have to worry about other children being around a monster like you.

The abuse is not going to ruin my life because I'm fighting it and getting help. People like you are the ones who need help, yet you're so sick that you think you're normal. I would hate to be in your shoes, because I believe in God, whether you do or not, and you will find punishment for what you've done.

I hope you rot in hell. Polly

After writing this letter, Polly felt she had at last been able to express her true feelings and she began to feel less troubled by her anger.

Anthony was abused by his uncle and as an adult felt very angry toward him. However, every time Anthony saw his uncle he felt like a frightened boy again and left as quickly as possible. Writing this letter helped Anthony express his anger and regain his power.

If I ever got hold of you I would kill you, but maybe that would be too good for you. Can't you see that you have turned my world upside down these past 14 years? What was up with you? Couldn't you get pleasure with someone your own fucking age? All you are is a dirty old man and I hope you rot in hell. Anthony

Shirley wanted to vent her anger and tell the abuser how harmful his actions were and how the trauma can affect the child, the adolescent, the adult. She wrote this letter.

Shirley's letter

Dear Abuser,

For many years I have hated you, and for many years I wanted to walk in on you when your store was full of people and vent all my hatred upon you, to humiliate you as you humiliated me. I wanted to scream out the hurt you caused and show you that we, the children of abuse, grow up but we don't ever forget.

Have you any idea of the damage you have done? Did you really think it was such harmless fun to grope a small child's body? Did you really think you could do that and leave a child's mind and soul untouched? If there is any shred of human decency left in you, and if you truly understood the damage you inflicted, you would never do such a thing again. So I am going to tell you about the damage you have done to me.

You polluted my mind with things I knew nothing about, things no child should have to know. In violating me you made me feel ashamed and dirty, and that sense of feeling unclean never diminished. I grew up both rejecting my body and yet desperately trying to control it. One of the greatest crimes you committed was that you caused me to doubt my self-worth. It was not I who was degraded, whose worth as a person was diminished. Now I can hold my head up knowing I did nothing wrong.

I felt guilty. You knew that children are told never to take candy from strangers, so you gave me candy after abusing me, knowing I wouldn't refuse it. Knowing that in taking it I would be doing something I knew to be wrong, thus ensuring my silence and my guilt. Was that all I was worth to you, a penny candy? In giving me that piece of candy, you put me in the wrong so I could never tell what you had done.

Are you so sure it was worth it? For a few minutes of sexual excitement, for a moment of power over a child, you inflicted so much harm, damaged my life and the lives of so many others. You will not be able to lay the blame on the child all your life. We, the abused, refuse to accept all the hurt, anguish and guilt you have tried to force upon us. We, the abused, can heal, we can find peace, we can be free; while you, the abuser, can never rest. You

must always hide from yourself, from your guilt, from your shame;
for if you knew their true measure they would surely overwhelm
you.

 I am on my way to freedom. Freedom from you, from all the
pain, guilt, hatred and fear you inspired. I am free now to love a
man without fearing him. Shirley

Luke felt angry about how the abuse he had made him hate
himself and question his sexuality. Writing this letter helped Luke
vent his anger and place the blame back on his abuser.

Luke's letter

 I've needed to talk to you for a while now. You're probably
wondering what about or maybe you know.

 Do you remember the drinking establishment, "The Red
Lion," where we used to live? That's where it all started. That's
where you started touching my penis, masturbating me, trying to
kiss me, telling your perverted stories, walking through the
apartment with virtually nothing on, always looking for an
opportunity. I know it didn't just happen to me.

 Can you remember how old I was? No, probably not. Your
only reason for doing it was your own sexual gratification. You
didn't even think about how it might affect me. I bet it never
crossed your mind what you were really doing—fucking up my life,
condemning me to wonder about my own sexuality. You left me
stranded. I'd never thought about sex until you started abusing me
and then all I knew was what you taught me—how to blame
myself. Every day I woke up hating myself for what I'd done. I
enjoyed what you did and I hate myself for that. I hate myself for
something you did. If you think back you'll remember I was only 11
years old and ever since I've taken responsibility for something you
did. I'll never blame another child the way I've blamed myself, the
way I still blame myself. So for past 15 years I've put the whole
experience down to me being homosexual but that's wrong, I'm
not. You sexually abused me. You were to blame.

 I want you to know that I'm not keeping this secret any
more. I've been living in a hell that you started because you
couldn't control your own sexual urges but you could control a
lonely 11-year-old boy. You're a bastard and I hate you. There's a
big difference now. You're going to be the scared one. Now it's your

*turn to worry about the future. The crime you committed is a
crime worse than any other. To kill someone is to take away their
life, that's straightforward by comparison. To abuse a child you
don't give them the release of death, you send them to death on
earth. What really upsets me is I know that I can't hurt you the
way I want to. I can't make you feel this pain.* Luke

Katarina wanted to tell her abuser, her brother, how he had
damaged her life. She wanted to express her anger and her sadness
at being unable to relate to him as a brother.

Katarina's letter

Brother,

*I was asked to write to you and, thinking about it, I agree
that it is a good thing to tell you what I think about you and what
damage you have done to me.*

*You have been so clever; not only abusing my body but also
making sure I would grow up with fear in my heart and no self-
esteem. For 20 years after the abuse I still thought of myself as
less worthy than other people. You made sure that if you were
around I felt like a worm about to be stepped on. I wanted to see
you dead, but my fear of you made it impossible to attack you in
any other way than in my mind. I was still helpless.*

*If only you had shown some form of remorse, treated me
with kindness when we were grown up. Although I hated you, there
was a part in me that desperately wanted to forgive you, to be
liked by you, to make a new start and become at last a brother
and sister in the way I had seen in other families. Yet I know if I
had told you what damage your abuse did to me, you would have
done no more than shrug your shoulders and say "So what?"*
Katarina

In her letter, Katarina went on to describe in detail how his abuse
had affected her whole life and expressed her anger to him for this.
Having talked about her abuse and worked through her feelings,
Katarina's feelings toward her brother have changed:

*Of course I am still angry. But it is not the same kind of anger any
more that I used to feel. The kind of anger I feel now is anger at
someone who has done me wrong, who knew it full well and did
not care. It is the healthy kind of anger, not the kind that is nothing*

*but blind fury. If I see him in the street, when I go back to my
hometown, I am now strong enough to look him in the eyes.*
Katarina

Regaining your power from the abuser

Some Survivors have no contact with their abusers, or their abusers
are now dead. Others may see their abusers occasionally or on a
regular basis, especially if the abuser is a family member. Thinking
about the abuser, whether he or she is alive or dead, can make
Survivors feel frightened, vulnerable or angry. Even Survivors who
feel very angry can quickly regress to feeling childlike, powerless
and frightened when they actually see their abuser, as Anthony
discovered. Some Survivors continue to see or hear their abusers
even though the abuser is dead, and these hallucinations can be
terrifying and paralyzing.

The exercise below is intended to help you overcome feelings
of fear about your abuser and to feel more empowered. It also
helps to reinforce the knowledge that what happened to you was
not right and that you were not to blame for being abused. Before
you start, keep in mind that the exercise is to be done on paper or
in your imagination, not in person with your abuser. This means
you are in control of what happens. Confronting your abuser in
imagination can be a powerful and liberating experience for
Survivors. Confronting your abuser in person is a very different
matter and can be dangerous to you, both physically and
psychologically. The exercise is not aimed at helping you confront
your abuser in person but at helping you feel more powerful by
understanding and expressing your thoughts and feelings about
the abuse and the abuser.

Exercise: Standing up to your abuser in imagination

1. What do you want to say?

    Think carefully about exactly what you want to say to your
    abuser. Do you want to express how you feel about the
    abuse? Do you want to tell the abuser how he has damaged
    your life? Write down exactly what you want to say as a
    series of short statements; for example, you raped me. I have
    a lot of problems because of what you did to me. You are
    responsible.

2. The abuser's response

   When the abusers are confronted about the abuse in person they rarely admit to what they have done. They usually deny that the abuse ever happened or minimize what really happened by pretending it wasn't sexual abuse but something innocent or loving. Some abusers blame the Survivor for what happened, often by suggesting the Survivor wanted the abuse or caused it to happen in some way—these may be the same things the abuser said to the Survivor as a child. Some abusers threaten the Survivor for speaking about the abuse and again, this may be a familiar pattern from childhood. Think about how your abuser might respond if he or she were challenged and write them down.

3. Think about how you could reply assertively and write down your replies.

   Learning how to challenge abusers' reactions by responding assertively (in the exercise, not in person) can help you feel more in control and more powerful in relation to your abuser. Keep your replies simple. Deny what isn't true and say what is true. Do not be sidetracked or think you have to justify how you feel.

Here are some examples of steps 2 and 3.

Abusers reactions	Possible assertive replies
Denying:	
I did not touch you.	Yes, you did. You had intercourse with me.
I don't know what you're talking about	Yes, you do, you made me touch your penis.
You are a liar/mentally ill/imagining it.	I am not a liar/mentally ill/imagining it, you did touch my private parts
You are suffering from "false memory syndrome."	No, I am not. You raped me.
Minimizing:	
I was only tickling you.	You did not only tickle me, you rubbed my genitals.

continued . . .

I was teaching you the facts of life.	You were not teaching me the facts of life, you sexually abused me.
I was only playing with you.	You were not only playing with me, you masturbated over me.

Blaming:

You enjoyed it.	You were responsible. You sexually abused me.
You kept taking your clothes off in front of me. You asked for it.	You were an adult and you sexually abused a child.

Threatening:

No one will speak to you again.	I am not to blame, you are responsible for the abuse.
I'll tell your parents what you've done.	You are responsible for the abuse, you are to blame.

4. Role-play confrontation

   After you have done this, try role-playing the confrontation with a friend. Get a friend to pretend to be the abuser and act out the confrontation. Practice all the abuser's possible reactions, however unlikely or upsetting they are, and how you would respond. You may find this is more difficult to do than you think. Although this is an imaginary confrontation, you may experience all the feelings of fear and vulnerability that you felt as a child. Keep practicing. As you feel more able to stand up to your abuser in your imagination, you will begin to let go of your fear and feel more powerful.

Confronting the abuser in person

Some Survivors feel they need to confront their abusers in person. This is not a necessary part of the healing process and can be very damaging if it is done at the wrong time, with unrealistic expectations or without the right preparation.

Survivors' expectations of what might happen can be wrong. They often think the abuser will be hurt and upset if they confront him, and assume he must feel bad about what he has done. As we have seen, abusers usually deny what they have done, however strong the evidence against them. If the abuser does admit to the abuse at all, he will probably minimize it. The abuser might also try to blame or threaten you. These reactions could be devastating if you are not prepared for them or if you still feel guilty, unsure about your memories and feelings or intimidated by the abuser.

We do not advise you to confront your abuser, but if you decide that you want to do this IT IS VERY IMPORTANT THAT YOU DO NOT DO THIS UNTIL YOU ARE FULLY PREPARED.

In this section, we will look at why some Survivors want to confront their abusers, how to prepare to confront your abuser and at what happened when some of the Wakefield Survivors took action.

Why confront the abuser?

Pam remembers how she talked to friends at work about her plans to confront her abuser.

> One of my colleagues said, "You only want to confront your father to split him and your mother up, to teach him a lesson." I replied, nearly in tears, "No, that isn't the reason I want to confront him. I want to get over the anxieties I have about men in general. I look at men I don't know and think of them as potential child abusers."
> Pam

Like Pam, some Survivors want to confront their abusers to overcome their fear of that person and of people in general. Some Survivors decide to confront their abusers to protect other children, especially when they know that he or she has already abused many victims.

> I knew my father had abused a lot of other members of my family and I suspected he was still doing so. I could protect my own children from him but how could I protect everyone else? I asked my sister to come with me to support me when I confronted him. Our aim was not to hurt him but to stop him from hurting anyone else. He did admit he had done some things to his daughters, which he regretted, but denied abusing anyone else. He said the others just wanted to make trouble and were out to get him. We told him we were watching him and that I was not going to keep quiet if he continued abusing. Kate

Kate saw other benefits from this confrontation:

> I did not say all the things I wanted to say, but I was surprised to find that I had passed the burden of guilt back to him, where it belongs. I felt strong. The power relationship between us changed after this. He seemed to avoid me rather than me having to avoid him. Kate

Sexual abuse occurs in secret. The abuser gets the child to comply by using some form of power (adult authority, manipulation, physical strength, threats), leaving the victim feeling powerless and controlled by the abuser. Often the victims feel they are under the abuser's power for the rest of their lives. Confronting the abuser can break the secret and take this power away from him or her. Although Kate had primarily gone to confront her abuser to protect other children, she also found the power relationship between them had reversed.

Exercise: Why do you want to confront your abuser?

1. Write down what you want to achieve by confronting your abuser.

2. For each aim ask yourself, "Is this realistic?" For example, if you want the abuser to say he is sorry, this isn't very realistic because he is unlikely to do so.

3. Ask yourself if there is a better or easier way to achieve your objective. For example, it might be better to contact Social Services or the police in order to protect other children. You may be able to deal with your anger just as effectively by standing up to your abuser in imagination.

Common reasons for wanting to confront abusers include:

+ to break the silence and with it, the hold the abuser may still have over them
+ to reverse the power relationship
+ to rid themselves of the fear they still have inside—the fear an abused child has of her adult abuser
+ to protect other children from the abuser
+ to help them get over their own fears and anxieties about people in general

+ to express their own anger and distress
+ to get the abuser to acknowledge what he has done and to see the harm he has caused
+ to clear the air and help resolve their feelings toward the abuser

Some of these aims are unlikely to be achieved. Abusers will rarely admit to the abuse so Survivors must be prepared for their reactions. If a Survivor hopes the abuser will acknowledge the harm he has done, she is likely to be disappointed. Make sure your aims are realistic and you have explored the alternatives before you decide to go ahead with the confrontation.

Preparing for a confrontation

We are not recommending that you literally confront your abuser, but if you are determined to do so, please make sure you are fully prepared and that you are not placing yourself in any danger. You will need to pay attention to the points below.

Your own feelings

It is important that you do not plan to confront your abuser until you have worked through your own feelings about the abuse. It would be best to have some counseling first or at least to have read this book and talked to others about the abuse. You need to feel certain that the abuse was not your fault and the abuser was responsible for what happened. The abuser may accuse you of being a liar, say you are crazy or blame you for the abuse. You will end up feeling much worse if you are in any doubt about what happened and who was responsible.

It is also important that you do not see the abuser if you are full of rage. The purpose is to talk to him, not to attack him physically. Attacking him could put you in physical danger and have legal consequences. It will also leave you feeling helpless and out of control again. Make sure you have first worked through the exercises in this chapter on expressing your feelings (talking to a cushion and writing letters).

Support

If you know of anyone else who has been abused by the same

person, ask that person or persons to confront the abuser with you. Go through all the preparations with them. If you have a partner or friend with you when you confront the abuser, make sure they understand they are there for support only. It will not help you feel empowered again if another person takes over and confronts the abuser or deals with the abuser's reactions. If you are going to confront the abuser alone, then have someone you trust in the next room. Afterward you will probably need someone to talk to about how you feel, so make sure there will be someone available to support you.

Practice

Be clear about what you want to say to your abuser, and be prepared for whatever response he might give. Use the exercise on standing up to your abuser in imagination to prepare yourself and practice again and again with a friend or therapist by role-playing the confrontation. Do not go ahead with the confrontation until you feel certain that you can handle whatever the abuser might say.

A few abusers break down, cry and say they are sorry when they are confronted. Survivors may then feel pity for the abusers and regret hurting them. It is the abuser that hurt you; if he is upset, it is because of what he has done. Remember that abusers manipulate their victims so they can sexually abuse them. The abuser may be crying because he is genuinely sorry or he may be crying to manipulate you into feeling sorry for him and therefore retracting what you have said. He may also be crying for himself because he is frightened of other people knowing what he has done or of being prosecuted by the police. You could respond by saying, for example

+ You are upset because of what you did.
+ Don't expect me to comfort you, you abused me.
+ Well, you should be upset about this.

Plan

Plan in detail where, when and how you are going to confront the abuser. Choose a place where you feel comfortable and safe, your home or neutral territory. Some Survivors choose to confront their abusers in a public place with a friend nearby for added protection.

VERY IMPORTANT: Do not confront someone who may be violent.

Pam's confrontation

Pam called her parents and told them to come see her that evening at 8.30 p.m.

We hadn't had contact for over two years. My immediate thought was—would I break down?

I gave my husband the job of making coffee to keep him out of the way—I had to do this alone. My mother sat beside my father in the family room, so I dismissed her immediately to the dining room. I then confronted my father with exactly what he'd done to me. He'd raped me and sucked my body. I told him how this had affected me, particularly over the past two years when I had had a nervous breakdown. I told him that I became agoraphobic and I couldn't have a sexual relationship with my husband because all I saw was my father's face. I told him I hated him so much.

He sat there for approximately an hour and listened to me. Then I told him I wanted to tell my mother in front of him to prove to her I wasn't lying. I'd actually told her about it at the time it first happened and many times since, but she'd dismissed me as a liar.

My father more or less made his admission of guilt by nondenial. But I was pleased, because normally you can't talk to him without him blowing his top. He was devastated and I thought, "Well, now you can walk around with it on your conscience for the rest of your life."

I told them both they were lucky to be alive walking out of my house, because all I wanted to do was kick their teeth in or stab them both to death. I hated them so much. Their reaction was that they didn't blame me. Pam

Pam's father did not admit his guilt, but he didn't deny it either. Pam had at last managed to express her anger and distress to her parents and this marked a turning point in her relationship with them and in her own feelings.

When they left, I felt like I'd been carrying a huge backpack and somebody had just taken it off me. I felt marvelous. I felt I'd really achieved something. All I ever wanted was a mom and dad who cared for and loved me. Up to the present, the change in them is

unbelievable but for the better, and I feel a lot better within myself.
There is life after abuse and this is what it took for me to find that
out. Pam

Pam's husband, Brian, describes the change in her relationship
with her parents after the confrontation.

The big turning point came when Pam decided to confront the
abuser, her father. She got twenty-four years of anger off her chest
in as many minutes. Now she is a changed woman, never to be
intimidated by her parents again. In fact, they are now somewhat
unnerved by her, and are at her beck and call. Since then there
has been some form of family relationship. On my part it is
toleration because they are Pam's parents. On her part . . . they
are always her parents in the end. Brian

Claire and Joan's confrontation

Claire and Joan are sisters who were both abused by their brother-
in-law, Tony, the husband of their eldest sister. They decided to
confront Tony because Joan was still feeling depressed and
powerless at the end of her group therapy and because they were
worried he might be abusing his own children. As Claire said,

I want to confront him, to show him how bad it is and to stop him
if he's still doing it. I don't want him to think he has escaped. I
want him to feel ashamed of what he did. Claire

The sisters held several meetings to discuss their expectations
about what might happen and to brief their husbands. The
meetings were also to plan what they wanted to say and to practice
assertive ways of dealing with all Tony's possible reactions. Claire
and Joan originally thought Tony would admit what he had done
and get upset. Without the meetings and practice they wouldn't
have been prepared for what did happen.

My younger sister Joan and I were to confront our abuser, Tony,
together. We were quite scared, but we felt ready to go ahead. We
both felt we needed to do this, and in a strange way I was looking
forward to it.
The scene was set at Joan's house. Her husband had left
the house but while we waited for Tony to arrive, we were wishing
that her husband had stayed. Later we were very proud of
ourselves for doing it alone. As we saw Tony walk down the path,

Joan decided to calm herself down by doing a few of the breathing exercises we had learned at group therapy.

Tony had no idea why we wanted to see him but we wasted no time. I was the first to speak and I told him that Joan and I were seeing a psychologist because of what he had done to us as children. Color drained from his face and I felt stronger. He said, quite annoyed, that he didn't know what we were talking about and that he'd never done anything to us. Joan had to spell it out and all the time he was denying it. He said he was only tickling us. By this time he was standing at the door and saying he was leaving. Joan suddenly became very strong and confident and continued to tell him how well we remembered where and when those awful things took place and he got very frightened and raised his voice.

He continued to trip himself up with his lies, and as he kept changing his story he seemed to get smaller and smaller, weaker and weaker. We felt more sure of his guilt than ever, now. We kept saying over again "Yes, you did it." He said we were both insane and he felt sorry for us. Then he used his last weapon when he said "I'll tell your mom and dad—what will they say about what you've done?"

Something clicked inside me—I had heard this before from him, all those years ago. Except this time instead of feeling guilty, I felt more sure I was doing the right thing and said, "Yes, what would they say to you, if they knew what you did to their children?"

We continued to surprise him by telling him we knew of two other women who had been his victims. We told him we could take him to court and that we were worried about his own daughters. He still denied everything and said he was going to get his wife, Rita (our sister). She arrived shortly, alone. He had told her what had been said and swore to her that he hadn't done anything.

When it was all over, I felt sorry for my sister Rita. I wanted to put my arms around her but I couldn't, because she still didn't say she believed us. I still felt we had done the right thing.

It was a big relief to know it was all over and I wouldn't have to do it again. I was full of confidence and thought we performed well. We couldn't have done it any better and we did it alone, without our men behind us. Now Tony knows how much he hurt us and spoiled Joan's life and now he's spoiled his own. It feels really great to put the guilt on to him. It's changed my life.

I don't blush very much these days. Each day I get a little more confident and like myself better. I released a lot of anger on that day and now I feel much calmer. It's changing Joan's life too. The very next day she went swimming and instead of rushing into the water, so that no one could see her body, she idled about for a while and could look at people in the water and hold her head up high. She didn't feel ashamed any more.

I don't feel like keeping it a secret any more. In fact, I want to tell all the family except mom and dad—not because of shame this time, but to protect them from feeling they let us down by failing to protect us from this pathetic person. Claire

Their sister, Rita, soon believed them and Claire and Joan made sure his own children were safe by contacting Social Services (chapter 17 describes the procedures for protecting children).

During the confrontations, Tony seemed to grow smaller and weaker to the sisters, while they felt themselves growing bigger and stronger. Claire and Joan had anticipated all of Tony's possible responses and practiced how they would reply, so it didn't matter that he denied abusing them. What was important was that they were able to confront him and show him and themselves that they were no longer ashamed and were not responsible for the abuse. Joan got her power back and immediately began improving. Her depression lifted and she began to feel more confident every day.

Joanne's attempted prosecution

Joanne had spent her childhood in fear of her stepfather, Ken, who was physically violent as well as sexually abusive. As an adult, she had told her mother and family what had happened to her, but was shunned by them and still felt she carried the blame for the abuse. Joanne decided not to confront her stepfather directly because he was a violent man. However, she still wanted Ken and her family to acknowledge that it was Ken, and not she, who was responsible for the abuse, so she went to the police and made a statement. Unfortunately the case was never brought to court because of lack of supporting evidence. Joanne was not disheartened by this, however, because Ken had been arrested and her accusation had been made public. She expressed her feelings by writing a letter without sending it.

Joanne's letter

Dear Ken,

Well, no doubt you are feeling very relieved at the moment after hearing that you're not going to be prosecuted after all, even though you sexually abused me for years. At the beginning of the Survivors' group I would have been devastated if I'd have known that the case wouldn't go to court, but now, much to my surprise, I don't feel bitter. I feel I've made my point to you. You now know how much I hate you and that if possible I would have seen you imprisoned once again. I felt a great deal of satisfaction when I heard that you'd had to have minor surgery through stomach pains due to the "stress and worry" you've been going through for the past ten months. I was glad to hear it; at least you've suffered in some way after all the suffering you caused me and all those around you.

For all those years I was absolutely terrified of you. Well, now I feel so proud and full of strength to have stood up to you. For the past year I've been the one who has had power over you. My actions have brought you worry and fear. For years you told me that if I spoke about it "no one would ever want to have anything to do with me ever again." How it delights me when I know you now realize that I can discuss this terrible "secret" with others and with members of our family. How false those threats were but as a child these and other threats seemed very real. It hurts to realize how commonly these threats are made by you and your fellow abusers.

I thank my lucky stars daily that I've received help. I'm relieved to say that I sincerely feel as if I've been "reborn" at the age of 31. At least you haven't ruined my entire life. I'll never forgive you for what you've done to me and the way you've ruined my life up until now with my husband and my own children. They have seen me during my periods of depression and sadness, though not any more. You can't hurt me any more. I'm finally rid of you. I don't feel I'll ever be able to forgive you, but I'm certainly on the way to forgetting about what you did and the problems you caused. I am now getting on with my life and, perhaps more important, I'm aware that my life is now more rich than yours.
Joanne

Joanne had anticipated all the things that could happen if she gave a statement to the police, so that even though the case was dropped before it got to court, confronting her abuser in this way helped Joanne regain her own power.

After the confrontation Joanne writes:

> He now knows he doesn't have a hold over me any more. He can no longer frighten me with the threat that everyone will blame me and reject me if I tell about the abuse.

Summary

Abusers do not fit a stereotype. They can be men and women of any age, class or race. They can have many different personality characteristics and lifestyles. The feelings Survivors have toward their abusers can be just as varied. They may have a conflicting mixture of feelings including hate, love, fear, guilt, concern, disgust, betrayal, pity and anger. The exercises suggested in this chapter can help Survivors to explore and understand their feelings toward their abusers; to express their feelings and so release some of their pain; and to regain their personal power.

Suggestions

+ Explore your feelings toward your abuser using the exercises described in this chapter (talking to a cushion or writing a letter to the abuser), or by talking to a counselor or therapist.

+ To help you regain your power from your abuser, try the exercise on standing up to your abuser in imagination.

+ We do not suggest you confront your abuser face to face. If, however, you have decided to do this, please be very careful and follow the guidelines in the chapter. DO NOT confront your abuser without full preparation—it will only cause you more emotional distress. DO NOT confront an abuser who is likely to be violent.

+ If you know or suspect that your abuser is currently abusing another child, protect the child by informing Social Services or the police, or get some advice by contacting one of the telephone helplines listed in Resources. Also see chapter 17, *Working toward Prevention*.

PART FIVE

Breaking Free

16

Overcoming the Problems

Before I went for therapy, I thought I would never feel strong enough to take charge of my own life. I wouldn't have believed it was possible for my life to change so much. Jane

You can learn to feel better about yourself and overcome the problems resulting from your sexual abuse. In this chapter, we look at how Survivors can break free from their problems and regain their own power. Survivors describe what it was about being in a group that helped them and how they feel after individual or group therapy. Some of the quotations and information in this chapter derive from research conducted on the Wakefield Survivor groups by clinical psychologist Sally Pinnell.

Getting help

We have seen how childhood sexual abuse causes adult Survivors to feel bad about themselves and experience problems in many areas of their lives. Some Survivors are only mildly affected by the abuse, but others hate themselves and feel their lives have been destroyed by it.

How can you begin to break free from the effects of the abuse and take control of your own life? Reading this book and working through the exercises is a start. Talking to a trusted friend or family member may also help by breaking the secret and allowing you to feel accepted by someone who knows what has happened to you. For some Survivors, this may be enough, but others will need to get more help by seeking individual therapy or joining a Survivors group. Before you decide you do not need further help, talk it over (in person or on a telephone helpline) with someone who can offer help. You may find it hard to go for help because you feel ashamed and worthless or think your problems are insignificant.

> I was afraid I would be wasting the psychologist's time. I was not worthy of nice people wasting their valuable time on a disgusting person like me. Eileen

Feeling unworthy is one of the effects of being sexually abused. You do deserve help.

> If you are being abused in any way, or have been abused, no matter how long ago it happened, please tell someone and get some help. You owe it to yourself. Joan

A list of helpful resources appears at the back of this book with suggestions of people or organizations you can contact. If the person you choose to speak to doesn't believe you, or responds inappropriately, then keep on telling until someone does.

How can anything help?

> I couldn't believe that just talking would help; it did, it does. I like myself. I did nothing wrong. Jocelyn

If you were sexually abused as a child, nothing can change that fact. What can change is the way you see yourself, the way you understand what happened during the abuse and the way you feel about yourself and others. Building a relationship with someone who knows your background and problems (rather than someone who just knows the "front" that many Survivors hide behind) can help you overcome problems in trusting others. As an adult, understanding the events of your childhood will help you see that you were not to blame for the abuse, you were not guilty. In time, the feelings of guilt, shame and self-blame will also change. You can conquer problems relating to your sexual identity, your sexuality and your sexual behavior by working on your feelings about yourself. Your feelings of powerlessness will fade as you learn to face your fears rather than avoid them, and begin to take control of your own life, your own problems and your own feelings. Your own power will grow as you assert yourself in the world and discover who you really are without the burden of shame and fear. Reading this book, going for therapy or joining a group can help you overcome your problems.

Writing

Writing is the thing I've found really helpful. Once I started writing I couldn't stop. It really surprised me—I could write better than I could talk. Claire

Writing can help you overcome your problems whether you are working on your problems alone or with the help of others. Survivors have found writing is especially helpful for remembering their experiences, exploring and expressing their feelings, facing their fears and accepting their experiences and themselves. In chapter 1, we suggested you do the written exercises at the end of each chapter. This can be difficult for some people, but many Survivors find this an important part of the healing process.

Some Survivors are too afraid to write down their thoughts. They are afraid that someone else will see them, or afraid that if the words are written down on paper they will have to face up to the fact that the events really happened.

Writing was terrifying. I would scrawl things down but I couldn't look at them, or else I would throw them away. Colleen

Many Survivors feel the need to throw away or destroy their writings at first. You could keep a stamped, addressed envelope ready and mail them to someone you trust (a therapist if you have one) as soon as you've written them. You can ask the person who receives the letters to read them or just to hold onto them until you are ready to read them again or show them to someone else.

I always used to burn my writings, but then I started mailing them to my therapist as soon as I'd written them. Mailing them still felt like I was getting rid of them again, but then they arrived at her office and it was there in black and white—not hidden any more. It was still my secret when I burned them, so I was pleased when I could let my therapist read them. I felt so much better that it wasn't hidden. Everything before had to be a secret—no openness at all. Lucy

You may find it difficult to begin writing.

It's difficult to get started. You're thinking about who is going to see it, but once you start you don't know where to stop. One of the girls from an earlier group has kept all her writings and says she can see how much she has improved. One girl says she writes down her thoughts when her mind is racing, and it helps her to stop thinking about it. I'm going to try that when I can't concentrate. Claire

Writing becomes a way of helping you cope with your thoughts and feelings and a way of releasing all the secret fears and memories.

At first I tended not to think about things so they wouldn't hurt as much. Now I think things out and write them down, not push them away. It's best to deal with things. I'm good at that now. Claire

Writing can help Survivors to remember more about their childhoods and to see the past in a new light.

So I started writing. It was really helpful. I could go back and remember. Once I started writing, I couldn't stop. It wasn't just about the abuse, it was about my whole childhood. By writing it down, I really could see why it wasn't my fault—why it happened and why I couldn't tell. That was the best part, it was a real help. Mavis

If you have not been able to do the written exercises at the end of the chapters, why not try again now? You may also want to try the exercises in the *Breaking Free Workbook,* which lead you step by step through a process of overcoming your difficulties.

Joining a Survivors group

After I saw my therapist three or four times, she suggested I join a group, but I didn't want to go. The idea of being in a group of other women really scared me. But I eventually said "Yes" and it was the best thing I've ever done. Jocelyn

Not everyone would like to join a group or has the opportunity to join one. We have found that Survivors benefit a great deal from being in a group and overcome their problems much more quickly.

Fears about joining a group

I saw my therapist four times before I joined the group. I was terrified of being in a group. I didn't want to speak to anyone else

about it. It was this secret between the psychologist and me and nobody else.

I was frightened of the group and didn't think it would help, but I would have given anything to go because I'd become so desperate. I don't know what I expected. I was so afraid of anyone knowing what had happened to me. I was so ashamed of it. It was my secret. What would they think of me? I thought they would blame me for letting it happen. Lucy

Many people are nervous or extremely frightened at the thought of joining a group. Sexual abuse occurs in secret, and the feelings of shame arise partly from keeping this secret. Widening the circle of people who know about the secret by joining a group can be very frightening, but feeling accepted by other people who know the secret can help reduce the feeling of shame.

I didn't want to go to the group at first because it meant increasing the number of people who knew what had happened to me. My psychologist said she could talk to me about how other Survivors feel, but it would be different for me to talk to the women myself, to actually go into a room with other Survivors, who know I have been abused too and have the same feelings.

I didn't know if I would get to the first group meeting until I actually got there. Walking into the room, I realized everyone was in the same boat. I didn't feel threatened when I walked in, but I didn't enjoy it. I felt I'd come this far and had to do it. Jocelyn

Survivors often fear that someone else in the group will know them or talk about them outside the group.

I am a professional woman and I had fears of joining a group in case someone from the group recognized me in the street and discussed me in public. Everyone would know what I had done. The group discussed confidentiality and the therapists asked every member present to respect each other. They said it was unlikely that anyone would discuss another group member in public because they had all suffered the same or similar experiences. This was reassuring and put me at ease immediately. Eileen

Many women say they should not be part of a Survivors group because they feel like a fraud. They think they shouldn't be in the group because they can't remember what happened during their abuse, or they think their abuse was not as serious as everyone else's.

The first week at the group, I knew I had been abused but not remembering much about it, I didn't know if it had really happened and that was my big fear. At first you feel everyone else is much worse than you and then you get it into perspective and realize that, whatever the form of the abuse, it has affected each of us. Jocelyn

Many Survivors feel that they are different from everyone else or that their abuse was different. In the group, Survivors become aware that they share many feelings in common and that whatever has happened to them, it is just another form of abuse.

> It may help you overcome your fears about joining a group if you can arrange to meet a Survivor who has already been in a group. You can talk privately together about what actually happens in the group, and the more experienced group member may be able to support you in getting to the first meeting.

In the Wakefield groups, there is no pressure to talk about what actually happened during the sexual abuse or who the abuser was. The initial emphasis is on how the abuse made the Survivors feel about themselves and how it affects their lives now.

We didn't give all the gory details of our abuse. We talked about the problems the abuse left us with. I had forgotten so much about my own abuse, but others in the group could remember, and a lot of things they said prompted flashbacks and memories in me. Jocelyn

The group then moves on to understanding and expressing their feelings about the abuse and to working out ways of overcoming their current problems.

Sticking with it

In the first session, the therapists explained how we were likely to feel worse during the first few weeks because discussing the abuse makes it more of a reality. Only by reliving the experiences could we face up to our problems and overcome our bad feelings. This was very true. I soon began to feel the past feelings of shame and self-disgust, and all the childhood experiences and emotions came flooding back to me. Having been warned about this was very helpful. Eileen

You may get to the first meeting but want to drop out after a few weeks. It's certainly not easy being in a Survivors group or in individual therapy. All the bad memories and unpleasant feelings that you have been trying to push to the back of your mind come to the surface. You need to face them again so you can accept them, share them, release the pain and power of the memories and start the healing process.

> During the group, you start thinking about your abuse all the time—when you're eating or cooking, you're still thinking about it. You wake up in the night thinking about it again, and you feel you should just hide it and try to forget about it again, but you know you've got to get it out and deal with it, you can't hide it forever.
>
> At first I thought, what have I done— I'm making things worse. I wished I'd never started. But now I realize I've got to get it out and face it and then maybe I can break free of it.
>
> I went through a phase of feeling really angry that I could have been so different if I hadn't been abused. It's been a horrible year. There was a lot to be uncovered and it wasn't nice. It's been very hard, but I've sorted it out now. Claire

Here is what Pam's husband had to say:

> Eventually Pam got help at a Survivors group, but it didn't end there. The more she went to the group for a while, the worse she became. For a few weeks there was no living with her. For two days after each group session, it was like living with a polecat with piles. I still cringe at the thought of those days.
>
> It was worth it, though. Pam is certainly a different person now compared to the one who started going to the Survivors group. She still has some hang-ups, but she is much more assertive and able in day-to-day life. Brian

There may be times when you want to give up and to blot it all out again. However, if you try to push your feelings away they will surface again or erupt in other ways, such as anxiety, depression or eating problems. Talk about your feelings and try to stick with it.

> It got a lot worse. It seems so long ago now since I've had a bad patch. But there were times when things were getting upside down. It was triggering memories that I brought home with me and were on my mind all the time. I was worse than before I went to the group. It seemed to last a long time, but it was probably just three or four days solid. It was as if it was all fighting to come out,

*and then it was all right. I called my psychologist and said I didn't
know if it was worth it, but then I went back to the group and
talked it through with them—that really helped.*

> *But I couldn't have stopped halfway. I knew if I got through
the first week, I would stick it out to the end. Jocelyn*

How the group helped

In the rest of this section, we look at what Survivors found most
helpful about being in a group.

Creating a safe environment

*If I had to think of one thing that helped me in the group, it would
be honesty. I really believe throughout my life I haven't been
honest with anybody, and I felt in the group from the beginning
that everyone wanted to be honest. We had all kept a secret, but
it wasn't a secret in there. I could go in there and say anything,
things I wouldn't have told anyone else, and I knew it was safe.
Jocelyn*

One of the most important things about a group is that it can create
a safe environment where Survivors can talk freely without putting
on a brave face. They can talk honestly about their innermost fears
and still feel respected and accepted by the other group members.
This helps them to overcome the feelings of guilt and shame. They
can also start to learn to trust others again.

*When I was in the group room, I started to feel better, but then I
had to go home and cope with the outside world. Even though it
was difficult, hard work and distressing, I felt secure there, even
more so than in individual work with the therapist. Colleen*

Sharing feelings and being accepted

*Before I joined the group, I tended not to think about things so
they wouldn't hurt as much. Getting things out in the open was
upsetting at the time, but you need to do that to continue and
make progress. You think it's going to hurt too much to get things
out, but it's worth it, even if it's difficult. I didn't realize how badly it
affected people. The women have done some awful things to
themselves, and I think I've gotten away very mildly. But it's nice to
know the other people know what you're going through and what*

you're thinking about. You feel you can trust them because they've gone through it. Claire

In the group, Survivors can share their feelings about themselves and still feel accepted.

I always thought other people were judging me. In the group you talk to other people who know exactly how you feel and accept you. Anita

I found the group very helpful, and I benefited enormously just by being with other people who had had the same experiences as me. I felt at ease with them. Anthony

I've only felt like me again since joining the group and getting everything out and hearing others say similar things. It's like looking in a mirror. There's a feeling in the group that other people are interested in what you've got to say. There wasn't an ulterior motive to what people were saying or doing. A couple in my group were very open and honest from the beginning, which made it easier for me. We jelled quickly. I could never eat anything before the group and after the group I could never go straight home.

One day I went into the group and said it felt lighter in the room and it was, as if everyone had suddenly unburdened themselves. We seemed to find that if you'd had a bad week, then the others had had similar experiences. We went through a period where we all had a lot of nightmares, or we were all angry at our mothers. We could relate to each other so well. Jocelyn

The group helped because I knew I was not alone. I had time to talk about myself. I felt respected, even after I'd disclosed my abuse, and the group helped me realize it was not my fault. It also helped to compare the way I'd coped with how the other men had coped. We acknowledged that each of us cope in different ways and we didn't judge each other negatively for turning to drink, drugs or self-harm. Luke

Talking to each other helps the Survivors let go of some of their bad feelings.

I feel better when I come out of a group meeting. When I arrive I feel tense and a little nervous, but once I've left the group and I'm walking down the street, I feel great. You have a chance to say what you feel. You may have been bottling it up all week, but when you get to the group you can talk about it. Mavis

The Survivors also learn to trust each other.

> *Most surprisingly, the group became very close knit and extremely supportive to each other, even during the first few weeks. There was a feeling of trust and a strong bond began to build among us. This was extremely helpful because no one felt inhibited in discussing very deep and intimate problems.* Eileen

They start to feel safe enough to allow their innermost feelings to surface and be expressed. Facing up to their feelings instead of blocking them off also helps Survivors feel less powerless and more in control.

> *As the group went on, I saw such a big change in me, in the way I thought about myself. When things cropped up that I couldn't cope with, they supported and helped me. They didn't tell me what to do, but they would give me ideas and we'd talk about it. I knew I had their support and I wasn't alone, whereas before I'd always been alone.* Lucy

Making the connections

> *As long as I can remember, I'd never liked myself, I was always moody, bad-tempered and angry. Since going to the group and letting my anger out, I'm not like that any more. I realized I was angry for a reason.* Jocelyn

Survivors grow up thinking of themselves as bad, crazy or different from other people. As adults they may still believe these things about themselves, and therefore feel worthless and depressed. They often do not connect their present feelings and problems with their earlier abuse. In the group they can see how the other group members have similar problems and begin to understand where their own problems come from.

> *I didn't know my shaking had anything to do with my abuse.* Mavis

> *I kept telling myself I haven't been affected, I don't need to go to the group. But I'm glad I did, because as the group has gone on I've realized the abuse affected me more than I thought. At first I told myself I was just going along for Joan's sake (my sister), but I'm getting a lot out of it for myself. I can see how it's affected me now. I thought if you were sexually abused it only affected you in a relationship with another man, but it causes all sorts of problems. I'd never thought about that at all.* Claire

Making friends

*I can't imagine a better group. We're friends and see each other
outside the group and call each other if we've got a problem or
are worried about each other. Lucy*

**Sharing feelings and being accepted by people who knew about
their sexual abuse helped Survivors learn to trust each other and
develop close friendships, often for the first time in their lives.**

*I used to feel there wasn't any point in living. It's hard to feel that
people like you if you don't really like yourself. I'm surprised how
well we all got along in the group. It's been good to be able to get
in touch with the group members between sessions, even though
we didn't at the beginning. Colleen*

*The relationship between Survivors in a group is like that between
men fighting a war in the trenches. They all have different
personalities and different likes and dislikes. In the outside world
they might never become friends, yet they have shared something
that forms a bond. They have gone through hell together, fought
side by side for every little victory one of them has achieved and
picked each other up in their setbacks and defeats. The bond
between men who have fought a war in the trenches will last long
after peace has come for all of them. Similarly, the bond between
Survivors is still there, long after each one of us has built a new life
and has found peace with herself at last. Ingrid*

The Survivors often stay friends after the group has ended.

*I'm talking about not going to the self-help group any more, but I
do want to meet and keep in touch with the other women,
because we have shared so much. Jocelyn*

Helping others

**Being in a group with other people who have had similar
experiences not only helps Survivors understand their own
problems, but also enables them to help other group members.
Helping others, while respecting their own needs, can increase the
Survivor's self-esteem and decrease their feelings of
powerlessness.**

*It was definitely good for me to listen to other people and feel I
could help, giving support as well as receiving it. It gives you*

confidence, and helps you realize things about your own situation.
Colleen

It also helped being able to help the others. You can understand how they feel and talk about how you coped. Helping someone else made me feel better about myself. Lucy

Overcoming the problems

How do people feel after they have been in individual therapy or in a Survivors group? How does it change them and their lives? Below, we look at some of the changes in the Wakefield Survivors.

Breaking free of the guilt and shame

I used to wonder sometimes if I would ever get over this feeling of guilt. Now I don't feel guilty about what happened—I can lay the blame at my stepfather's door. The group has been wonderful for me—I don't know what would have happened to me if I hadn't been referred to clinical psychology. Jane

I used to cope by taking overdoses, but since starting the group, I don't do that any more. I am not ashamed any more and I am no longer afraid of my abuser. I am now enjoying life to the fullest. Anthony

Understanding how an abuser plans and sets up the situation where he can abuse helps Survivors put the responsibility for the abuse onto the abuser and in time break free from their own feelings of guilt.

Meeting others who were also sexually abused as children took away the terrible isolation. For the first time, I talked to people who understood how I felt and why. When I listened to them, I thought, "They could not have stopped their abuser; why did I feel guilty all my life that I didn't find a way to stop mine?" The shame and guilt began to go after our first group meeting. Katarina

Sharing their experiences with others and being accepted enables Survivors to feel less ashamed and able to talk without shame about their abuse to their friends and family.

I was so afraid of anybody else finding out. Now I feel like I want to tell more people. Claire

Some time soon I'll tell my mom. Before, I really worried about anyone knowing, but now the world could know as long as it helped them and helped me. Lucy

Along with the decrease in the feelings of guilt and shame comes an increase in self-esteem: Survivors feel better about themselves as people and accept they have rights, too.

I feel better about saying what I think. It doesn't matter so much how people see me. I feel more confident that I am doing the right thing. I hadn't realized how much time I spent trying to please people and ultimately not succeeding. I take more time now to stand back and assess situations rather than jumping in. Jane

Better relationships

I've got more confidence, although I still have a ways to go. I'm starting to get along with other people again. I'm going out a lot more. I never used to go out at all, while my husband was working out of town. Mavis

I'm more open with people—I want to be friends now. Jocelyn

Therapy enables Survivors to feel better about themselves and overcome their lack of trust. This enables them to begin forming relationships with other people. As we saw earlier, Survivors who attended groups were also helped by forming close relationships within the group.

Before the group, I was afraid of making relationships, and I thought that anyone who looked at me would know what had happened to me. I thought I was such a terrible person. I didn't want to go out before. Now it's nice to go out socially. Lucy

Survivors learn to trust their therapist or each other first. After that they can begin to develop other relationships. After working on their feelings toward their abusers, they can also improve their relationships with their sexual partners, or begin to form new sexual relationships with people they can trust.

Lucy had been terrified of men, but after the group she became engaged and is now married.

Overcoming sexual problems

For years I had sex promiscuously, fucking from the neck down, trading sex for a moment's attention, for a hug even. This was followed by several years of total dislike of sex after the birth of my first child. I gradually learned to share my feelings, fears and needs with my husband, and to help him share his with me. As we learned to communicate within other "safe" areas of our relationship, to communicate with our hearts and minds, we were more able to communicate with our bodies. We learned to give each other privacy and to support one another. Gradually we were able to give one another the confidence we each needed to let ourselves be vulnerable. Sex can be about love and now for us it can be as free and liberated, as erotic or as close and comforting as we both want it to be. Shirley

Survivors often have sexual difficulties resulting from earlier abuse. They can work on these problems with a therapist or in a group by learning to accept their bodies, to love and respect themselves and to trust and relate to other people. Survivors often do not know what is "normal" sexually. It can help to discuss this in a group and learn more about sex and sexuality. Learning to enjoy sexual intimacy may not happen early in therapy, because it is important to deal with issues relating to self-esteem, body image, trust in others and communication with your partner (if you have one) first. Shirley's account shows it is possible to overcome problems around sex and develop a close and loving sexual relationship.

Feeling powerful

Now I feel I am in control. I know I still have weaknesses and I will continue to work on them. I am not a perfect person, but I now acknowledge that I also have talents and a lot to offer. I am so thankful to Jehovah God that he has brought and directed me through the right channel, so at last I can feel like me and know who I am. Kate

Having no control about what happens during sexual abuse often leaves Survivors feeling powerless in their later lives and unsure who they are. During therapy, Survivors learn to face their fears and overcome their feelings of powerlessness. Many return to work or start new jobs.

I quit my job after I had a panic attack in the cafeteria. Before the group, I didn't think I would ever be able to get another job. I don't know when the change started, but near the end of the group I got a job working behind a bar. The first time I tensed up and began shaking, but the owner said I did fine. I enjoy it now. I feel better about myself since I started at the bar. Mavis

Releasing the tension that holds back the fears and becoming aware of their own worth and abilities often gives Survivors renewed energy and a feeling that they can take control of their lives again.

When you're worried and stressed, you have no energy. Now I feel full of life and energy. I could conquer anything at the moment. I think much more of myself and have more confidence. I have so many things I want to do now. I don't see how I'll have time to fit everything in. I feel like making a fresh start. I want to go to the community college and take a course. Claire

Becoming aware of their own self-worth and learning to take control of their lives often helps Survivors rid themselves of problems with drugs, alcohol or eating.

A lot of the problem was my weight, and once I lost weight I felt a lot better about myself. But I never could have done it without the group. I began to feel I was worth something—that I had something to offer as a person. People were interested in me and I could have pride in myself. Before the group, it didn't seem like there was any point in losing weight, and I was frightened of men so it worked in keeping them away. If I hadn't come to the group I would have lacked the confidence to say to myself: "You're doing this for you, because you want to lose weight and feel more confident." Colleen

Assertiveness training helps Survivors understand that they have rights and teaches ways to express them. As Survivors overcome their fears, understand why they felt so bad about themselves and come to feel they can cope with their life and stand up for their rights, the feelings of powerlessness fade.

Mainly I feel happy with myself and fairly confident. I'm trying to be assertive. Now I can give my opinion again. I feel as if I've got the vivacity that I had when I was seventeen. I feel like I can handle most situations. Obviously I have ups and downs, which is good—it's just like anybody else. Colleen

Finding yourself

I was so scared of the change, of letting go of my image, my "front." But I'm just me—released from the pain and guilt. It's so great just to feel comfortable with myself at last. Clancy

Talking about your sexual abuse, understanding and accepting what really happened and breaking free from your problems can release the person you are underneath. Instead of hiding behind the "front" you present to the world, you can find your true self and live your life as you want to.

Before I joined the Survivors group, I felt confused about who I was. Now, through opening up, being honest, revealing the "secret," I have found me, and I like what I am. I am not bad, inferior, a person of no importance, or worth. The anger and frustration and hate that I thought was me has been sorted out. It has been painful, it has been hard, but I was abused 23 years ago and since then I have been living a lie. Now I feel free, free and lighter, I have been released. This "secret" held me down and eventually it dragged me down, but now it cannot hurt me any more. I survived it. Now I can hold my head up, I don't have to pretend any more. I am not afraid. No one has a hold on me. The anger and frustration are gone. It's the feelings inside me that have changed. I was always running away from me and I don't need to any more. I couldn't believe that just talking would help, it did, it does. I like myself. I did nothing wrong. Jocelyn

Reference

"An exploratory study of the process of change during group therapy for adult survivors of childhood sexual abuse," Sally Pinnell, M.Sc. Clinical Psychology Dissertation (1989), Academic Unit of Psychiatry, University of Leeds, 15 Hyde Terrace, Leeds L2S 9LT, England.

17

Working toward Prevention

I n this chapter, we look at what you can do to help prevent the
sexual abuse of children. Child sexual abuse is common, and
becoming aware of the prevalence of sexual abuse may make you
feel depressed and powerless. Taking action to help prevent further
abuse can help you feel empowered again. You can play an
important part in the prevention of sexual abuse if you want to.

Before you think about carrying out any of the suggestions in
this chapter, work through your feelings about your own abuse
and overcome any problems the abuse has created in your life. You
may want to put your energies into looking after, and trying to
protect, other people, but you are important, too. You deserve an
opportunity to be yourself and fulfil yourself in your own life. We
recommend you receive help for yourself before you think about
helping others.

The spread of sexual abuse

Sexual abuse occurs in secret. Abusers abuse children in secret and
manipulate them to keep quiet so they can go on to abuse more
and more children. Research and clinical work show that abusers
can abuse many children over many years.

Survivors often end up feeling powerless, and some go on to
form adult relationships with other abusive people who physically,
emotionally or sexually abuse them and may also abuse their
children. Survivors' own childhood experiences may leave them
unable to appropriately protect their own children from abuse. A

257

small number of abused people go on to abuse children themselves. Each abuser can therefore create a spreading wave of further abuse and distress.

How can we prevent sexual abuse?

To stop the spread of sexual abuse, we need to break the silence. For each child or adult Survivor who can talk about her abuse there is an abuser who can be prevented from harming other children. For each abuser who is prevented from having access to children, there may be dozens of children protected from abuse and saved from years of suffering. Children who disclose and receive help do not have to go on to develop problems that can last throughout their lives. Children who are believed and protected do not have to carry forward the feelings of shame, self-blame, betrayal and powerlessness. Adults who disclose can receive help for themselves, overcome their feelings of powerlessness and learn how to protect their own children from abuse.

People can work for the prevention of sexual abuse by teaching children how to protect themselves, watching for signs of abuse and listening to children. It is possible to begin the process of prevention of sexual abuse at a grassroots level by breaking the secret, talking about sexual abuse, encouraging people to listen to their children, learning ways to protect children and acting to prevent abusers from having access to children.

In this chapter we suggest ways of responding to adults who disclose their own childhood abuse to you. We describe how people can protect the children in their care from sexual abuse, and how they should respond if they suspect abuse or if a child discloses to them. We also look at what you can do to prevent your own abuser, or any abusers you are aware of, from having access to children. The work that the Wakefield Survivors are doing toward prevention is described. The final section of the chapter looks at wider issues involved in the prevention of sexual abuse.

Listening to adults

Most of the Wakefield Survivors begin to talk openly about their own abuse after they have been through therapy. Often their friends or other family members tell them they have also been abused. In breaking your silence, you can help others to break their secret, to receive help and to prevent further abuse. Listening to adult Survivors who want to talk about their abuse is the first step in helping them break free from their pain and shame. It also means they are more likely to learn how to appropriately protect their own children and so a new generation may be saved from abuse. The Survivor may also act to prevent their abuser (or abusers) from harming other children.

> I started talking among my friends and acquaintances about my own abuse and about the therapy I was receiving. More and more of them disclosed their own sexual abuse to me. Almost every one of my women friends experienced some form of sexual abuse as a child. That was when I realized I could not remain silent. I remember too vividly my own despair when my need to be listened to and understood found nothing but deaf ears. Ingrid

What do you do if an adult discloses to you? The first thing to remember is that there is no need to panic and feel you have to do something right away. A child who is being abused needs immediate protection, but with an adult Survivor the abuse has usually happened in the past. In some cases, the abuse may still be ongoing and the person will need support and acceptance until she is able to stop the abuse.

When people begin to talk about their own childhood abuse, just listen, believe them and accept them. Let them tell you as much or as little as they want to. Make it clear you believe them. They may want to meet again to talk about it. Do not feel that you have to be responsible for the person, but do let them know they need to keep on talking about it, recommend they read this or another book on sexual abuse and encourage them to get some professional help. Look at the Resources section at the end of the book.

Protecting children

At least 10% of children are sexually abused. You can learn how to protect children around you from abuse and how to support children who have already been abused. Each child that you help in this way can be saved from a lifetime of problems. It can also be a step toward the prevention of abuse of other children, because it may lead to the identification of another abuser. Some abused children also become abusers themselves; receiving help at the time of their own abuse can stop this cycle.

The only sure way to prevent children from being abused is to ensure they are not available to an abuser. Children are sexually abused because an abuser has access to them, not because of anything that the child does. Never leave children alone, even briefly, with anyone who is known, or suspected, to be an abuser.

In this section we will look at how you can watch for signs of abuse in children, how you can encourage a child to disclose abuse to you, what to do if a child discloses to you and how you can teach children to protect themselves.

Signs of abuse

Children often show they are in distress by changes in behavior. Finding out why they are behaving "badly" or differently from usual may uncover sexual abuse. You can encourage children to talk about how they are feeling and what is disturbing them and give them an opportunity to disclose any abuse. Children who are being sexually abused do not usually tell anyone what is happening to them, but they may show signs that they are in distress or that they are being abused. Some of these signs are described in chapter 6, *Silent Ways of Telling*, and listed in Table 3. Remember, however, that children who show these signs are not necessarily being sexually abused. The behavior changes could be caused by some other disturbance in their lives, such as a divorce or death in the family, or physical or emotional abuse. Sexual abuse is suggested if a child has more sexual knowledge than you would expect for his or her age or is acting in a sexually inappropriate way. Disturbed behavior indicates that something is wrong and the child needs a trusted adult to find out what is happening to him or her. If you are concerned about a child, ask for advice from one of the telephone helplines or encourage the child to talk to you.

Listening to children

To encourage your children to talk to you, show them you have time for them and want to listen. Make sure they know you will protect them and not punish them if they tell you about any inappropriate sexual behavior. Children may not talk about abuse directly. They may say, "I don't like Mr. Smith," or "I don't want to stay at Grandad's any more." Try not to dismiss what they say. Ask why they don't like that person or why they don't want to stay somewhere or go with someone. If a child feels uncomfortable with someone, respect their feelings. If you are receptive, your child will be more likely to talk.

This is Kate's advice on how to protect your children:

Talk and listen to your children. Their feelings count. If they don't like someone's company, ask yourself why. Don't force them to go with people they don't like, or dismiss their feelings by saying they're awkward or acting up.

Don't put down children by calling them a baby if they are afraid of something or someone. If boys or girls are afraid, there's a reason—find it out. Believe your children. Don't dismiss their worries or fears or dislikes. Kate

What do you do if your child tells you he or she has been sexually abused?

+ Don't panic. Try not to show how upset and angry you are.
+ Listen to him or her.
+ Believe the child. Tell the child you believe him or her.
+ Tell the child he or she is right to tell, and don't blame the child in any way.
+ Tell him or her you will not let it happen again. Make sure the child is not left alone with the abuser.
+ Tell the child you may need to tell someone else to get help to protect him or her. Explain to the child what you are going to do and why. Do not allow the child to feel he or she has no control over what is going to happen. Contact either the social welfare office in the area where the child lives or the local police Child Abuse Unit.
+ Do not threaten to kill or harm the abuser. This may make the child feel guilty or frightened.
+ Make sure the child gets some help to work through his or her confused feelings about the abuse. Ask your doctor for a referral to a clinical psychology clinic or call the Child Abuse Hotline in your area.

If a child discloses to you, you will probably feel upset, angry or shocked. Try to get some support for yourself. Remember that with appropriate help now, the child will not necessarily develop immediate or long-term problems.

When I began to talk freely about sexual abuse, my daughter had the confidence to tell me that it had happened to her three years before, when she was five years old. Because she could tell me so early in life and because I know what help she needs to overcome her shame and guilt, I know that she will grow up without the mental scars that a continued silence would have produced. Ingrid

Teaching children to protect themselves

It is difficult to identify an abuser unless you know they abused a child. They don't look different from anyone else and outwardly may appear to be respectable members of the community. You can't be with your children 24 hours a day for the rest of their lives, so it is important to teach children how to recognize situations that are dangerous or simply uncomfortable.

I don't want to frighten my child

Many people worry that by teaching children about the dangers of sexual abuse they will make them frightened and mistrustful of all adults. If the subject is approached in the right way it doesn't need to be a problem. We don't need to teach children to fear and distrust people; we can teach them positive skills to help them feel safe. We can teach them that their bodies belong to themselves and they don't have to let anyone touch their body in a way they don't like. We teach children how to cross the road and protect themselves from the dangers of traffic without making them too fearful to ever step off the pavement or get into a car. We can also teach children how to protect themselves from sexual abuse without making them fearful of every adult.

What to teach your children

Teach your children that they have the right to feel safe and that they can talk to you openly, whatever happens to them. Tell them that you will believe them and not be angry with them if they tell you about being touched or feeling uncomfortable with someone. Teach them their bodies belong to them and they have the right to say "No." Show you mean this by giving them a choice about physical contact. Ask if they want to give you or anyone else a kiss or hug, but do not insist. It may be embarrassing if your children refuse to kiss someone, but support them if they do this. Explain to friends and relatives that your children have the right to choose who they kiss and hug. Teach the difference between surprises, like presents and parties, and secrets. Tell them they should not keep secrets, even if they are told to, and to talk to you or another

trusted adult if anyone asks them to keep a secret. Make it clear
that the rules apply to everyone, including family members.

You can also teach general safety rules about not talking to
strangers and not going into other people's homes without
permission, for example. It will be easier for them to talk about
sexual abuse if they know the words for body parts and sexual
acts. Teach them some basic sex education. Make clear the
difference between sex and sexual assault so they do not grow up
afraid of touching themselves or of appropriate sexual activity.

Remember that young children take what you say literally. Be
as clear as you can and check that the child has understood you.

> When I was very small, my mom told me not to take candy from
> strangers. I thought it was because they might be poisoned. When
> an old lady on a bus offered us some candy and my mom said it
> was all right to have one, I was really impressed that my mom
> could tell who had poisoned candy and who didn't. Shirley

You can start to teach very young children about protecting
themselves at a level they can understand. Show them they have
rights by giving them choices about physical contact and in other
ways, such as allowing them to choose which book to read at
bedtime or which clothes to wear. Play "What if . . ." games, with
questions such as, "What would you do if the baby-sitter asks you
to keep a secret?" Keep talking to your children about protecting
themselves; don't do it just once. There are several good books on
how to protect your children (see the reading list at the end of this
chapter). Some of the Wakefield Survivors drew up a list of things
you can teach your children to keep them safe from abuse. This list
appears in Table 9 (page 265).

Stopping the abusers

> Now I'm questioning myself as to whether or not I should do
> something about the abuser to put a stop to it all, to protect my
> own daughter and other children in the family. If he died, I wouldn't
> have all these decisions to make. I ought to do something about it,
> but can I? Am I letting my own daughter down if I don't? What
> would it achieve anyway? One year in prison, then out. Could I be
> the one to put him in prison? Perhaps he would die in prison. He
> would certainly suffer, but I don't want him to suffer even though it
> would be his fault because he's an abuser. I would still feel

responsible. But then I would feel responsible if he abuses anyone else. It could be partly my fault if he abuses any more children because I didn't do anything. But how could I hurt my mom? Kate

Deciding to take action can be difficult. Kate was racked with indecision. Her father had abused her and her nine brothers and sister, his grandchildren, nieces and many others. She didn't want to hurt her father or her mother by exposing his activities, but she couldn't sit back and let him abuse even more children.

Abusers rarely abuse one child. They may abuse dozens throughout their lifetime and often continue abusing in their old age. After group therapy, Survivors begin to talk about their abuse to their friends and family and often find others were abused, too. Forty per cent of the Wakefield Survivors know of at least one other child abused by their own abuser. Abusers keep on scheming, planning, and creating opportunities to abuse more children.

What can you do about it?

What can you do to prevent your abuser from abusing other children? The most important thing is to ensure that abusers do not have access to any children. You can help protect children from abusers by informing the child-protection authorities, by confronting the abuser or by going to the police.

If you know, or have strong suspicions, that an abuser is currently abusing a child, inform Social Services (ask for the Child Protection Officer) or the police (ask for the Child Abuse Section) immediately. If you can, provide them with the abuser's birth date and the child and with as much other information as you can. Give your own name if at all possible. This will be kept confidential and not given to the abuser or his family. You can do this anonymously by telephone or letter, but then you will not be able to provide any further information that might be needed, nor will you receive any feedback on the investigations. At the very least, phone one of the helplines at the back of this book and discuss the problem with them.

Child sexual abuse is happening all around us. To protect the next generation we must act every time we have suspicions. You will rarely be certain that your abuser is still abusing. If your abuser has children of his own or has access to children, these children are at risk and you should inform Social Services, whether or not you know for certain that he is abusing them. Social Services

Table 9: Teaching Your Children to Feel Safe

Teach them the following:

+ They have the right to feel safe and they should tell someone if anyone makes them feel afraid or uncomfortable.
+ That you will believe them and not be angry if they tell you of an incident when they have been touched or felt uncomfortable.
+ Not to keep secrets. Not telling about surprises is OK; for example, presents and parties.
+ They are allowed to disobey an adult if they are in danger. It's OK not to be polite to protect themselves.
+ How to say "NO," shout "STOP," and run away.
+ Differences between good touch and bad touch. Bad touch is anything that makes you feel uncomfortable, confused, uneasy.
+ What their private parts are (their breasts, buttocks, genitals). No one should touch their private parts, unless it's a doctor or a nurse and a parent is with them. It's OK for them to touch themselves.
+ They should not touch the private parts of an adult or older child.
+ They have the right to say "NO" if anyone touches them in a way they don't like or makes them feel uncomfortable. They don't have to kiss or hug anyone young or old if they don't want to. They have a right to say who touches them and how. "It's my body—I decide."
+ If a person touches them in a way they don't like, or if they feel uncomfortable or uneasy about anything, they should tell an adult they trust. If that person doesn't believe them or help them, they should tell someone else and keep telling until someone does help.
+ To tell an adult if they think they are being followed.
+ Not to talk to strangers, or go anywhere with strangers.
+ To be wary of special favors, bribes and blackmail.
+ That they can ask about other people's puzzling behavior; for example, "Why does Uncle George want to play the funny game?"
+ How to use the telephone and memorize their own telephone number and that of a trusted person.
+ Rules about invitations into another person's home when playing outside.
+ A password to use if an unfamiliar person has to get them from school.
+ About sex education; differences between sex and sexual assault.
+ That these rules apply to everyone, including the family, teachers, baby-sitters, and others.

will then investigate the case.

In some cases, the abuser is still around but there are no children in his immediate environment. In these circumstances, some of the Wakefield Survivors have decided to confront their abuser to let him know they are watching him, and to tell him they are informing people around him, especially those with children, of his past offences. *DO NOT* confront your abuser without fully preparing yourself as described in chapter 15, *Abusers*.

Some adult Survivors, such as Joanne in chapter 15, give statements to the police and attempt to prosecute their abusers to prevent them from abusing others. Check with the local authorities regarding statutes of limitations on these matters (that is, how long after the abuse prosecution may be instigated.) There may also be difficulties finding enough supporting evidence for the case to go to court. If you want to consider prosecuting your abuser, talk to a professional about it or phone the police and discuss it with someone from the Child Abuse Unit. You can ask to speak to a policewoman if you prefer.

A.C.T. (Abuse Counseling and Training)

Wakefield Survivors help prevent further sexual abuse by breaking the secrecy around their own abuse, by protecting their own and any other children around them and by ensuring their abusers do not harm any more children. Some Wakefield Survivors wanted to do more than this. They formed an action group called A.C.T. to help other people who have been abused and to do further work toward the prevention of abuse. A.C.T. members attended counseling courses, counseled other Survivors and worked to increase public awareness of child sexual abuse. Being sexually abused can make you feel helpless and out of control; A.C.T. members found working toward prevention helped them feel more powerful.

Working with survivors

I was glad to pick up the suggestion the psychologists made to meet some of the women who were on their waiting lists. Before therapy starts, many Survivors feel the stigma of shame and guilt very strongly and it helps them to meet another Survivor who has been through therapy and who not only will understand them, but also reassure them that life will be much better after receiving the help they so desperately seek.

Many Survivors hate themselves before they receive therapy. Meeting someone and liking someone who had the same experience of being abused makes it easier for them to begin to like themselves. Katarina

A.C.T. members met with Survivors who have been referred to Wakefield Clinical Psychology Service to talk to them about their own experiences. Some A.C.T. members ran self-help groups for Survivors.

We set up a Survivors' Support Group. Initially this was an idea Lucy and I had to help one Survivor overcome her fear of groups. We started with just two Survivors and every week added one more of the new Survivors who would be in the next therapy group. Slowly they got used to each other, slowly they lost the fear of a group, although at times it still came back. Now they talk openly about the effects of the abuse and are able to encourage the new Survivors who still have to overcome their insecurities about being in a group. Katarina

A.C.T. members attended some Survivors group sessions run by the psychologists. They encouraged group members to continue when they became distressed because they were confronting their memories and feelings. A.C.T. members also attended sessions on specific topics to talk about how they had learned to cope with their problems.

A.C.T. members were also involved in therapy groups for abusers—providing the abusers with a victim's perspective on abuse and challenging their beliefs.

A.C.T. members ran nurseries for the children of other Survivors so they could attend a group, worked as volunteers at a local domestic violence drop-in center and met with and advised other groups of Survivors. They were involved in campaigning for awareness and the prevention of sexual abuse by giving media interviews and by contributing to this book.

You may want to join or set up a group to work toward prevention but do not feel you have to do this. Some Survivors benefit from the therapy groups and afterward just want to get on with their lives. They deserve to put their past behind them at last and to fulfil their lives in whichever way they choose.

Recovered memories
and "false memory syndrome"

The last few years have seen a lot of publicity about "false memory syndrome." Some of the information has been misleading or inaccurate and many people are now confused about what "false memory syndrome" refers to. Survivors have felt upset and angry because of things they have read or heard. Some have told us they are afraid they will no longer be believed. Others have been told that they have not really been abused but are suffering from "false memory syndrome." To prevent further misunderstanding and disbelief, people need to know what "false memory syndrome" refers to, and to whom it could apply.

"False memory syndrome" is not actually a syndrome or a medical diagnosis. The term was first used by the False Memory Syndrome Foundation in the United States in 1991. The foundation use the term to describe people who have *not* been sexually abused who somehow come to believe that they have been abused and who create memories of events in their childhood that did not occur. The term "false memory syndrome" should *not* be applied to people who have actually been abused and it cannot apply to people who have always had some memories of their abuse. "False memory syndrome" does not describe people who knowingly make false accusations of abuse. False allegations of abuse can be made, but are no more likely than with any other crime. The false memory societies take the view that it is not possible to forget about childhood sexual abuse and therefore believe that anyone who recovers memories of abuse must have "false memories." Therapists have been accused of inducing these "false memories" in clients with no memories of sexual abuse who came into therapy with other problems.

A great deal of evidence supports the fact that people can block out or forget traumas, including childhood sexual abuse, and remember the events later. As we have discussed previously, memories of childhood sexual abuse can be triggered by events such as the birth of a child. Survivors sometimes recover memories of abuse while in therapy, perhaps because their memories are triggered by talking about their lives or because they feel safe enough to allow the memories back into awareness. Recovering memories of abuse does not mean the memories are false. However, therapists cannot say how accurate memories are and they cannot diagnose sexual abuse from a person's symptoms. All memories can be distorted so recovered memories, nightmares and flashbacks are not necessarily accurate recollections of the past. There may be other information (for example, siblings may have witnessed the abuse or been abused by the same person) that can be used to corroborate the accuracy of memories, but some people may never know for sure what has happened to them.

It may be possible for some people to come to believe they have been abused when they have not; however, there is no evidence that this is a widespread epidemic as the false-memory movement has suggested. The idea that "false memories" are widespread has been fueled by sensational newspaper reports. Parents who have been accused of abusing can easily speak out in the press to proclaim their innocence and blame therapists for persuading their adult children that they had been abused. However, newspapers run the risk of being sued for libel if they publish allegations of abuse without hard evidence, and therapists cannot speak out about particular cases because they are bound by strict rules of confidentiality. Only one side of the story is presented, and once again victims' voices are less likely to be heard.

Support for the idea that "false memory syndrome" is an epidemic has been described as a backlash against breaking the silence about sexual abuse. It has been suggested that "false memory syndrome" has gained such popular acceptance because society finds it easier to believe in widespread false memories than in the widespread sexual abuse of children. To be falsely accused of abusing a child must be terrible, and we need to be aware that this happens occasionally and do our best to prevent it. However, accusing victims of having "false memory syndrome" can also be an ideal defense for people who have sexually abused children. We hope this information will increase understanding and thereby help Survivors to continue to speak out.

Wider issues in prevention

Why is the sexual abuse of children so widespread? Why is it mostly men who abuse? These questions need to be addressed if we are to create a safe society for children. We can begin to answer these questions by looking at issues such as the general treatment of children and women in our society, the different expectations for males and females and the effects of pornography.

In our society, children are devalued. Emotional, verbal, physical and sexual abuse of children is a daily occurrence. Children are powerless, and some adults feel it is acceptable to exert power and control over children in whatever way they want to. There are differences in the ways that boys and girls are brought up. Girls learn that to be valued they must be nurturing to others and not show anger. Girls and women who are victimized therefore usually turn their anger and distress in on themselves and become depressed, self-destructive and vulnerable to further abuse. Boys learn that to be valued they must appear to be powerful and not show any weakness. Boys and men who are victimized are more likely to turn their anger and distress outward and try to regain their power by victimizing others, particularly those they see as less powerful than themselves. This means men are more likely than women to become abusers and women are more likely to become victims.

Women have less access than men to money, jobs and influence. However, women are the ones who shoulder the emotional, practical and financial burden of childcare. The lack of legal protection afforded to women and children and the lack of access to money, housing, childcare facilities, and so on, put women in a position where they are powerless and vulnerable. This makes it difficult for women to leave men who are violent or sexually abusive to themselves or their children.

Pornography, pin-up girls and the use of women's bodies in advertising contribute to a climate in which women are not respected and are seen as sex objects. Child pornography encourages abusers to believe it is normal and acceptable to have sex with children. Pornography, especially child pornography, is used by abusers to fantasize about abuse, and this helps them rationalize their abuse. Having sex with children in other countries on sex tourism trips also encourages the belief that the sexual abuse of children is acceptable.

We can address these issues by making changes individually in terms of how we relate to others and bring up children.

We can all play a small part in reshaping a society in which it is possible for children to be abused and for women to be regarded as of less importance than men. Each individual, whether she has been a victim of abuse or not, can try to influence those people close to her. It is not just the work of feminist movements or psychologists writing books and giving lectures. Parents can teach their sons to respect girls as equals and that it is not unmanly to show care, concern, sensitivity and understanding toward others, male and female alike. They can teach their sons and daughters to value their rights and the rights of others. Women can begin to put a stop to being treated as nothing more than ornaments who are not to be taken seriously. Wives can insist on being treated as having equal rights. Daughters can insist on being listened to in their wishes and plans for their own future. Ingrid

We need change in government policies and distribution of resources. Abused children and adults need immediate help to overcome problems arising from the abuse. Professionals who work with children should be trained to recognize the signs of abuse and to deal with disclosure. Schools should teach children assertion skills and how to protect themselves from abuse. Abusers need treatment to confront them with the damage they are inflicting on others, to help them overcome their motivation to abuse children and to stop them continuing to abuse children. This is particularly important for children who are victimizing other children, to stop them from embarking on a lifetime of abusing.

Summary

We can all play an important part in the prevention of sexual abuse. Just as individual abusers can start a spreading wave of sexual abuse, the fight against sexual abuse can spread out from individuals who are aware and want to keep children safe. You can empower yourself and help prevent sexual abuse by listening to and helping children and adults who have been abused, by learning how to help children remain safe and by ensuring your own abuser does not harm other children. You can make changes in your own life in the way you treat children and allow yourself to be treated. People can organize to campaign for more resources for the treatment of victims and abusers, and to control pornography and material that degrades women and children.

Survivors have suffered in silence for too long. Now it is time to speak out. Breaking the silence helps you break free from the influence of your past and can also help reshape a society where sexual abuse is common.

Suggestions

✦ It is important for you to sort out your own problems and feelings before you help others, so do get help if you haven't already. If you want to work toward the prevention of sexual abuse, follow the suggestions in the chapter.

✦ If you know or suspect a child is being abused, follow the instructions given in the chapter on how to protect the child. Look for signs of abuse in children. Listen to children who try to talk about their abuse. Teach your children how to protect themselves from abuse.

✦ Ensure your abuser and any other abusers you become aware of are not able to harm other children by following the suggestions given in the chapter.

Resources

If you are a child who is being sexually abused or you suspect a child is being sexually abused, contact one of the agencies or telephone helplines listed at the back of the book.

If your child has been sexually abused, your doctor or social worker can arrange for therapy for the child to help him or her overcome any emotional issues arising from the abuse.

Further reading

Adams, Caren. *No More Secrets: Protecting Your Child from Sexual Assault.* San Luis Obispo, CA: Impact Publishers, 1981.

James, Beverly. *Treating Traumatized Children: New Insights & Creative Interventions.* New York: Simon & Schuster, 1990.

Mandell, Joan G., and Linda Damon. *Group Treatment for Sexually Abused Children.* New York: Guilford Press, 1989.

The Journey Continues

18

Many Survivors wonder whether they will ever overcome their problems or if they will always be haunted by their problems and their past. Others wonder if they will slip back to where they were. We have already seen how the Survivors in this book began their journey to healing. Seven years later, six Survivors who contributed to the first edition of this book tell us about their current lives and the changes they have made. All six Survivors were in group therapy in the late 1980s or early 1990s.

Ingrid

Ingrid was sexually abused by her brother. She has now put the past behind her and has completely changed her life.

> It is now more than a decade since I had therapy and my life could not be more different than before I joined the Survivors group. My confidence has improved greatly, as has my ability to think positively. I no longer expect bad things to happen and no longer think anything negative that happens to others is my fault.
>
> I found the strength to divorce my husband after fourteen years and leave a loveless and empty marriage. Finally free from restrictions, I earned a degree with the Open University and studied psychology for six years. After receiving my degree, I started an advanced degree course in philosophy and am now in my third year. After fourteen years with my ex-husband as a housewife with small part-time jobs, I returned to the work force,

*working first as a secretary and later as office manager. I bought
an old house and started to rebuild my life completely.*

*My life is very happy and fulfilled now. I will get married in
three weeks and know this time the marriage will last. We have a
partnership of equals in which not only love, but also respect,
friendship and mutual consideration for each other's needs are
important. Before therapy I would not have been able to have a
relationship like this because I did not feel equal to anybody.*

*I no longer have sexual problems but thoroughly enjoy the
physical side of my relationship. Being touched and touching my
partner does not recall memories of abuse any more. I feel a
freedom to do what I want and to be anything I want to be. I have
learned to love my body and myself and am happy. Ingrid*

Kate

Kate was sexually abused by her father and other family members.
She has overcome the effects of the abuse and has worked to
prevent further abuse within her own extended family and
elsewhere.

*I have worked in residential care and on projects. I have earned a
certificate in counseling skills. I have told my mother about the
abuse and so no longer need to protect her. I have also confronted
a pedophile who married into the family. I am no longer a
Jehovah's Witness and actually view the six years that I was as
quite an unhappy time in my life. When I think back, I realize I was
treated kindly by a few, but unkindly by others. I strongly feel that I
was robbed of my feelings and made to feel unworthy by some of
them, and I was not taken seriously when child-protection issues
arose. I now feel healed, loved, worthy and I feel like myself. Kate*

Fiona

Fiona experienced a childhood of neglect and emotional, physical
and sexual abuse within the family and sexual abuse by many
other nonfamily members. Fiona was barely literate when she
came into therapy, but she worked hard to overcome the effects of
the deprivation and abuse she suffered and has now managed to
create the life she wanted for herself.

*I am a qualified trainer and I have earned my post-graduate
diploma in counseling. I have continued to help other Survivors by*

facilitating a support group. I have learned to drive, which for me was a great achievement due to my phobia. I also practice karate and have reached my brown belt (3rd Kyu). My relationship with my daughter is good. I do not overprotect her and she has appropriate freedom in terms of relationships (boyfriends). Relationships are better. I no longer use sex as a coping strategy. I am more assertive, I manage my anger well and I am a calmer person. I no longer have any obsessive behaviors or anxieties. I feel strong and can face anything. Fiona

Jane

Jane was sexually abused for ten years by her stepfather. She turned her life around and now approaches her life from a position of strength while accepting that there will always be challenges.

Professionally I have taken on projects that I am interested in and that are fulfilling. I have been able to say what I am unable to do and ask for support when I feel I need it. I am in a successful relationship with a man who says he enjoys being with an assertive woman and I believe him. We are happy in a relationship that is sharing, caring and supportive. We don't live together, choosing to respect each other's space and acknowledge our respective children's needs. I am surviving being a parent, although I find my role as a parent challenging. It is difficult to maintain secure boundaries and confidence when dealing with a teenage daughter who struggles with being assertive.

I am much more self-aware and can cope with experiences, feelings and situations much better. I know what will help me cope if I feel I need help. I feel confident and assertive. I am comfortable with myself and can give myself permission to make mistakes. Without the healing, I wouldn't have achieved any of this. Jane

Eileen

Eileen was sexually abused for many years by her uncle. She pursued a successful professional career for many years and is now able to use her retirement to further her self-development.

I am more positive about what I want in life and no longer live in a soap opera where I am play-acting that I am a confident, happy person. The obsessive behavior is still as strong as ever; for example, opening cans at the base to avoid any dust on top, folding tea towels with the pattern on the outside, toilet seats down after use, coat hangers facing the same way on the rail. These don't cause me a problem, so I don't feel I need to change them.

During the years since I finished therapy, I have joined day and evening college classes and have taken various courses, including plumbing, welding and furniture restoration. Because normally men take these courses, it would not have been possible for me even to consider taking them in the past. I feel comfortable doing them now. I feel more able to cope and get on with my life. I can even smile these days and mean it. Eileen

Pam

Pam was sexually and physically abused by her father and sexually abused by another family member. Her first husband also physically abused her. Pam has now achieved the professional qualifications she needed to pursue the career of her choice.

I was married throughout my therapy, but I have since divorced. I am now a career mom, totally independent financially. I've struggled to get my career on track as a single parent, but I've achieved it. I have qualified as a counselor and also as an adult-education teacher/trainer/lecturer. I have been fortunate enough to work with Survivors and with schizophrenic and P.T.S.D. (post-traumatic stress disorder) clients. All of this work has enriched my life greatly. I have achieved more than I thought was possible when I was surviving my abuse and recovering. I am continually moving my goal posts in order to meet a new challenge. I have recently started writing my own book about my life, my experiences and post-therapy changes.

I have learned that I love my son immensely and that he is the most important thing in my life. I didn't believe in myself as a mother; now I am a mother first. I'm not infallible; I'm human. I do my best and this is acceptable. This is the commitment I made to my son when I made the decision to have a child. I'm proud of the fact that I can combine a career, motherhood and run a home on my own. I've now got a wonderfully supportive relationship with my parents. I am a strong person and, I think, self-aware. I've become a professional, independent woman. I know what I'm capable of. I know my limitations. I'm much more assertive and confident, although this does wane at times. I've moved away from the

*dependent, unconfident, emotionally unstable person I once was,
whose thoughts revolved around abuse. I'm now more confident,
emotionally stable and satisfied. I feel fantastic.* Pam

These women all describe how they feel better about themselves,
are more confident and act more assertively. Relationships of all
kinds are better for them. Since therapy, they have all felt strong
enough and free enough to pursue qualifications, careers, job-skills
training or interests for themselves. They have all rebuilt their lives
and have become truer to themselves.

Ingrid, Kate, Fiona, Jane, Eileen and Pam also reflect on what
helped them in therapy and what has helped them since.

*Being with others who had been through the same problems as I
had is what helped me the most. I remember listening to another
Survivor talking about her feelings and thinking, "That is what I
feel!" and feeling relief at not being an outsider any more. Although
I had talked to many health professionals in my attempts to
receive help before I finally found the Wakefield Survivors group, I
never before had the feeling that I was truly understood or that I
could share my feelings and thoughts.*

*Since therapy, I have learned to see myself as valuable
person with the same rights as anybody else and because I
express this in the way I behave, this is also how I am treated by
others. I have learned to speak about my feelings, my thoughts
and worries to those close to me. I have become confident and
able to trust people. Having trust in people and not being
disappointed reinforces the ability to trust.* Ingrid

*Most important for my recovery was the one-to-one counseling
and group therapy I experienced at the Wakefield Psychology
Service and the genuine support I received from Charles Fortte
(who then worked for the Gracewell Foundation). Without his help
I don't think I would have ever told my mother. He also gave me
an insight into offenders, which proved very valuable to me and to
others as well. Healing is a continuing process. I feel that
throughout my life I have been fortunate enough to meet many
people and experience many different situations that have helped
me to heal. I have also been helped by books and articles,
attending training courses, work colleagues, friends and some
family members.* Kate

Being able to talk and explore the abuse and how it affected me without being judged was a great help. Being supported and respected by my therapist and the Survivors group members and being able to look at alternative ways of behaving was also very helpful. I now work as a counselor, and in my profession it is important to continue my journey of self-awareness and growth. Fiona

The healing initially involved being given time and space, being made to feel valued and worth helping, feeling I had something to offer as support for others and recognizing and accepting support when I needed it. Being given the time and space to talk about my feelings and emotions allowed me to release feelings I had held in for years. I was then able to put them aside and explore what I felt about a lot of other issues. The healing has continued and I know when I need space and I have friends who can give and receive support. Jane

The counseling was a godsend, having spent fifty years denying that the abuse had happened to me because it was too painful to admit (even to myself) that the physical, mental and sexual abuse was reality. The group therapy and hearing other people's stories made me realize that I had lived a very lonely life believing that I was the only person in the world who had been abused. Eileen

The support of other group members really helped me. The relationships that were forged in therapy have continued. I feel lucky that these people are friends, close friends whom I can be open and honest with. We talk about all kinds of things. We still support each other through crises. We socialize together and laugh together. The relationships I now have with these people are as close as friends can be.

Every time I hit a crisis my eating disorder emerges as something I can control while everything else seems out of my control. The healing process comes into play every time I encounter a crisis. I sit back and analyze, assess its impact, release the feelings, identify the options and put these into action. Once the crisis is overcome or dealt with, my eating disorder goes away again. It's almost a friend. I can deal with crises now because I learned to take control and to focus on the things that are important. Group therapy enabled me to analyze my life and take time out to re-evaluate what is meaningful. Pam

All the Survivors emphasize the importance of receiving support from others whether in individual counseling, from other Survivors or from family and friends. This helped them to stop feeling worthless and alone. Feeling valued, understood and sharing their feelings without being judged also helped them overcome problems. Being able to give and receive support continues to help them deal with difficulties that are part of everyday life.

Does the abuse play any part in these Survivors' lives now?

Survivors often ask if they can ever truly put their abuse behind them. Eileen describes how she used to feel that her past was always with her, and Ingrid felt haunted by constant reminders of her abuse. How much are they affected by the abuse now?

> *The abuse is no longer at the forefront of my thoughts and it is rare that I think about it at all. So much has happened in my life and I have changed so much that it almost seems like a totally different life I once led. I used to walk down the street, see someone wearing glasses and think "my abuser wears glasses," or heard a certain phrase and thought of him. Almost everything reminded me of my abuser and the abuse I suffered. Thoughts used to come uninvited and were almost constant reminders of a past I so much wanted to forget. The problems I had as a result of the abuse overshadowed every aspect of my life, but now they are gone. When I met my abuser again five years ago, I felt no fear and no inferiority. My fragile body image used to crumble when he was close, but this time I felt no different, it was as if he had not been there. I am free. Ingrid*

> *My own childhood abuse has no negative effect on my current life. The large number of problems I endured in my childhood gives me experience that helps me in my current work with clients. My past feelings and defenses give me great insight which I use constructively in my work with counseling clients. Fiona*

> *As a parent, I am concerned about child-protection issues. I feel that many children are given inappropriate freedom without any experience of how to cope with it. I find it difficult to reconcile what my daughter's friends are allowed to do with what I feel is*

appropriate. This makes it harder to maintain firm boundaries with my daughter under such pressure from her friends. Jane

Until the therapy, I always felt that the abuse was within, without and around my life continually, every day. Now the abuse is in the past. Even though I will never forget the abusers and their actions, it is now behind me and I can get on with my life. The feeling of being trapped in my own body with a nightmare past no longer haunts me. I am extremely protective with my three grandchildren (girls). We play-act what they would do and how they should react if they were approached by strangers, and discuss the differences between good touching and bad touching. Eileen

I'm a better person because I know how it feels to be trapped, abused, beaten, betrayed, unloved. My own understanding of abuse has enabled me to pursue a worthwhile career—I now teach professionals on issues of child abuse and adult Survivors. I don't think about the abuse at all unless I'm training other people about the subject. I am a parent who wants my child to feel loved and appreciated. I want to give him the best I possibly can. Most of all I want him to have happy memories of his childhood and I want to be there for him. There was a time when I could never imagine getting out of bed on a morning and the abuse not being there, but it's happened. It's not there, it's no longer my waking thought. I don't think about the abuse any more. I enjoy life. I didn't think there could be life after abuse, but there is. Pam

Ingrid, Kate, Fiona, Jane, Eileen and Pam now feel free from the burden of their pasts. They have all begun to use their awareness about abuse in constructive ways. Jane, Eileen and Kate have described using their experiences to increase awareness of child abuse and child protection. Ingrid has since worked with victims of violence and Pam and Fiona have found their own past experiences help them in their chosen careers.

Breaking free from your past and overcoming your problems is an ongoing process. Growth, healing and developing self-awareness continue throughout life. These women have all continued to grow. They continue to use the skills they have learned and now see their abusers as "in the past" and not part of their current lives. They have all made many positive changes and moved forward in their lives and they know that for all of them, and all of us, the journey continues.

Resources

A doctor, nurse, social worker or other professional can assist you in getting help from a clinical psychologist or other therapist. Do not be afraid to ask to see a woman if you feel uncomfortable talking to a man (or vice versa).

The national address or phone numbers for various organizations are listed below. For information on local sources of help, contact the national office or try your local telephone directory. Please include a stamped, self-addressed envelope for written replies.

General Resources / Organizations

Committee for Children
2203 Airport Way S., Suite 500
Seattle, WA 98134-2027
(206) 343-1223
http://www.cfchildren.org

Giarretto Institute
also: **Adults Molested as Children**
232 E. Gish Rd. 1st Fl.
San Jose, CA 95112
(408) 453-7611 or (408) 453-7616
http://www.giaretto.org

Incest Survivors Anonymous
P.O. Box 17245
Long Beach, CA 90807-7245
(562) 428-5599

Incest Survivors Resource Network, International
P.O. Box 7375
Las Cruces, NM 88006
(505) 521-4260
http://www.zianet.com/ISRNI

Parent Child Abuse America
P.O. Box 2866
Chicago, IL 60609
(312) 663-3520

Parents Anonymous
675 Foothill Blvd., Ste. 220
Claremont, CA 91711
(909) 621-6184
Hotline: (800) 421-0353
http://www.parentsanonymous.natlorg

Parents United International
615 15th St.
Modesto, CA 95354-2510
(209) 572-3446
http://www.ainet.com/parents-united

People Against Rape
P.O. Box 5876
Naperville, IL 60567-5876
(800) 877-7252

Prevent Child Abuse America
P.O. Box 2866
Chicago, IL 60609
(312) 663-3520
http://www.preventchildabuse.org

Stop It Now!
P.O. Box 495
Haydenville, MA 01039
(888) PREVENT
http://www.stopitnow.com

Survivor Connections
52 Lyndon Rd.
Cranston, RI 02905-1121
(401) 941-2548
http://www.angelfire.com/ri/survivorconnections

Survivors of Incest Anonymous
P.O. Box 21817
Baltimore, MD 21222-6817
(410) 282-3400
http://www.siawso.org

Voices in Action
P.O. Box 148309
Chicago, IL 60614
(800) 7-VOICE-8
http://www.voices-action.org

Hotlines

Boys Town
1-800-448-3000
http://www.boystown.org

Childhelp USA & Canada
1-800-422-4453
National Child Abuse Hotline
http://www.childhelpusa.org

Children of Alcoholics Foundation
(212) 595-5810 x 7760 or 7764
(referrals to national and local self-
help counseling groups and
treatment centers)

Clearinghouse on Family Violence,
  Health & Welfare
1-800-267-1291

National Directory of Hotlines and
  Crisis Interventions Centers
  Covenant House Nineline
(800) 999-9999 (24 hour hotline for
runaways and their families)

National Domestic Violence Hotline
1-800-799-7233

Rape, Abuse & Incest National
  Network
1-800-656-4673

Male Survivors

Male Abuse Survivors Support
  Forum
Web site:
http://www.angelfire.com/nc/asari
an/frames.hmtl

Men's Resource Center
12 S.E. 14th Ave.
Portland, OR 97214
(503) 235-3433

MensNet
Web site:
http://www.magi.com/~mensnet/
netsite.htm

National Organization on Male
  Sexual Victimization
P.O. Box 20782
West Palm Beach, FL 33416
(800) 738-4181
http://www.nomsv.org/

Professional / Educational

The Abuse Institute
14622 Ventura Blvd. No. 748
Sherman Oaks, CA 91403-3600

American Professional Society on
  the Abuse of Children (APSAC)
497 S. Dearborn St., Ste. 1300
Chicago, IL 60605
(312) 554-0166
http://www.apsac.org

Association for the Treatment of
  Sexual Abusers
10700 SW Beaverton Hillsdale Hwy.,
No. 26
Beaverton, OR 97005-3035
(503) 643-1023
http://www.atsa.com

Defense for Children
  International—United States
14907 Berry Rd.
Accokeek, MD 20607-3115
(301) 292-2450

International Society for Prevention
  of Child Abuse and Neglect
  (ISPCAN)
401 N. Michigan Ave., Ste. 2200
Chicago, IL 60611
(312) 578-1401

National Center on Child Abuse
  and Neglect
U.S. Department of Health and
Human Services
P.O. Box 1182
Washington, D.C. 20013
(800) 841-3366
Web site:
http://www.calib.com/nccanch

National Coalition against Sexual
  Assault
125 N. Enola Dr.
Enola, PA 17025
(717) 728-9764
http://www.ncasa.org

National Committee to Prevent
  Child Abuse
21 Tamal Vista Blvd., Ste. 209
Corte Madera, CA 94925
(800) 626-9671
http://www.childabuse.org

Odyssey Institute Corporation
5 Hedley Farms Rd.
Westport, CT 06880
(203) 255-4198

One Voice, National Alliance for Abuse Awareness
1835 K. St. N.W., Ste. 960
Washington, D.C. 20006
(202) 462-4688

Paul and Lisa Program
P.O. Box 348
Westbrook, CT 06498
(860) 767-7660

Safer Society Foundation
P.O. Box 340
Brandon, VT 05733-0340
(802) 247-3132
Web site:
http://www.safersociety.org

Society's League against Molestation
c/o Women Against
Rape/Childwatch
P.O. Box 346
Collingswood, NJ 08108
(800) 491-WATCH

Village of Childhelp
P.O. Box 247
14700 Manzanita Park Rd.
Beaumont, CA 92223
(909) 845-3155

Women in Transition
21 S. 12th St., 6th Fl.
Philadelphia, PA 19107
(215) 564-5301
http://www.libertynet.org/~wit

Canada

S.A.F.E. (Self Abuse Finally Ends) in Canada
659 Dundas Street
London, Ontario N5W 2Z1
(519) 649-5462
www.wwdc.com/safe/

Internet Resources

Usenet groups

alt.support.abuse-partners
alt.sexual.abuse.recovery
alt.sexual.abuse.recovery.d

Web sites

Abuse/Incest Support:
http://incestabuse.miningco.com/
health/incestabuse/

Anonymous Sexual Abuse Recovery:
http://www.worldchat.com/public/
asarc/

Partners and Allies of Sexual Assault Survivors Resources List:
http://idealist.com/
wounded_healer/allies.shtml

POSitive Partners of Survivors
(chat room):
http://clubs.yahoo.com/
positivepartnersofsurvivors

Further Reading

General Readings

Adams, Caren, and Jennifer Fay. *Free of the Shadows: Recovery from Sexual Violence.* New York: New Harbinger Publications, 1990.

Ainscough, Carolyn, and Kay Toon. Surviving *Childhood Sexual Abuse Workbook.* Tucson, AZ: Fisher Books, 2000.

Allender, Dan B. *The Wounded Heart: Hope for Adult Victims of Childhood Sexual Abuse.* Colorado Springs, CO: NavPress, 1990.

Barnes, Patty Derosier. *The Woman Inside: From Incest Victim to Survivor.* Mother Courage Press, 1991.

Bass, Ellen, and Laura Davis. *The Courage to Heal: A Guide for Women Survivors of Child Sexual Abuse, 3rd Edition.* New York: HarperPerennial Library, 1994.

Butler, Sandra. *Conspiracy of Silence: The Trauma of Incest.* Eugene, OR: Volcano Press, 1996.

Davis, Laura. *Allies in Healing: When the Person You Love Was Sexually Abused as a Child, a Support Book.* New York: Harperperennial, 2000.

Dolan, Yvonne. *Resolving Sexual Abuse.* New York: W.W. Norton & Co., 1991.

Engel, Beverly. *The Right to Innocence: Healing the Trauma of Childhood Sexual Abuse.* Westminster, MD: Ivy Books, 1991.

Finney, Lynne. *Reach for the Rainbow: Advanced Healing for Survivors of Sexual Abuse.* New York: Perigee, 1992.

Ford, Clyde. *Compassionate Touch: The Body's Role in Emotional Healing and Recovery.* San Francisco, CA: Publishers Group West, 1999.

Gannon, J. Patrick. *Soul Survivors: a New Beginning for Adults Abused as Children.* New York: Prentice Hall, 1989.

Hall, Liz, and Siobhan Lloyd. *Surviving Child Sexual Abuse: A Handbook for Helping Women Challenge Their Past, 2nd. Ed.* Falmer Press, 1993.

Hancock, Maxine. *Child Sexual Abuse: A Hope for Healing.* Wheaton, IL: Harold Shaw Pub., 1997.

Kritsberg, Wayne. *The Invisible Wound: Healing Childhood Sexual Abuse.* New York: Bantam Books, 1993.

Kunzman, Kristin A. *The Healing Way: Adult Recovery from Childhood Sexual Abuse.* San Francisco, CA: HarperSanFrancisco, 1990.

Landry, Dorothy. *Family Fallout: A Handbook for Families of Adult Sexual Abuse Survivors.* Safer Society Press, 1992.

Maltz, Wendy. *The Sexual Healing Journey: A Guide for Survivors of Sexual Abuse.* New York: Harperperennial, 2000.

McClure, Mary Beth. *Reclaiming the Heart: A Handbook of Help and Hope for Survivors of Incest.* New York: Warner Books, 1990.

Poston, Carol. *Reclaiming Our Lives: Hope for Adult Survivors of Incest.* New York: Bantam Books, 1990.

Napier, Nancy. *Getting through the Day: Strategies for Adults Hurt as Children.* New York: W.W. Norton & Co., 1994.

Nestingen, Signe, and Laurel Lewis. *Growing beyond Abuse: A Workbook for Survivors of Sexual Exploitation or Childhood Sexual Abuse.* Bulverde, TX: Omni Recovery Press, 1996.

Rutter, Peter. *Sex in the Forbidden Zone.* New York: Ballantine, 1997.

Sands, Christa. *Learning to Trust Again: A Young Woman's Journey to Healing from Sexual Abuse.* Grand Rapids, MI: Discovery House, 2000.

Sanford, Linda. *Strong at the Broken Places: Overcoming the Trauma of Childhood Abuse.* New York: Avon Books, 1992.

Affirmations/Meditations

Brady, Maureen. *Daybreak: Meditations for Women Survivors of Childhood Sexual Abuse.* New York: HarperCollins, 1991.

Farmer, Steven, and Juliette Anthony. *Healing Words: Affirmations for Adult Children of Abusive Parents.* New York: Ballantine Books, 1992.

Male Survivors

Hunter, Mic. *Abused Boys: The Neglected Victims of Sexual Abuse.* Westminster, MD: Fawcett Books, 1991.

King, Neal. *Speaking the Truth: Voices of Courage and Healing for Male Survivors of Childhood Sexual Abuse.* New York: Harperperennial, 1995.

Lew, Mike and Ellen Bass. *Victims No Longer: Men Recovering from Incest and Other Sexual Child Abuse.* Scranton, PA: HarperCollins, 2000.

Rhodes, Richard. *A Hole in the World: An American Boyhood. Tenth Anniversary edition.* Lawrence, KS: University Press of Kansas, 2000.

Sonkin, Daniel Jay. *Wounded Boys, Heroic Men: A Man's Guide to Recovering from Child Abuse.* Holbrook, MA: Adams Media, 1998.

Tobin, Rod. *Alone and Forgotten: The Sexually Abused Man.* Ontario, Canada: Creative Bound, 1999.

Teen Survivors

Bean, Barbara, and Shari Bennett. *The Me Nobody Knows: A Guide for Teen Survivors.* San Francisco, CA: Jossey-Bass, 2000.

Lee, Sharice A. *The Survivor's Guide: A Guide for Teenage Girls Who are Survivors of Sexual Abuse.* Newbury Park, CA: Sage Publications, 2000.

La Valle, John. *Everything You Need to Know When You Are the Male Survivor of Rape or Assault.* New York: Rosen Publishing Group, 1995.

Children and Parents

Girard, Linda Walvoord, and Rodney Pate. *My Body Is Private.* Morton Grove, IL: Albert Whitman, 2000. Reading level: Ages 4-8.

Hagans, Karthryn, and Joyce Case. *When Your Child Has Been Molested: A Parent's Guide to Healing and Recovery.* San Francisco, CA: Jossey-Bass, 2000.

Kleven, Sandy, and Jody Bergsma. *The Right Touch: A Read-Aloud Story to Help Prevent Child Sexual Abuse.* Bellevue, WA: Illumination Arts, 1998. Reading level: Ages 4-8.

Kraizer, Sherryll. *The Safe Child Book: A Commonsense Approach to Protecting Children and Teaching Children to Protect Themselves.* Old Tappan, NJ: Fireside, 1996.

Wooden, Kenneth. *Child Lures: What Every Parent and Child Should Know About Preventing Sexual Abuse and Abduction.* Sarasota, FL: Bookworld, 1995.

Professional Reading

Giarretto, Henry. *Integrated Treatment of Child Sexual Abuse: A Treatment and Training Manual.* Palo Alto, CA: Science & Behavior Books, 1992.

Salter, Anna C. *Treating Child Sex Offenders and Victims: A Practical Guide.* Newbury Park, CA: Sage Publications, 1988.

Schetky, Diane H. *Child Sexual Abuse: A Handbook for Health Care and Legal Professions.* New York: Brunner/Mazel, 1988.

Ryan, Gail D. Juvenile *Sexual Offending: Causes, Consequences, and Correction.* San Francisco, CA: Jossey-Bass, 1997.

About the Authors

Kay Toon and Carolyn Ainscough met at Leeds University in 1983 when training as clinical psychologists, joining forces thereafter to work for the Wakefield Health Authority and other community organizations. For the last eight years they have presented training workshops on sexual abuse throughout the United Kingdom, given papers at national and international conferences and been interviewed for newspaper articles, radio and television programs on topics related to sexual abuse. Carolyn Ainscough and Kay Toon are also the authors of *Surviving Childhood Sexual Abuse Workbook* (Fisher Books, 2000).

Index